Lost Generations

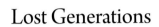

Corpus Christi College
Cambridge *c*.1900

Lost Generations

*The lives of those members of the College of Corpus Christi
and of the Blessed Virgin Mary, Cambridge who died undertaking
military service during the First World War, 1914 to 1919*

Peter Martland

WITH AN INTRODUCTION BY
Sir Hew Strachan

Corpus Christi College
UNIVERSITY OF CAMBRIDGE

First published in Great Britain in 2023 by
The Master and Fellows of
Corpus Christi College, Cambridge

A CIP record for this book is available from the British Library

Book design/typography by Dale Tomlinson
Typeset in Arno Pro

Copy-edited by Linda Randall

Printed and bound in the United Kingdom by Henry Ling Ltd,
The Dorset Press, Dorchester DT1 1HD

ISBN 978-1-7393938-0-9

Contents

Foreword

On 9 July 1755, a combined force of nearly 1,500 British regular soldiers and American provincials, including a young George Washington, approached Fort Duquesne, held by the French and located on the forks of the Ohio river. The British column had successfully advanced through tough terrain, and during the morning crossed and recrossed the Monongahela river without incident. That afternoon, however, it was hit by a smaller force of French and Native Americans. Sent out from Fort Duquesne, they took control of high ground to the British flank and used the cover provided by the thick woods to pour fire into the British close-order formations. The fight lasted three hours but eventually the British broke in panic. Two-thirds of their number were killed or wounded. It was a catastrophic start to the North American element of what we now know as the Seven Years War.

The commander that day, and the British commander-in-chief in North America, was Major General Edward Braddock. Braddock achieved the highest military rank of any Corpus alumnus before the twentieth century. Born in Perthshire in 1695 and himself the son of a general, he came up in 1710 as a Fellow Commoner before abandoning Cambridge for the army a few months later. He died from the wounds he received on the Monongahela and so was unable to answer the charges of incompetence that followed his defeat. Although historians have amplified them, some of his contemporaries were more forgiving. James Wolfe, himself to fall in more heroic fashion at Quebec four years later, blamed not Braddock but the poor quality of the soldiers under his command.

Even if he was more infamous than celebrated, Braddock is the exception to prove a rule. Before the First World War, Corpus would not have described itself as a military college. Nor, for that matter, would any other college in Cambridge or Oxford. This did not mean that would-be soldiers did not go to university. Douglas Haig, the commander-in-chief of the British Expeditionary Force in France and Flanders from 1915 to 1919, went up to Brasenose College, Oxford, before pursuing his chosen career as a soldier. But the typical Corpus man of the nineteenth century opted for more peaceful pursuits, the majority becoming schoolmasters or clergymen. Many of those whose careers Peter Martland has so painstakingly reconstructed in this volume were the sons of priests and had themselves planned to take holy orders if they had been vouchsafed a longer life than the Great War permitted them.

Those who were alive on 4 August 1914, the day that Britain declared war on Germany, were conscious of its epoch-making quality, not just for the nation but also for themselves. Nonetheless, it would be wrong to see August 1914 solely as a bolt from the blue, a change of direction without any precedent. Corpus's then-Master was Robert Townley Caldwell, a mathematician whose father had commanded the 92nd (Gordon) Highlanders. Caldwell himself commanded the 3rd (Militia) Battalion of the Gordons, with whom he served between 1887 and 1895, and he was proud enough of his credentials as the colonel of a Highland regiment to present to the College the ram's head snuff mull occasionally to be seen in the Senior Combination Room. In August 1914, with the vacation in full swing, he was not in Cambridge but in his Aberdeenshire home. A month later, he died there as the result of a car accident.

As a Corpus undergraduate, Caldwell had joined the Cambridge University Rifle Volunteers in 1864. Two years later, by which time he had been elected a Fellow of the College, he was commissioned as a captain, and he went on to command No. 1 or A Company (to which Corpus members belonged) and then became the second in command of the corps in 1871. He was the Commanding Officer of the University Rifle Volunteers between 1882 and 1885.

The Volunteers had been raised in response to the French invasion scare of 1859, and one of its two prime movers, the Reverend William Emery, was also a Corpus Fellow. The task of the Volunteers was to give 'each individual … a thorough knowledge of his weapon [the rifle], and so to qualify the force to act efficiently as an Auxiliary to the Regular Army and Militia'. The corps soon took on the attributes of another undergraduate club, with target-shooting as its sport, and with a round of reviews, field days, and social activities. Both as second in command (when he seems to have been *de facto* Commanding Officer for much of the time) and Commanding Officer, Caldwell sought to bring a more military bearing to the Volunteers and, as the College's Bursar, used both New Court and the Hall for drills and dinners. Caldwell saw the corps through and past a phase in its existence when enrolments fell and its members were accused of playing at soldiers. By 1885, its strength stood at 325, of whom 260 were deemed 'efficient', and it represented about 10 per cent of the undergraduate body. In 1900, when its strength reached 789, or about 25 per cent of the undergraduate population, it raised a company for service in the South African War.

In 1908, the Secretary of State for War, R B Haldane, created the Territorial Force from the Militia and Volunteers, to act as a reserve for home defence. He assumed that the Regular Army would form an expeditionary force for overseas service, either in the empire (most probably India) or in Europe (as proved to be the case in 1914). As a result of Haldane's reforms, the University Rifle Volunteers became the Officers Training Corps, tasked with producing officers for both the Regulars and the Territorials. Every university created a Military Education Committee to liaise between it and the War Office, and to take charge of military studies. Collectively, the universities constituted the Senior Division of the Officers Training Corps, while schools made up the Junior Division. The adjutants of the units of the Senior Division were themselves Regulars and those undergraduates who joined them were required to attend fifteen parades a year (or thirty if they had not been in the Junior Division at school), complete an annual musketry course, and attend annual camp. In return, they were each paid a gratuity of £35 a year if they continued with their military commitments after going down.

Alongside infantry, the Cambridge University OTC also established cavalry, artillery, engineer, and medical units, so diversifying the training it offered and moving away from the more limited expectations of the University Rifle Volunteers. Its establishment was now 1,000, in a student body that totalled 3,760 in 1910. However, both the OTCs and the Territorial Force in general struggled to recruit to their establishment. The Cambridge OTC mustered 600 in its first year of existence but that still represented a significant proportion of undergraduates, just under 20 per cent. Haldane, although he opposed conscription or national service for the Regulars (not least because his party – the Liberals – would not have tolerated it), was in favour of compulsion for the Territorials. So too were many senior figures at Cambridge, including two heads of houses. In January 1913, they wrote to the national press to propose a compromise between an under-strength Territorial Force and conscription. They wanted to require efficiency in the OTC or Territorials as a condition of graduation for all students who were British nationals and who were physically fit and aged under thirty. They claimed that sixty-five members of Senate supported the plan and by May 1914, despite the opposition of the *Cambridge Review*, 1,719 members supported the demand that Senate discuss the proposal that military training be a requirement for those wishing to proceed to a degree. Senate already supported the OTC in lesser ways, permitting absence on military exercises to count towards residence and appointing a Directory of Military Studies for the University.

The outbreak of war brought these debates to a halt but they show the University's attention to military service in the run-up to 1914. In 1912, the War Office had prepared a scheme for the rapid commissioning of the University's cadets. On 3 August 1914, the day that Britain sent its ultimatum to Germany, the Corps' headquarters in Market Street was besieged by would-be volunteers, including many who had shown no previous interest in military affairs. More expansive premises were required and Corpus offered itself as a temporary base for the Board of Military Studies until early September. The Board's military committee sat at the high table in Hall for three sessions a day, conducting oral examinations of those applying for commissions. On the undergraduate tables before them were ranged the papers of the various branches of the army; the secretarial staff worked in the Old Combination Room; and another college room was allocated for medical examinations.

The pace slowed from September and the Board moved its operations to other locations. By 15 September 1916, it had handled 3,432 applications. Of nearly 4,000 cadets struck off the OTC's strength between 1908 and 30 September 1915, 2,842 were known to have secured commissions in the army, and this total does not include those who joined the Royal Navy or colonial units or who served in the ranks.

Over 74 per cent of those commissioned in the army in this way served in the infantry. So too did the vast majority of those whose lives are recorded by Peter Martland. We do not know how many of these Corpus men had previously served in the OTC but it is reasonable to suppose – given university averages – that a quarter to a third had done so. It may well have been more. While the big colleges, like St John's and Trinity, were able to form their own single-college companies in the University Rifle Volunteers, Corpus seems to have consistently punched above its weight, despite its small size, presumably responding at least in part to Caldwell's leadership.

We now know that joining an infantry battalion as a subaltern was not a safe option. Of those who donned a uniform in the First World War, 12 per cent died, but that percentage rose according to branch of service and age. Army officers had a death rate of 15.2 per cent, but that includes senior officers who were less exposed to mortal danger; the death rated reached 16.8 per cent for those in the Royal Flying Corps. These losses were disproportionately borne by products of public schools and universities, with some Oxford and Cambridge colleges reporting death rates as high as 18 per cent of those who served. That proportion rose the nearer to the outbreak of war that an individual matriculated. Twenty-nine young men went up to Corpus in October 1913 and eight of them were killed in the war. So, in absolute terms, 27 per cent died and, since not all will necessarily have joined up, the figure could well have been over 30 per cent of those who served.

These were appalling losses and Peter Martland does full justice to their impact, individually and collectively, on the life of the College. But he has done Corpus an even greater service because he has identified all those from the College who served and survived. Given that 88 per cent of those who served came home, their numbers massively outweighed those whom we commemorate on war memorials. The percentage of deaths as a proportion of those who served may be higher for a community like Corpus (and Peter Martland has done the work to make that calculation more precisely).

One of the new Corpus undergraduates in October 1913 was Basil Liddell Hart. In 1933, by which time he had already forged a formidable reputation as a military theorist and writer, not least through his works on the First World War, he concluded of the conflict:

It was one of the most valuable experiences of our lives, offering to the fortunate survivors lessons in life that no substitute could have provided to the same extent, tending to the development of sympathy and understanding, correcting the 'cash nexus' of modern civilisation, and laying the foundations of a philosophy of life for those who chose to build up on them. I know for my own part I am more glad of that experience than anything else I have known.

Many with similar experiences expressed themselves in comparable terms. Liddell Hart served as an infantry subaltern on the Somme in 1916 and never returned to Corpus to finish the History degree on which he had embarked. Others did come back from the war and yet more came up to the College who had gone directly into the army on leaving school. The post-war College was reframed by those who had passed through the Great War and survived. They carried with them the legacy that Liddell Hart described. He was elected an Honorary Fellow in 1965 and died in 1970. I remember coming into College as an undergraduate that year and seeing the flag at half-mast. In the following year, Chris Andrew urged me to read Liddell Hart's posthumously published history of the Second World War for an essay I was due to write for him.

When, in 1975, I was elected a Research Fellow by the College, two veterans of the Great War were still active presences, albeit as Life Fellows. Archie Clark-Kennedy, former Dean of the London Hospital, had been an infantry officer in India and Mesopotamia, before completing his medical training and ending the war as a doctor with a field artillery brigade on the Western Front. He remembered how, in the advance of September 1918, the drivers of the guns would fall from their horses as they succumbed to influenza. Robert Thouless, the psychologist who graduated in 1914 and served as a Signals Officer in Macedonia, had tried – as became fashionable among those who grieved after the war – to understand whether the dead could communicate with the living. In 1942, he wrote *Straight Thinking in War Time*, an illustration of how the influences of one war were reflected in the consideration of its successor.

John Thomson MacCurdy, elected into Fellowship in 1926 and a psycho-therapist whose ideas were shaped by Freud, had died long before – in 1947. But his contribution to the war effort was even more immediate and also longer lasting. In 1917, the year in which he became a Medical Officer with the American Expeditionary Force, he published *The Psychology of War*, with a foreword by W H R Rivers, the man who treated both Siegfried Sassoon and Wilfred Owen at Craiglockhart Hospital. MacCurdy followed it up the following year with *War Neuroses*. He and Rivers were pioneers in the field of what was then most commonly called shell shock but is today dubbed post-traumatic stress disorder. They concluded that susceptibility to the condition was dependent on social class. The more sensitive and educated the officer, the more vulnerable he was, not least because his sense of duty was also high. By contrast, the private soldiers whose lack of exposure to 'civilising influences' led them to manifest their responses to the consequences of combat in more physical ways that they defined as hysteria. MacCurdy's and Rivers's rank-dependent interpretation held sway in the interwar years.

Today, MacCurdy is regularly honoured as the benefactor whose endowment provides Fellows with a free glass of wine after dinner in Combination and enables the Old Members' dinner named in his memory. The First World War happened over one hundred years ago but its effects are still to be seen in many other, often unobtrusive, ways in both the College and the University. Peter Martland's moving commemoration of those who died, and those who also served, gives that legacy immediacy and vividness, transporting us to a College and a society very different from our own.

SIR HEW STRACHAN (m.1968)

PROFESSOR SIR HEW STRACHAN MA PhD (Hon) D.Univ (Paisley) FRSE FRHistS FBA is a distinguished British military historian, well known for his studies of the British Army and of the First World War. He matriculated into Corpus Christi College, Cambridge in 1968 to read the Historical Tripos and was later elected to a fellowship. He is a former Admissions Tutor and Senior Tutor and is now a life fellow of the College. Between 1992 and 2000 he was Professor of Modern History at the University of Glasgow. He then became the Chichele Professor of the History of War at All Souls College, Oxford. Sir Hew is currently Professor of International Relations at the University of St Andrews, a trustee of the Imperial War Museum and patron of the Western Front Association.

Acknowledgements

Many individuals and institutions have knowingly or unknowingly helped make this book possible. To express my appreciation to everyone is I fear impossible, so to anyone missing from these acknowledgements, please do not feel aggrieved but also accept both my apologies and thanks. My thanks must however go first and foremost to the Master of Corpus Christi College, Cambridge, Professor Christopher Kelly, and to the College Fellowship for the support and encouragement I have received and for giving me access to the College Archives. I must also thank the College Archivist Genny Silvanus and her predecessor Lucy Hughes for their unstinting assistance in pointing out potential sources, both before COVID and furlough put a stop to archival access and since. In addition, I must thank other members of the College including the Masters' Executive Assistant Christoph Hartwig, Professor Peter Carolin, Dr Charles Read, Tim Rossiter, Dr Patrick Zutshi, Professor Sir Hew Strachan, His Honour Judge Mark West, Dr Christopher Thouless, David Mickelthwait, and Angus Knowles-Cutler. Phil Tomaselli and Dr Nicholas Hiley, two great historians and rooters around in archives, gave sterling help and unstinting support as did Richard Bonney. In addition, I must also acknowledge the input of several descendants of alumni who saw war service including those whose names are recorded on the war memorial: specifically, former College Master Stuart Laing, Ralph Cobham, Julian Elkington, The Rt Hon the Lord Etherton QC Kt PC and Thomas Hooley. Furthermore, I must add my thanks to Fiona Colbert, the biographical librarian at St John's College, Cambridge. Appreciation is also extended to the staff of the Cambridgeshire Collection for access to the G C H Culley album. Also, to Sue Besnard, churchwarden of St Gregory's, Goodleigh, Devon for the photograph of the Arthur Milton Lewis memorial stained-glass window and to Liz Gorst, administrative manager and PA to the rector of St John the Baptist Church, Busbridge, Waverley, Surrey for the photograph of the John Edward Templeman Barnes memorial stained-glass window and entry in the memorial book. Overseas help came from Vicki Stegall and the Yencken family in Australia, and from Glen Hall of Sarina, Australia. Finally, many thanks to those wonderful school archives and archivists who gave their time to provide invaluable data and who showed great interest in this project. These were Jennifer Law of Bishop's Stortford College, Catherine Smith of Charterhouse School, Godalming, Surrey, Dr C S Knighton of Clifton College, Bristol, Peter Henderson of The King's School, Canterbury, Alison Schreiber of King William's College, Isle of Man, Charlotte McCrory of Oakham School, Gary Collins assistant archivist at Rugby School, Rachel Hassall of Sherborne School, Robin Brooke-Smith of Shrewsbury School, Ginny Dawe-Woodings and Graham Seel of St Paul's School, London together with my friend and Corpus contemporary Christopher Ramsey, headmaster of the Whitgift School, Croydon, and his colleague Bill Wood, the school archivist. This list of thanks would not be complete without expressing my sincere thanks to Fiona Gilsenan, head of communications at Corpus Christi College, our wonderful copyeditor Linda Randall and designer Dale Tomlinson. These together with myriad other sources have made this book possible. To each and all my sincere and grateful thanks. All copyright where known is hereby acknowledged. If anyone has been missed in this respect, apologies. If errors are spotted or additional information can be provided do get in touch. Of course, all the errors belong to the author.

PETER MARTLAND (m.1982)

Abbreviations

ADC: aide-de-camp
BA: Bachelor of Arts
BChir: Bachelor of Surgery (the primary medical degree in Britain)
BEF: British Expeditionary Force
CB: Companion of the Order of the Bath
CBE: Commander of the Most Excellent Order of the British Empire
CF: Chaplain to the Forces
CH: Companion of Honour
CIE: Companion of the Indian Empire
CMG: Companion of the Order of St Michael and St George
DD: Doctor of Divinity
DFC: Distinguished Flying Cross
DPH: Diploma in Public Health
DSO: Distinguished Service Order
FGS: Fellow of the Geological Society
FRAeS: Fellow of the Royal Aeronautical Society
FRCP: Fellow of the Royal College of Physicians
FRCS: Fellow of the Royal College of Surgeons
FRGS: Fellow of the Royal Geographical Society
FRIBA: Fellow of the Royal Institute of Architects
FRS: Fellow of the Royal Society
FRSL: Fellow of the Royal Society of Literature
FSA: Fellow of the Society of Antiquaries
GBE: Knight Grand Cross of the British Empire
GCVO: Grand Cross of the Royal Victorian Order
GOC: General Officer Commanding
KBE: Knight Commander of the Most Excellent Order of the British Empire
KStJ: Knight of the Order of St John of Jerusalem
Kt: Knight
LittD: Doctor of Letters

LLB: Bachelor of Laws
LLD: Legum Doctor (Doctor of Laws)
LRCP: Licentiate of the Royal College of Physicians
LSA: Licentiate of the Society of Apothecaries
MA: Master of Arts
MB: Bachelor of Medicine
MBE: Member of the Order of the Most Excellent Order of the British Empire
MC: Military Cross
MD: Doctor of Medicine
MRCP: Member of the Royal College of Physicians
MRCS: Member of the Royal College of Surgeons
MVO: Member of the Royal Victorian Order
OBE: Officer of the Most Excellent Order of the British Empire
OTC: Officers Training Corps
PC: Privy Councillor
QC: Queen's Counsel
RAF: Royal Air Force
RACD: Royal Army Clothing Department
RAMC: Royal Army Medical Corps
RFC: Royal Flying Corps
RMO: Regimental Medical Officer
RN: Royal Navy
RNAS: Royal Naval Air Service
RNVR: Royal Naval Volunteer Reserve
TD: Territorial Division
TF: Territorial Force
VD: Volunteer Officers' Decoration

Introduction

sic itur ad astra
('thus one journeys to the stars')
A quotation from Virgil's epic poem *Aeneid*.
It forms the personal inscription on the gravestone of
Private Noel James Stanway Patch (m.1892),
47th Battalion (6th Reinforcement) Infantry, Australian Imperial Force.

This book is formed of sixty-nine biographies of the men of Corpus Christi College, Cambridge who as members of the British and Imperial armed forces died during or just after the First World War. Of these, sixty-two names were inscribed on the College war memorial. To these must be added seven further names discovered during the research undertaken for this work; in 2023 these names were added to the memorial.[1] The book also contains an appendix listing all those members of College known to have undertaken military service during the years 1914 to 1919, together with such details of their lives as survives.

*   *   *

The chapel of Corpus Christi College, Cambridge contains two memorials commemorating the College's dead from the world wars of the first half of the twentieth century. They take the form of stone tablets attached to the chapel wall to the right of the altar. The First World War memorial is (with one exception) a simple alphabetical naming of the dead. Today, after the passage of so much time, no one in the College knows anything about these people unless that is, like the former Master Stuart Laing, one of your ancestors is among them. This gives the names a certain anonymity which is, some may argue, a fitting way to commemorate the College's losses. However, as part of our marking the centenary of the First World War, it is perhaps even more appropriate for current and future members of College to know something of the individuals who left behind little else but their names on a stone memorial. For although they died long ago, they remain connected to us by place, if not by time.

It is worth remembering that these men (Corpus was an all-male institution until 1983), just like their twenty-first-century counterparts, either hoped to or did come up to the College to complete their education, gain a degree, and discover some of life's pleasures before taking up personal and professional responsibilities. Some were young (some just teenagers) and had hoped to come to Corpus straight from school, but never did. Others were part way

---

1. For reasons lost to history the names of Lieutenant-Colonel Duncan Burgess (m.1871), Acting Sergeant George Henry Bournes (m.1893), 2nd Lieutenant William Francis Meyrick Coningham (m.1909), Captain Arthur Milton Lewis (m.1913), 2nd Lieutenant Donald Charles Goolden, Lieutenant William Arthur Roberts and College servant Private Edwin George Cracknell were not inscribed on the war memorial when it was carved in 1923. This omission was rectified in 2023.

through their courses when war broke out and left without completing their degrees. Many were old members, of whom some were middle aged and married with families. Whoever they were, due to the exigencies of war and conflict, they all sadly perished long before their time, far from home and family, often in terrible circumstances.

*   *   *

I first came to know the College memorials as a student in the early 1980s and my knowledge (slight though it was) developed over the years. My interest in the First World War memorial was rekindled in 2014 when undertaking research into College life in the years just before and during that war. I knew nothing of the people named on the memorial, when they lived or attended the College, or what they studied, or what happened to them. That all changed when I began the research resulting in these biographies and the accompanying photographs.

At the start, it proved a bit of a detective story, as little else but the names on the memorial appeared to have survived. The College Archives contain few papers regarding its planning, design, or erection, or criteria for the inclusion of names. That said, the Chapter Book (which contains the records of the Governing Body) has just a tantalising amount of information. For example, the decision on 20 January 1920 to erect 'as a memorial to members of the College who died on service during the war, a tablet be affixed to the exterior North wall to the Chapel'.[2] Although unrecorded, the College also decided to pay for the memorial rather than appeal to the alumni for funds. In 1921, the Chapter Book further records the tasking of the Master and Tutor with the drawing up a list of names to be inscribed on the memorial. Further, in January 1924, it notes the decision to send a photograph of the war memorial to the nearest relative of all those named. Surprisingly, no account or date for its unveiling or dedication appears to have survived, but it is likely to have been on or around Armistice Day 1923.

The lack of data regarding the memorial was disappointing, but a trawl of the multitude of sources held in the College Archives revealed many other treasures. In addition to the Chapter Book, I was able to access the Admissions and Praelectors Books, which contain details of each student's admission, matriculation, tripos subject and results, and finally graduation. I was also able to review contemporary student sources, such as surviving copies of the College magazine *The Benedict*, published between 1898 and 1928 (excepting the war years), together with the Chess Club minute books and its termly group photographs (the only contemporary College photographs with names attached). The latter revealed many of the subjects as they looked during their time at Corpus. The same was true of the Boat Club minute book, which gave details of their achievements on the river, the races in which they participated, their crews, and positions in the boat. For the immediate pre-war period, it was possible to marry this information with images in three photograph albums compiled by Robert Oke

---

2. The location for the tablet was changed at a later and now unknown date.

(m.1902), George Charles Henry Culley (m.1911) and the Australian brothers Edward Druce and Arthur Frederick Yencken (both m.1911). At the University level, the wartime editions of the journal the *Cambridge Review*, with its rolling reporting of alumni military happenings, proved extraordinarily helpful. For details of the pre-1900 members of College, the online University of Cambridge alumni database proved a rich source of information.[3]

I also discovered modern published biographical works relating to two individuals, the Reverend Charles Edmund Doudney (m.1889) and Louis Mander Stokes[4] (curiously, among the oldest and youngest listed), together with other readily available published sources. Of these, one of the most important was the 'Admissions 1822–1950' section of Patrick Bury's *The College of Corpus Christi and of the Blessed Virgin Mary: A History from 1822 to 1952* (1952). The online Commonwealth War Graves Commission database proved invaluable, as were the surviving armed forces records held at The National Archives (TNA), Kew. In addition, use was made of a broad range of online sources including www.familysearch.org, local newspaper archives, rolls of honour compiled by schools and other universities, together with regimental, local history and myriad other websites. Several entries have benefited from the input of descendant family members and other sources.

The key source for this book was *The War List of the University of Cambridge 1914–1918* (1921) compiled by Gordon Vero Carey.[5] Drawing on the *Cambridge Review* data and other sources, *The War List* contains extremely basic details of those members of the University known to have undertaken service in the British and Imperial armed forces. *The War List* was compiled on a college-by-college basis and formatted alphabetically. Given its publication so soon after the Armistice, this methodology is understandable. Unfortunately, it does not help the modern reader appreciate the extraordinary age spread (the oldest was born in 1847 the youngest in 1898) or levels of cohort recruitment. However, with *The War List* it became possible to construct the appendix to this book, which has been reworked as a listing by matriculation year. It also contains much additional biographical information together with the names of those missing from the original list.

This research revealed significant wartime record-keeping errors making *The War List* and Bury's 'Admissions' data less than reliable with many of those admitted to the College but not matriculated due to military service missing from these lists. As far as possible, this gap has now been filled, bringing the listing more into line with the College war memorial and the listings in the *Cambridge Review*. However, a further gap in the data makes the appendix only partially successful and that is the omission of those who saw war service but

---

3. This source is freely available at www.venn.lib.cam.ac.uk.
4. J. Horne (ed.), *Best of Good Fellows: The Diaries and Memoirs of the Reverend Charles Edmund Doudney, MA CF (1871–1915)* (1995), and R A Barlow and H V Bowen (eds.), *A Dear and Noble Boy: The Life and Letters of Louis Stokes 1897–1916* (1995). Louis Stokes was admitted to the College as a pensioner in January 1916. He should have matriculated in October 1916, but never did.
5. This important work is freely available online at www.archive.org/details/warlistofuniversoocareuoft/page/64/mode/2up.

waited until after the Armistice to apply to come up. Clearly, many freshmen matriculating in the years 1919, 1920, and 1921 fall into this category.[6]

Inevitably, given the fog of war, its reliance on contemporary data, and rushed publication, *The War List* has come down to us with significant errors and omissions. Wherever possible, these issues have been corrected. Furthermore, the text is both terse and brief and employs a range of sometimes baffling initials, abbreviations, and contractions. In this work, these imperfections have been corrected, making the information more intelligible, readable, and informative.

*   *   *

At the time of their deaths, the ages of the College war dead ranged between 18 and 67 years. This means, unsurprisingly, they had quite diverse lives, experiences and war service. Many (in fact quite a disproportionate number), reflecting the late nineteenth- and early twentieth-century patterns of College admissions, were the sons of Anglican clergymen. Several were themselves clergymen, acting as Chaplains to the armed forces. A small number were members of the medical profession and an equally small number were professional soldiers. However, they were mainly amateurs, though pre-war membership of school or the University Officers Training Corps (OTC) or their predecessors was not unusual. A few served in the imperial forces of Canada, Australia, and India. Overall, they served in many theatres of war including Gallipoli, Mesopotamia, East and West Africa, the Balkans, in the naval action at Jutland, but mainly on the Western Front in France and Flanders. A small number died of sickness or as the result of accidents and two are known to have taken their own lives. However, perhaps the saddest and most disturbing group of casualties are the youngest cohort, several of whom were killed as the result of flying accidents or in air combat. As a group they are composed of not quite a quarter of the Corpus war dead and had been admitted to the College just before or during this conflict. Some came up for a short time to await their commissions, whilst others went straight from school to the armed forces. By the end of that terrible war, they were all dead, forming what can only be described as a 'ghost cohort', a tragedy of what might have been.

If this book is to serve a purpose, then it must be to shine a light onto the lives of those men of Corpus who more than one hundred years ago put down their pens and gave up, as one writer put it, 'those careless, happy student days' for the sake of country, family, professions, and way of life. However, they did more than that, for when they went off to fight as fate would have it, they also gave up their lives and futures to defend what they believed in, that is to say for us. For that reason alone, they are worth honouring and remembering.

PETER MARTLAND (m.1982)
Cambridge, 2023

---

6. According to the Admissions Register, in the years between 1919 and 1921, a total of eighty-seven students with birth years prior to 1899 were matriculated. All of these could, potentially, have applied to come up after war service. Of course, several of those matriculating in the early post-war years had been offered places and were therefore admitted to the College during the war.

THE
CORPUS CHRISTI COLLEGE
CAMBRIDGE DEAD
OF THE
FIRST WORLD WAR

The First World War memorial in the chapel at Corpus Christi College, Cambridge.
In 2023 seven additional names were cut into the memorial.

1871

BURGESS, **Duncan**, **Lieutenant Colonel**, MRCP FRCP (1850–1917), Royal Army Medical Corps (Territorial Force).

At the time of his death, Duncan Burgess was one of the College's most senior serving military officers. He was born in 1850 at Dreggie, Grantown (now Grantown-on-Spey), Morayshire, Scotland, the son of Gregor Burgess. According to Bury, he matriculated into Corpus as a scholar in 1871 (the University alumni website mistakenly has 1872) having previously studied mathematics at Aberdeen University; at Cambridge in 1875, he was 13th Wrangler (MA 1878). He subsequently studied medicine, first at the London Hospital (MB 1882), then Würzburg, Germany and finally in Vienna, Austria-Hungary. He was elected to a Fellowship in 1875, became an MRCP in 1887 and an FRCP in 1905. During his years as an active Fellow, he supported undergraduate activities and in 1889 contributed two guineas (£2.10) towards a new College eight.[7]

In 1905, Duncan Burgess became Professor of Medicine at Sheffield University and Senior Physician at the Sheffield Royal Hospital.[8] He retired in 1915 upon reaching the age of 65.

He returned to medical duties during the First World War when he was officer in charge of the 3rd Northern General Hospital, a large Territorial Force medical facility based in Sheffield. It had a staff of fifty-seven officers (all surgeons or doctors) and 1,360 other ranks. The hospital was probably the Sheffield Royal, simply taken over (or partly so) by the military. His *British Medical Journal* obituary notes: 'He performed his military duties with great devotion for nearly two years, and in all probability the additional stress materially hastened his final illness.' On 18 January 1917, the *Sheffield Daily Telegraph* reported: 'General regret will be felt in Sheffield at the death of Dr Duncan Burgess which took place last night at his residence, Broomfield House, Glossop Road. He had been ill for about nine months and for some weeks confined to the house. His death was due to heart failure.' It was said he died from overwork, aged 67.

---

7. His brother James Rose Burgess was also an undergraduate at Corpus (m.1877). On graduation, he became a schoolmaster but died in 1902.
8. On taking up this appointment, he left the College, but excercised his right to remain a Fellow under the old College statutes.

The local press published several tributes. One of Burgess's medical students wrote of him:

> Those of us who attended his lectures will never forget his genial personality, his racy stories and the kindly interest he took in our studies. He was never too busy to point out a case of special interest, or to give an instructive bedside clinic, and some of the things he taught us will remain in our memory throughout our medical careers. To some of us, who are only at the bottom of the ladder, he has left a brilliant example of what perseverance and plodding will do. He was a great physician, a great teacher and a true friend to those who came in contact with him. We shall never forget him, and what he did for us in our careless, happy student days.

A friend and neighbour wrote:

> The large number of doctors and other friends who attended the funeral showed the respect and affection of one who at all times was an honourable, sympathetic and courteous colleague and friend. I do not know any doctor who was more popular with the medical profession than he was. Clever and distinguished, he was always modest, unassuming and never self-assertive. He was one of those who did good by stealth and did not let his left hand know what his right hand did. Many are the kindnesses Dr Burgess did professionally and to the poor and needy, though known only to the recipients. His considerable kindness and courtesy to his patients at the Royal Hospital were the outcome of his sympathetic and truly kindly nature and were much appreciated by them. At a boys' class in a Sunday School the teacher asked who was the beloved physician, one of the boys held up his hand and exclaimed 'Dr Burgess, sir'. Although Dr Burgess made no open profession as a Christian, yet a great part of his life was most certainly in line with Our Lord's teaching, which, after all, is the important thing.

Duncan Burgess was buried with full military honours. He left the balance of his estate (£2,600) to the College. There is an obituary in both *The Lancet*, 1/1917, Vol. 189 (4874), p. 167, and the *British Medical Journal*, 27 January 1917, p. 141. See also Bury, p. 224. In 2023 his name was added to the College war memorial. He is recorded in *The War List*.

1889

DIXON-WRIGHT, Reverend Henry Dixon, MVO (1870–1916), Chaplain, RN. Henry Dixon-Wright was born at 3 St George's Villas, Bickerton Road, Upper Holloway, London on 25 April 1870, the son of Martha née Box and Henry Wright, a printing and law stationery manager. The family were originally from Tewkesbury, Gloucestershire; however, his father moved to London and in 1869 married governess Martha Box. A second child, William, was born in 1871, and by 1881 the family lived in Highgate, where Henry attended Highgate School.

Henry matriculated into Corpus in 1889 (where he was known as Henry Wright), read the Classical Tripos and graduated with a BA in 1892 (MA 1904). During his time at the College, he was a member of the Chess Club and on graduation studied at Ridley Hall, was ordained deacon in 1893 and priest the following year. He served two London-based curacies and in 1897 moved to Guildford before taking an appointment as English chaplain at Las Palmas in the Canaries.

His career took a significant turn in 1899 when he was appointed a Royal Navy Chaplain. Early naval appointments were uneventful: HMS *Resolution* in the Channel Fleet, followed in 1900 by HMS *Ramillies* the flagship of Rear Admiral Lord Charles Beresford the second in command of the Mediterranean Fleet. In August 1903, Henry was appointed to HMS *Bedford*, a Monmouth class armoured cruiser serving in the 2nd Cruiser Squadron in the Channel Fleet until 1906.

In June 1904, whilst serving on *Bedford*, he married Annie Louisa Paton née Lawrie. The couple had two children, Henry John Dixon-Wright (b.1905) and Frank William Dixon-Wright (1911–1942) who was later Wing Commander, DFC, RAF, 115 Squadron and killed in action in 1942, aged 31. In 1911, Henry changed his surname to Dixon-Wright (*London Gazette*, 8 September 1911).

In 1906, Henry was appointed to HMS *Egmont* as Chaplain for the Malta Hospital and in 1907 became Chaplain at the Royal Naval College in Dartmouth. During this time, he prepared both the Prince of Wales (the future Edward VIII) and his younger brother Prince Albert (the future George VI) for confirmation. In the year 1911 to 1912, he acted as Chaplain to the King and Queen on their journey to and from India for the Delhi Durbar and was awarded the Royal Victorian Order, 4th Class.

At the outbreak of war, Henry was appointed Chaplain to HMS *Albemarle* and assigned to the 3rd Battle Squadron in the Grand Fleet as part of the Northern Patrol. They were subsequently transferred to the Channel Fleet to bombard German submarine bases along the Belgian coast, before once again returning to the Grand Fleet. *Albemarle* went into refit in October 1915 and Henry was appointed Chaplain to HMS *Barham*, one of the newest battleships in the fleet.

Henry Dixon-Wright died on 1 June 1916 of wounds received in action on HMS *Barham* during the Battle of Jutland (31 May to 1 June 1916), aged 46. During the battle, *Barham* was hit by six large calibre projectiles. They killed four officers and twenty-two men and wounded one officer and thirty-six men.

In a biographical note, the Reverend David Youngson records that although Henry lay severely wounded with a shattered spine and leg, he was praying for victory. He was brought back to Orkney and died the day after the battle, one of nine Chaplains who were killed. He was aged 46 and left a widow with two infant sons. He was buried at the Royal Naval Cemetery, Lyness, Hoy, Orkney.

DOUDNEY, Reverend Charles (known as Charlie) Edmund (1871–1915), CF 4th Class, Royal Army Chaplains Department, attached to the 18th Brigade, 6th Division.

Charlie Doudney was one of four sons and three daughters of the Reverend David Alfred (1838–1912) and his wife Georgina Doudney née Fry (1837–1936); his mother was a descendant of prison reformer Elizabeth Fry. His father was an evangelical minister and editor of *The Gospel Magazine*. Charlie was born in Cumberland and attended Hastings Grammar School (now Ark Alexandra Academy).

The Doudney family had an association with Corpus that went back three generations and he matriculated into the College in 1889 as a pensioner to read the Mathematical Tripos. According to a note in the Admissions Register, his referee was Sir James Colquhoun Bart and he intended to study mathematics probably aiming at an honours degree. An additional comment notes: 'Was candidate for entrance scholarships and thought a <u>very good character</u> then.' The University records indicate that he did not achieve honours in mathematics, or any other subject, and must have taken an ordinary degree. Overall, he makes only two appearances in the list of the largely voluntary internal examinations, gaining a second class in an 1891 examination on the Acts of the Apostles, and in 1892 was awarded one guinea in books for English reading. As an undergraduate, he was a member of the Boat Club and rowed in College eights, fours, and sculls. After graduating with a BA in 1892 (MA 1896) he trained at Ridley Hall, was ordained deacon then priest in 1894, serving as a curate until 1896. His brother Herbert William (1873–1963) (m.1892) was also ordained priest before serving in Australia.

Charlie was the husband of Joanna Clara (known as Zoe) Schroeder née Poulden (1876–1958) of Oxford; the couple had four daughters, Esther Eirene (b.1900), Noelle Mary (1904–7), Joy (b.1908) and Désirée Gowler (1913–2003).

In 1896, Charlie Doudney went to Australia as a missionary and was vicar of Orroroo, South Australia until 1898. Thereafter, he was rector of Port Augusta,

South Australia, then Christ Church, North Adelaide, and finally of Gawler St George, South Australia. In 1906, the family returned to Britain and a living at St Luke's Church, South Lyncombe, Bath, where he served between 1907 and 1915. During this time, he gained a reputation for his interest in wireless telegraphy. He was also a good rifle shot, taking part in Bisley as a member of the Australian team and in individual contests.

In January 1915, he became an army Padre and saw service in the Ypres Salient. Determined to conduct his ministry in his own way, he ignored instructions from the church hierarchy to stay out of the firing line. In July 1915, whilst home on sick leave, he preached a sermon later published in *Keenes Bath Journal*. In it, he said:

> There was an article in a daily paper, two or three months ago, describing the work of chaplains at the Front, and dividing chaplains into three kinds. First (it said) there are those chaplains who endeavour to carry out the Church's order in all details at the Front, and who lay more stress upon the exact nature of the service and what robes they wear than upon the men they are ministering to. Secondly, there are the amanuenses, who spend their time helping the troops, looking after their material comforts, writing their letters and procuring cigarettes for them. Lastly, there are those whom the writer calls missionaries – filled with the highest possible ideal, which at all times they hold before the men who are fighting. I must say I have come across some chaplains of the first two types; but nearly all I have met belong, most decidedly and definitely, to the class of missionaries who do not rest until they have brought the highest ideal into the hearts of the brave men who are fighting. Certainly, we do try to help with the writing of letters and in the concerts and games, but this is apart from our real work, which is to deliver the message of the other world.

Simon Harold Walker discussed his ministry in a University of Strathclyde student essay (n.d.) entitled 'Saving Bodies and Souls: Army Chaplains and Medical Care in the First World War'. He wrote:

> Charles Doudney ... brought to the role a wealth of medical experience. Prior to the war, Doudney had served as a chaplain in South Australia in remote locations which led him to act in many roles including local religious leader, mediator and medic. Indeed, on his first day to his new parish in Australia Doudney assessed several patients including a lad with a broken leg and a woman going into labour. Doudney, like so many other chaplains brought these skills and enthusiasm to his role in the First World War and relished in finding ways to care for soldiers above and beyond his traditional remit which eventually included him moonlighting as the resident radiographer along with his regular duties. Yet this focus of care was not limited solely to the wounded and sick. Doudney was also renowned for keeping a keen eye on the physical state of the medical staff, often advising overtired staff to rest or taking over less taxing medical duties, such as bandaging, to encourage respite.

Charlie Doudney formed a part of a small group of like-minded Anglican Chaplains active in and around the Ypres Salient at this time. His successors were friends and colleagues Reverend Neville Stuart Talbot MC DD and Reverend Philip Thomas Byard (Tubby) Clayton CH MC. These two put many of the ideas into practical effect, including the creation of Talbot House as a Christian rest centre for the troops in Poperinge (named after Neville's brother

the Reverend Gilbert Talbot, another friend who was killed shortly before Doudney). This became the basis for the ex-servicemen's charity Toc H.

On 16 October 1915, Charlie Doudney died of wounds at No. 10 Casualty Hospital, Abecle, Flanders, aged 44. He had been on his way to bury eight soldiers at Ypres when he was hit by shrapnel and his bowel perforated. Tragically, Charlie was due to return home on leave the following morning. When it was apparent that he was dying, a colleague, the Reverend Frederick Macnutt, who was at the clearing station, ministered to him afterwards writing:

> We did so hope that he would pull through, and everything that skill could do was done. When it became apparent that he was passing, the Archdeacon, the sister and I knelt down and commended his spirit to God and gave thanks for his life and ministry, and especially for his splendid service over here. The end came very quietly and peacefully, and as he was passing we repeated the words: 'Blessed are the dead that die in the Lord, from henceforth, yea, saith the Spirit, they rest from their labours, and their works do follow them.'

The Reverend Charles Doudney, the first beneficed clergyman to be killed in the war, is buried at the Lijssenthoek military cemetery. The personal inscription on his gravestone reads: *In Christo et in pace* (in Christ and in peace). He was an active freemason and is commemorated on the Masonic First World War website. There is a memorial tablet commemorating him in St Luke's Church, Lyncombe, Bath. It concludes: 'A soldier of Jesus Christ'. The National Archives, Kew[9] has an officer file WO 339/34023 and a medal card WO 372/6/69936. See also J Horne (ed.), *Best of Good Fellows: The Diaries and Memoirs of the Reverend Charles Edmund Doudney, MA, CF (1871–1915)* (1995).

9. Hereafter TNA.

Corpus May boat 1892.
Charles Doudney is seated second left. Seated to his left is future brother-in-law and
Rowing Blue (1893) Edward Henry Mansfield Waller (1871–1942) who later became
Bishop of Madras (now known as Chennai), India.

1892

PATCH, Noel James Stanway, Private (2699) (1874–1917), 47th Battalion
(6th Reinforcement) Infantry, Australian Imperial Force.

Noel Patch was born in Wrentham, Suffolk, the
second son of the Reverend Henry Patch (m.1850,
St John's) and Hero Elizabeth née Blaiklock. He was
educated at Worthing College, Sussex, matriculating
into Corpus in 1892, graduating with a BA in 1895.
During his time at the College, he was a rower. He had
an elder brother John David Henry Patch (m.1891, St
John's) who was ordained a priest and died in 1962,
aged 89, at Newton Abbot, Devon.

Noel Patch emigrated to Australia in about 1896
and farmed at Plane Creek (later known as Sarina),

Queensland. Two of his younger brothers also emigrated to Australia and like Noel saw military service during the war. Thomas Walter, who was a farmer, served with the 4th Light Horse Field Ambulance, 5th Australian Division, Australian Imperial Force in Egypt and on the Western Front. He survived the war and returned to farming in Sarina. Their brother, Captain Henry Patch, served with the 4th Battalion South Lancashire Regiment and the Royal Flying Crops. He died of wounds on 19 October 1917 as a German prisoner of war aged 23, just six days after the death of his brother Noel; neither of Noel's younger brothers came to Corpus or Cambridge.

In *More than just a Name* local historian Glen Hall commemorates the men of Sarina who went off to war; Noel Patch is described as 'well known in the area' and as 'a very civic minded man who did a great deal of good in early Sarina'. It notes that in 1913 he became shire clerk and agent for the Queensland State Savings Bank. According to his Australian Imperial Force attestation papers, he enlisted on 25 March 1916, aged 42. He was a single man, named his mother as next of kin, and asserted he was agnostic. After basic training, he was attached to the 47th Battalion as part of the 6th Reinforcement, embarking for Britain on 27 October 1916 and arriving in January 1917. Noel spent the next eight months with the 12th Training Battalion on Salisbury Plain, Wiltshire.

His unit embarked for France on 5 September 1917, where it became a part of the 47th Battalion. Three days later, the Battalion was ordered to Belgium and took part in the 3rd Battle of Ypres, known as Passchendaele. On 13 October 1917, whilst serving as a signaller, Noel Patch was killed in action, aged 43; he had been in action less than a month. The Battalion war diary notes 'At 5:45 am enemy heavily shelled Battalion Headquarters killing 24 and wounding 10 men. Nearly all were Signallers, Runners and Scouts, which upset all arrangements for communications. Many reliable lives were lost that will be hard to replace.'

Noel Patch was buried in the Passchendaele New British Cemetery, West Vaarlanden, Belgium. The personal inscription on his gravestone is a quotation from Virgil's epic poem *Aeneid* – *sic itur ad astra* ('thus one journeys to the stars'). Noel Patch is commemorated on the war memorials in Winchelsea, England and Sarina, Queensland, Australia. He is also remembered at the Australian national war memorial.

See also Glen Hall, *More than just a Name: In Memory of the 114 WWI Diggers Honoured on the Sarina Cenotaph* (self-published, n.d.).

1893

BOURNES, George Henry (Acting Sergeant), Corporal (1873–1921), 10th (Service) Battalion Royal Fusiliers, attached to the Intelligence Corps. He had previously served with 1st Battalion Royal Scots (The Royal Regiment), the Royal Engineers, the 1/6th Battalion Duke of Wellington's (West Riding) Regiment and the Labour Corps. An online history of the Intelligence Corps explains this curious military affiliation: 'To begin with, around 50 men were recruited into the Intelligence Corps. These came not only from within the army, but also from the Metropolitan Police and civilian life. At first, the unit was officer-only. As a cover story, the officers' batmen were nominally enlisted in the 10th (Service) Battalion, The Royal Fusiliers.'

George Henry Bournes was born at Buckmount, Clara, King's County (now Co. Offaly), Ireland on 4 July 1873, the son of Elizabeth Hartley Isabella and George Smith Bournes. His father was a timber merchant and the family moved to London when George was an infant, settling at Eastdown Park, Lewisham, London. George was one of thirteen children, most of whom died in infancy; at his death in 1921, he was survived by two unmarried sisters. George was educated at the Blackheath Proprietary School and in the 1891 census, aged 18, he self-describes as a student of theology. Two years later, he matriculated into Corpus. It took him until 1898 to graduate with a BA, aged 25. He was ordained deacon the following year and between 1899 and 1900 served as a curate in Bethnal Green, London, but was never ordained a priest.

There was some confusion in the few surviving military records over the spelling of his name (Bourns or Bournes). His history and occupation in the pre-war years is unknown. However, it is known that George saw active service during the war. According to the Medal Rolls, he served initially with 1st Battalion Royal Scots, though again record-keeping confusion leads to the view he served in France with a Territorial Battalion of the Royal Scots. He later served with the 1/6th Battalion Duke of Wellington's (West Riding) Regiment (Territorials) and then with the Labour Corps. After the Armistice, he served with the Intelligence Corps during the allied occupation of Germany.

George was based in Cologne where public records show he died on 31 March 1921 asserting the cause of death to be 'of sickness', aged 47. However, regimental records show he died of a self-inflicted gunshot wound, killing himself 'while the balance of his mind was disturbed'. He is buried in the Commonwealth War Graves Commission Cemetery, Cologne, Germany. It is not known if the College or his family knew of the cause of death. The records show that three years later his sisters returned his medals to the regiment. The personal inscription on his gravestone reads 'Kept in deep and loving memory by his sisters.' His name appears on *The War List* but not marked as died on active service. In 2023 his name was added to the College war memorial.

LANG, Henry (Harry) Astell, Major (1874–1915), second in command 4th Battalion Worcestershire Regiment, an element of the 88th Brigade, 29th Division.

Harry Lang was born at Biggleswade, Bedfordshire in 1874 the youngest son of the late George Lukis formerly of the Indian Civil Service and his wife Louisa Wynward. He had a sister Daphne.

He was educated at Summerfields School (now known as Summer Fields School), Oxford where he played football and cricket and then Marlborough College. He came to Corpus in 1893 but left after a single term to become a career soldier.

Harry was commissioned into the 2nd Battalion Worcestershire Regiment and between 1899 and 1901 saw action in the South African War, during which he was wounded and awarded the Queen's Medal with four clasps. Thereafter, he was ADC to the Governor of Malta and subsequently served in India and Burmah (Myanmar). In an obituary, the cricketing annual *Wisden Cricketers' Almanack* said of him: 'He did a deal of big-game shooting in Nepal, Kashmir and the Tirai and secured several exceptionally good heads of gond, barasingh and sambhur, besides tigers, leopards and bears.'

He then transferred to the 4th Battalion (in which William Barker – see below – also served) and after the Ottoman Empire entered the war took part in the Dardanelles campaign. On 24 April 1915, Lang landed with his regiment under fire at Cape Helles, Gallipoli and later took part in the three Battles of Krithia. He was Mentioned in Despatches and on 6 June 1915 was killed in action, aged 41. In a regimental account of events, it was said: 'That night [6–7 June] another counterattack was met and repulsed, then the enemy's efforts died away and the captured trenches remained thenceforward in British possession. But the success had been dearly gained. Many of the surviving officers and men of the 4th Worcestershire had been killed, including the second-in-command, Major H A Lang.'

In a letter to the family, his Colonel, Douglas Edward Cayley, wrote:

> Major Lang had been one of the mainstays of the Battalion. A good polo player, a sound cricketer, an all-round sportsman and a most able soldier, Major Lang was a fine type of Regimental Officer. Since the landing he had proved himself invaluable, always cool, clear-headed and of the most amazing bravery. His help to me has been more than I can acknowledge; what the Battalion will do without him I don't know.

He was buried in Twelve Tree Copse Cemetery, Gallipoli, Turkey.
The personal inscription on his gravestone refers to Psalm 25 which begins 'Unto thee, O Lord, do I lift up my soul'. He is commemorated on the Lingfield, Surrey and St Peter & St Paul's Church, Lingfield war memorials.

1894

BARKER, William, Major (1873–1915), 4th Battalion, attached to the 9th (Service) Battalion Worcestershire Regiment.

William Barker was the only son of Kathleen Anna and the late Surgeon Lieutenant Colonel Frederick Charles Barker of Rajkote-Kattiarwar, Bombay (now Mumbai), Indian Military Service. The family lived at Charlton Marshall, Blandford Forum, Dorset.

He was born in Bombay on 24 November 1873 and educated first at Elizabeth College, Guernsey and then, between 1889 and 1891, at Dulwich College. He matriculated into Corpus in 1894 and was a member of the Boat Club, rowing in the 1896 scratch fours. William graduated with a BA in 1897 and subsequently became a professional soldier.

According to the Dulwich College obituary, in May 1900 he was gazetted 2nd Lieutenant and posted to the 4th Battalion Worcestershire Regiment (the same Battalion as Harry Lang). A year later, he was promoted to Lieutenant and in 1908 to Captain. He served in Bermuda, Barbados, Malta, Egypt, and India, being Adjutant of Standing Camp, Ranikhet, India during 1910. Following the outbreak of war, he was attached to the 9th Service Battalion of his regiment and in June 1915 went with it to the Dardanelles. On 10 August 1915, he was severely wounded leading his men into action at Suvla Bay and died on HMHD *Gascon* at sea enroute to Malta on 15 August 1915.

De Ruvigny's *Roll of Honour*[10] adds the following:

> He was shot early in the day and fell into a small sap; when the Turks had been driven back, Private Hollins of his company returned to look for him, and, later, was joined by Private Coombs. Our troops had then retired, and they were surrounded by the enemy, but without the latter's knowledge of their presence in the sap. When it was dark, they with difficulty took Major Barker down to the foot of the hill where they remained until daylight, when they managed to bring him into our lines and handed him over to stretcher bearers.

He was buried at sea and is commemorated on the Helles Memorial, Gallipoli, Turkey. TNA have a medal card WO 372/1/235399.

---

10. The Marquis De Ruvigny *Roll of Honour* (5 vols.) (reprint 2003; originally published in 1922).

1898

HAMILTON, James, 2nd Lieutenant (1879–1916), 4th Battalion Border Regiment (Territorial Force).

James Hamilton was the seventh child of George and Isabella Hamilton of Middlesbrough. His parents were borderers, George was a clerk in the Customs Service and several of the children became teachers. His younger brother Thomas (m.1900, King's) taught in South Africa and later helped develop dairy production in Southern Rhodesia (present-day Zimbabwe).

James attended the Wesleyan School in Middlesbrough and Queen Elizabeth's Grammar School, Darlington (now Queen Elizabeth Sixth Form College). In 1896, he matriculated into Durham University as an arts student and Foundation Scholar, graduating with Second Class Honours in Classics in 1899.

In 1898, he matriculated into Corpus as a pensioner, became an Open Scholar in 1900 and graduated in 1901 with a BA in the Classical Tripos. During his time at the College, he was a member of the Boat Club and rowed at bow in the Michaelmas 1899 and Lent 1900 boats. Of this, *The Benedict* (Lent Term 1900) noted: 'Hamilton at bow is very light, but has a fairly even swing, is not springy and nippy enough for a bow, washes out badly.'

After Corpus, James taught first at the King's Hospital School, Dublin and then at Blackburn Grammar School (also known as Queen Elizabeth's Grammar School). He then had a brief spell at the Grammar School, Hampton-on-Thames (now Hampton School) after which he became second master at Heversham Grammar School (now part of Dallam School), Westmorland (now Cumbria) where he remained until 1915. As a teacher, he was something of an all-rounder, offering Latin, Greek, History, English, and French.

In July 1915, James joined the 4th Cumberland and Westmorland Battalion Border Regiment. Although this Battalion spent the war years in India, some of its members were attached to other units and saw war service in France; among them was James Hamilton. It is likely he served with 1/5th Battalion, although his medal card records him with the 4th Battalion. In September 1915, he joined the Inns of Court Officers Training Corps, and in January 1916, was commissioned 2nd Lieutenant in the Border Regiment.

His Battalion was deployed in France with the 151st (Northumbrian)

Brigade in the 50th Division alongside Battalions of the Durham Light Infantry. He joined the Battalion which had already engaged in various actions including the Somme Campaign. His Durham University obituary notes: 'the final weeks of this protracted campaign were grim and unrewarding, with scant gains, massive casualties and plummeting morale'. The Battalion was engaged in a series of actions over the autumn known as the Battle of the Transloy Ridges. It faced a huge ancient but strategically important burial site known as the Butte (or 'mound') of Warlencourt that commanded the road to Bapaume. This became the focus of numerous attacks which saw losses of around 1,000, giving it a totemic status among those attempting to capture it. In one, on 5 November 1916, James Hamilton, fighting alongside the Durham Light Infantry and Northumberland Fusiliers, was killed, aged 37. His death was officially reported on 18 November.

He was buried in the Warlencourt British Cemetery, Pas de Calais, France, alongside those who attacked with him that day. The personal inscription on his gravestone reads 'Risen with Christ'. James Hamilton's life is commemorated in the rolls of honour and war memorials of Middlesbrough and Darlington Grammar School (now Queen Elizabeth Sixth Form College).

HEWITT, Reverend Frederick Whitmore (1880–1915) CF 4th Class, Royal Army Chaplains Department, attached to the 20th Infantry Brigade.

Frederick Hewitt was the son of Stanley and Louisa Hughes Hewitt. His father was an underwriter and the family lived at Newson Square, Earl's Court, London. At the time of his death, Frederick was married to Blanche Ethel Mary née Quentin of Heatherley, Camberley, Surrey.

He was born in, Kensington, London on 5 March 1880 and according to the 1881 census lived in Ealing, Middlesex and in the 1891 census at Kingston Vale, Surrey.

Frederick was educated first at Temple Grove School, East Sheen, Surrey then, between 1894 and 1896, at Charterhouse School, Godalming, Surrey and finally at West Wratting.

He matriculated into Corpus as a pensioner in October 1898 and was a member of the Chess Club, holding office first as Secretary then President. Frederick was the subject of an affectionate article in *The Benedict* (Easter Term 1901), which concluded:

Two years [after Charterhouse] he became a member of the College of which he is now so distinguished and elegant an ornament. Here he might have been expected to indulge in his beloved cricket and soccer: but more arduous tasks were in store for him. The mossy path of pleasure was to be abandoned for the dusty 'grind' of virtue. Whatever may the loss to his College on the field, on the river his services have been invaluable. He rowed 4 and 7 in the Lent boats of 1899 and 1900 respectively, and 7 and 6 in the May boats of the same years. In October 1899 he was elected Boat Club Secretary, and in the following year Captain, the traditions of which he has worthily maintained. In July 1900 he rowed at 4 in the London Rowing Club, Thames Challenge Cup crew at Henley and was also stroke of their Wyfold Four. In October that same year he rowed in the 'Varsity Trials' for something over a fortnight. At the present time he is rowing once more at 7 in the May Boat – may good luck attend his crew!

Frederick did not forget his old club, and in 1905 sent three guineas (£3.15) toward the purchase of the Henley Boat. He graduated with a BA in 1901 (MA 1908) and, in 1903 (following the recommendation of the College), ordained as deacon and priest in 1904. Between 1903 and 1910, he held two curacies and after 1910 he was vicar of St Mary's Church, Brixton, Devon.

On 10 July 1915, Frederick Hewitt was commissioned as Chaplain to the Forces 4th Class, Royal Army Chaplains Department and in August 1915 was posted to the BEF in France and Flanders, attached to the 20th Infantry Brigade. He was killed in action by shellfire on 27 September 1915, aged 35; one of 179 Chaplains who were killed in the war. Charterhouse Roll of Honour has the following: 'He was instantly killed by the bursting of a shell while tending the wounded of the 9th [Battalion] Devons[hire Regiment] at the Battle of Loos, near Vermelles 27th September 1915 aged 35.' Frederick Hewitt was buried at Vermelles British Cemetery, Pas de Calais, France and the personal inscription on his gravestone reads 'Thy will be done'.

Frederick is commemorated on the Brixton war memorial, Brixton, Devon and the Charterhouse war memorial. TNA have an officer file WO 339/42601 and a medal card WO 372/9/161930.

MARTIN, **Edward Nugent Meredyth, 2nd Lieutenant** (1881–1916), 5th Battalion Royal Irish Lancers attached to the Machine Gun Corps (Cavalry).

Edward Nugent Meredyth Martin was of Anglo-Irish, Co. Carlow heritage, although he was born in Cornwall on 9 May (Ancestry.com mistakenly says April) 1881. He was the son of Eustace Meredyth Martin (1816–92), a barrister, traveller, and writer, and his second wife Jane née Lobb. His father's published works include *A Tour through India in Lord Canning's Time* (1881), *A Visit to the Holy Land, Syria and Constantinople* (1883), and a children's novel *Round the World* (1883). Edward was the grandson of the Reverend Edward Martin LLD, formerly the dean's vicar St Patrick's Cathedral, Dublin.

He was the youngest of five children from his father's second marriage and one of three who came to the College. Bury lists them as Eustace Meredyth Martin (m.1893) who read law and Roland Eustace Meredyth Martin (m.1896), who tragically died in College on 2 December 1896, aged 18. He attended Eastbourne College from 1894 to 1898, and in 1899, according to a news report in the *Eastbourne Gazette*, remembered his old school as he and a fellow former student presented the Volunteers with a prize cup for a shooting competition.

Edward Martin matriculated into Corpus in October 1898 with a view to obtaining a commission in the army. He clearly enjoyed his time and contributed to College life with his musical skills (violin and piano). He was also a member of several clubs and societies, including the Chess Club and as an athlete proved a stalwart of the Boat Club of which he was a committee member, a freshers coach, and rowed at five in the 1898 May and 1899 Lent and May boats. *The Benedict* (Lent Term 1899) noted he played football, describing him as: 'a good tackler and kicks well but sadly lacks pace'. In 1899, he tried rugby, *The Benedict* said of this: 'Martin has taken up the game with great enthusiasm and marked success. [He] is a good tackler and saves splendidly.'

Edward did not graduate and left to join the armed forces soon after the outbreak of the South African War. Edward was commissioned into the 3rd Battalion West Riding Regiment but transferred to the 5th (Royal Irish) Lancers. He served throughout the conflict, gaining the Queen's South Africa and King's South Africa medals. In 1903, he was back in England having resigned his commission. Thereafter, for more than a decade, he resided in Sussex pursuing country sports, competing in horse races as an amateur jockey (with more than a touch of Siegfried Sassoon, another 'foxhunting man'), and living the life of a country gentleman.

With the coming of war in 1914, he re-joined his regiment and was later attached to the 5th Squadron, Cavalry Brigade Machine Gun Corps. Formed on 26 February 1916, the unit combined machine gun sections taken from 2nd Dragoons, 12th Lancers and 20th Hussars. Also in 1916, he was posted to Ireland and took part in the suppression of the Easter Rising; when the rebels posted the original Proclamation of the Republic on the doors of the Dublin Post Office, it was Martin who removed it. On the reverse of the original proclamation, now in a museum, is the following inscription: 'This proclamation was torn down by Edward Nugent Meredyth Martin late of the Irish Lancers then of the Imperial Yeomanry from the doors of the Post Office in 1916.'[11] His brother Eustace Meredyth Martin, although not recorded in *The War List*, apparently saw military service and survived the war.[12] Edward Martin was killed in action whilst supervising a digging party on 30 September 1916 in the aftermath of the Battle of Flers-Courcelette towards the end of the Somme Campaign. He was aged 35 and is buried at Peronne Road Cemetery, Maricourt, Somme, France.

1899

COOPER, **Henry Weatherly Frank**, **2nd Lieutenant** (1881–1917), 7th Battalion Royal Fusiliers.

Henry Cooper was the only son of Thomas Henry Cooper MRCS LRCP of Hampstead and his late wife Emily Eliza. He was the eldest grandson of Luke Dowel Smyth MD of Bingham, Nottinghamshire and E E Smyth, of Dunnaweil, Tunbridge Wells. He was educated at the Priory School, Bedford School, and Tonbridge School where, in January 1898, he joined the Upper Sixth and in 1899 became a school praepostor (prefect).

He won an Open Classical Scholarship at Corpus and was awarded at the 1899 Tonbridge Summer Examination, the Latin Prose and English Essay Prizes and the first Judd Leaving Exhibition of £80.

---

11. Although this event has been recorded by several sources, current research has failed to identify the museum in which this artifact is held.

12. Nor have any papers relating to military service been located at TNA.

During his time at the College, he was active in the Corpus Debating Society, first as Secretary and subsequently Vice-President. In 1902, he graduated with a BA in the Classical Tripos. He then spent two years with the Indian Civil Service and when he did not achieve the success he was seeking, went to the Lycée de Carnot at Dijon where in July 1905 he took a diploma in French. His Tonbridge obituary says of him:

> He was a man of great ability and very considerable linguistic powers, and, thanks to his period of study at Dijon, his knowledge of French was so sound that he was able, we are told, to pass himself off as a Frenchman. He was no athlete in the strict sense of the term but had a passion for rock climbing and Alpine work generally, and when war broke out was on a climbing expedition in the Pennine Alps.

Between 1905 and 1916, he held several positions as a schoolmaster at Boxgrove School, Guildford, Sedbergh School, St Ronan's, West Worthing, Ovingdean Hall, and finally Stoke House, Guildford. He had decided to establish his own preparatory school when war broke out.

In May 1916, he enlisted in a Public Schools Battalion, passed into an officer cadet unit the following November, and was gazetted on 1 March 1917. He joined the 7th Battalion Royal Fusiliers at Dover and on 12 April left for France. The Arras Offensive began three days earlier and the Battalion was quickly engaged. On 29 April 1917 in fighting near Arras, he received a severe wound to the chest and died the same day, aged 36. Henry Cooper was buried at Duisans British Cemetery, Etrun, Pas de Calais, France, and the personal inscription on his gravestone reads 'Soon, soon to faithful warriors comes the rest Alleluia' (a line from the hymn *For all the Saints, who from their labours rest* by William Walsham How). He is commemorated on the Cooper family grave and memorial in St John's Church, Hampstead in the following terms: 'In Memory of Henry Weatherley Cooper BA Camb 2nd Lieut Royal Fusiliers Who for King and Country Was Wounded And Fell Asleep April 29th, 1917, Aged 36.'

LEEKE, Henry Alan, Lieutenant (1880–1915), D Company 9th Battalion Royal Warwickshire Regiment.

Henry Leeke was the only surviving son of Henry (1846–1922) (m.1865, Trinity) and Catharine Herbert née Fullerton of Seaford, Sussex; the couple had six other children and at the time of his death the family were living at Leamington. He is described on the Commonwealth War Grave Commission site as 'A well-known athlete in field events at Cambridge.' Henry Leeke's grandfather, the Reverend William Leeke (m.1826, Queens') of Holbrooke Hall, Derbyshire was a Battle of Waterloo historian and at 17 the youngest ensign at Waterloo.

Henry Alan Leeke was born on 15 November 1879 at Weston Hall, Stafford, the son of a pioneering British hammer and shot put athlete who was an Athletics Blue for the hammer in the years 1868 and 1869 and, between 1868 and

1872, three times Amateur Athletic Club champion.

Henry was educated at Leamington College and matriculated into Corpus in 1899. During his time at the College, he was a member of the Chess Club, the Boat Club, and the College Debating Society; in 1900, he spoke in favour of physical education in a paper entitled: 'The importance of physical training to all on the verge of manhood'. He rowed at four in the 1899 Michaelmas and 1900 Lent boats, and in 1901, trialled for the University. According to *The Benedict* (Lent Term 1900), the 6 feet 4½ inches 'Leeke rowed hard, but has not had time to learn all the intricacies of rowing; should make a useful oar in time, when he has learned to use his weight and great length of body, and to sit up.' In the Michaelmas Term 1900, rowing at six and weighing in at an impressive 13 stone 8 pounds he tried, according to *The Benedict*, 'hard at times and then rowed an excellent blade; he must learn to pick his body up more smartly off the stretcher and watch the time more carefully'. He also played rugby: 'Leeke (forward) tackles fairly successfully, but has not learnt how to accommodate his length to the requirement of the "scrum"'. The following year, his training diet was described as 'beef (cold), ginger beer, savoury omelettes and old port'. A *Leamington Spa Courier* obituary said he was 'a man of magnificent physique'. With these credentials, Henry Leeke won several Athletics Blues in the shot and hammer, winning both events in 1903.

After Corpus, Henry continued his athletics career, winning the 1906 Amateur Athletic Association hammer. He came second in the shot on three occasions between 1903 and 1910 and was English Amateur Champion for both events. He was also associated with the London Athletic Club. Henry was one of the first British athletes to take up the discus and he set a British record in 1908. At the 1908 Olympic trials, Leeke won the freestyle javelin with a throw of 135 feet 8½ inches (41.37 metres), but as the method used is not known, this mark was never recognised as a UK record.

Henry Leeke participated in the 1908 London, White City Olympic Games, competing in six different throwing events: the shot put, the discus, the Greek discus, the freestyle javelin, the javelin, and the hammer. However, he did not make the finals in any of these competitions and his ranking is unknown.

Also in 1908, he married Catherine Herbert née Fullerton of Thrybergh Park, Yorkshire. They had two children and resided in Hill, Leamington, Warwickshire. Pre-war, Henry was active in local affairs as a churchwarden, a local councillor, and a member of the Board of Guardians.

In September 1914, Henry Leeke was commissioned into the 9th Battalion Royal Warwickshire Regiment and became a machine gun officer for D Company. However, while serving in France he was taken ill and returned to England where he died on 29 May 1915 of meningitis in the Thornhill Isolation Hospital, Aldershot, aged 35. According to the *Leamington Spa Courier*, he had joined the armed forces: 'because he felt it his duty to go and set the example to others: as truly as any man dies on the battlefield Mr Leeke gave his life for his country'. In a 5 June 1915 obituary in both the *Cambridge Review* and the *Derbyshire Advertiser and Journal* a contemporary noted: 'He was immediately popular at Cambridge and in his regiment, and also in the neighbourhood of Hill, near Rugby, where he lived and did useful public work.' The *Leamington Spa Courier* noted the comments of a fellow officer, Captain Duncan Coates, who observed: 'He was the finest, straightest and best of Englishmen. Having everything to lose he willingly gave his life for his country. Every man in the Battalion loved and honoured him.' The 1901 *Benedict* biography concluded: 'His geniality is all pervading, and his dignity unimpeachable; like Chaucer, when he walks alone he walks swiftly, and though he has a career behind him that might suffice for a decently ambitious man, his friends foresee that he is one who has a still more distinguished position before him.'

Henry Leeke was buried in Aldershot military cemetery. TNA have officer files WO 339/20522 and WO 372/12/50489 together with a medal card WO 372/12/50489.

The grave of Henry Leeke in Aldershot military cemetery.

1900

BULLOCK, Gervase Frederic, 2nd Lieutenant (1881–1917), 11th Battalion South Wales Borderers.

Gervase Bullock was the son of Minnie Bullock née Weir of Ealing, London and the late Frederic D'Olbert Bullock LLB, a former sessions judge with the Bombay Civil Service.

Gervase was born in Punjab, India on 24 March 1881 and educated first at Temple Grove School, East Sheen, London and then, between 1895 and 1900, at Malvern College where he gained a scholarship and was head of School House. He was variously in Lower V-Remove, a minor scholar, a school prefect, and finally head of house. A sportsman, he played in the football XI, shooting VIII, and cricket XI. He was also a Lieutenant in the Volunteers.

Gervase matriculated into Corpus in 1900 and continued to play football as *The Benedict* (Michaelmas Term 1900) reported: 'Bullock in the centre has kept the forwards well together and has shot consistently well.' In Lent 1901, he trialled for the University team, though the critical eye of *The Benedict* noted he was 'A dangerous forward on his day, having plenty of pace and shooting power. Keeps the wings well together, but occasionally has an off-day as regards shooting.' He also played lawn tennis and graduated with a BA in 1903.

The November 1917 *Malvernian* obituary contains the following information. He was in Ceylon (now Sri Lanka) when war was declared and came home to join the Inns of Court OTC as a Private. In January 1916, he was commissioned in the South Wales Borderers and went to the front in the following June. Gervase was killed in action on 31 July 1917 at Pilkem Ridge, on the first day of the 3rd Battle of Ypres, known as Passchendaele, aged 35. A brother officer wrote of him:

> He was killed instantly by a sniper. He was in charge of the company at the time, and by his gallantry and coolness won the admiration of everyone. He was very highly esteemed by all, and his men positively loved him, and would have followed him anywhere. He died doing his duty nobly and well, as he had always done. I never knew him do a mean or ungentlemanly thing. He was a delightful friend and companion … He was a thorough sportsman; it was the very essence of his character.

He has no known grave and is commemorated at the Ypres (Menin Gate) Memorial, West-Vlaanderen, Belgium. A contemporary family death notice concluded: 'how can man die better' (a line from Thomas Babington Macauley's 1842 collection of narrative poems *Lays of Ancient Rome*).

1901

HANNA, John Henry, 2nd Lieutenant (1884–1917), 19th St Pancras Battalion London Regiment (Prince of Wales's Own Civil Service Rifles).

John Henry Hanna was born on 18 July 1884 in Whitehaven, Cumberland (now Cumbria), the son of William Hanna, a schoolmaster. He attended St Bees School, Cumberland before matriculating into Corpus in 1901.

During his time at the College, he was a Classics Scholar, a Bishop Green Cup winner and the holder of other prizes including the Latin Declamation Cup. In his final year, he was student sub-librarian. John was also a sportsman, rowing and playing rugby for the College. *The Benedict* (Michaelmas Term 1901) noted: 'J H Hanna rowed at 2 (8 stone 8 pounds) in trials.' The following year it reported: 'J H Hanna (three-quarter-back) knows the game well and plays with judgement and pluck: a neat kick and a good tackler.' The Michaelmas Term 1903 edition commented: 'J. H. Hanna, at back, tackles excellently and stops rushes well; is rather uncertain about his kick, and must learn to pick up the ball more neatly and quicker.' John graduated with a BA in June 1904.

In the 1911 census, John was a single man aged 28 living in Watford, Hertfordshire, and working as Classics master at Watford Grammar School. According to the St Bees Roll of Honour he enlisted in 1914, served as a non-commissioned officer and was wounded. In June 1917 he was commissioned 2nd Lieutenant with the 19th Battalion London Regiment and was killed in the action at the Menin Road during 3rd Battle of Ypres, known as Passchendaele, on 20 September 1917, aged 33.

He has no known grave and is commemorated on the Ypres (Menin Gate) Memorial, West-Vlaanderen, Belgium. He is also commemorated on war memorials in St Chad's, Ladybarn, Greater Manchester, Faringdon (the old Town Hall), Oxfordshire and St Bees School, St Bees, Copeland, Cumbria. TNA have an officer file WO 374/30763 and a medal card WO 372/8/247336.

1902

SMITH, Reginald George, Captain (1883–1917) (Bury and *The Benedict* have his name as George Reginald, but his Canadian officer file shows he was Reginald George Smith and a letter to his mother (also in the file) is signed Reg, the Commonwealth War Graves Commission also has Reginald George as does his

gravestone), 47th Battalion 10th Infantry Brigade, 4th Canadian Division. Formerly 77th Battalion Infantry Western Ontario Regiment, Canadian Expeditionary Force.

Reginald George Smith was born at The Crockleys, Marsten, Tortworth, Charfield, Gloucestershire on 2 November 1883, the son of Sarah Ann and Daniel Smith, a farmer. He attended Wotton-under-Edge Grammar School (now Katharine Lady Berkeley's School) and matriculated into Corpus in 1902. Reginald's student life, his love of sport and the countryside featured in *The Benedict* (Lent Term 1905). In a whimsical piece, the writer noted:

> On a horse, with a spaniel, with a gun, with a rifle or a trout-rod he is a familiar figure in all that countryside; away from it confined to a Grantchester grind he still gives play to his sporting instincts in a way-side mouse hunt or in a pursuit of the wily roach with a walking stick; even the daws and starlings on the sacred walls of Bene'ts – what, why, clatter and whistle when they see him leaning pensively out of his window after a Sunday 'Brunch'.

At Corpus, Reginald read the Classical Tripos, though he evidently did little by way of scholarship. Instead, he became a founder member of the Honest Cods, a drinking society created by Llewelyn Powys (m.1903) and active between 1904 and 1907. As if to make up for the work deficit, George was a noted all-round sportsman; he also played billiards and won the high jump in the College Sports against Keble College, Oxford. He was awarded a cap for cricket and colours for soccer. Of the latter, *The Benedict* (Michaelmas Term 1903) noted: 'G. R. Smith (Centre Half) has had a difficult place to fill but has done so with credit to himself. Uses his weight well but is too fond of shots from the halfway line. Tackles and passes well though rather slow.' He was a member of several College clubs and societies, including the Chess Club, the Corpus bridge four and the choir. Unusually, one November day he figured in the Cambridge Police Courts where he was fined for discharging a firework on Parker's Piece! Reginald's interests were eclectic; for example, he was present at the famous ghostly 'séance' in Old Court during the Michaelmas Term 1904 at which, as *The Benedict* observed: 'he looked with the calm eyes of a man, who is willing to believe what he sees; and it did not concern him much that he saw nothing'. For more on this episode, see Bury, pp. 105–7.

Reginald Smith's great love was the river, and as a member of the Corpus Boat Club he excelled as an athlete. He obtained Lent and May colours in his second year and was Second Boat Captain in his final year. His rowing career is

chronicled in the Boat Club minute book. He weighted 11 stone 8 pounds (he was also, according to his Canadian officer file, 6 feet 2½ inches), rowed at six in the 1904 May boat and bow in the November 1904 first scratch fours (Ronald Edward Wilson (see below) rowed two), coaching the losing trial eight in December of that year. Reginald stroked the famously successful 1905 Corpus Lent First Boat that, on day one, over-bumped Selwyn at the Pike & Eel; on day two, bumped Emma II; and on day three, 'the crew accomplished a most remarkable feat, by going up four places in one night'. In fact, the boat overbumped First Trinity III to become the sandwich boat and went up very fast on the Lady Margaret Boat Club (known as LMBC) II. On the fourth day, they 'got a splendid start', bumping Trinity Hall II in twenty-three strokes. *The Benedict* portrait explained this crowning achievement: 'he stroked the Corpus Lent boat [1905], which achieved the phenomenal feat of gaining nine places in four nights' racing'. This remarkable success took the Boat Club into the First Division.

In the 1905 May bumps, *The Benedict* described his rowing as: 'a powerful oar with good reach'. Reginald Smith also stroked the Henley boat that year. The affectionate *Benedict* portrait concluded with several ironic and prescient observations:

> Taking his stand upon a modified hedonism he is ready to face the slings and arrows and other missiles of misfortune with a calm fortitude. He never sits on the fence – though he is acquainted with railings! – and never changes his colours – though his colour changes sometimes at – what? whom? why, at times. His social proclivities are strong (his winter vacation being one long string of dances, 'walking outs' and parties). He takes an interest in literature and in athletics. But as the constellation of Ursa Major never sets in the heavens, so in his broad nature there ever stands out clear and steadfast a love of the outdoor world, a devotion to animals and a power of fraternising with all true children of nature.

He graduated with a BA on 17 June 1905 and emigrated to Canada where he became a schoolmaster at Ashbury College, Ottawa. In 1909, he joined the Canadian Civil Service, eventually becoming Private Secretary to the Minister of Labour. In 1914, he was appointed Secretary of the Canadian General Council of Boy Scouts.

On 11 February 1916, Reginald Smith was commissioned 2nd Lieutenant in the 77th Battalion Western Ontario Regiment, Canadian Expeditionary Force and on 19 June 1916, embarked from Halifax on the SS *Missanabe* bound for England. On 27 July 1916, he wrote in a detailed letter to his mother (a typescript is with his officer file) from the Canadian military base at Bramshott, Hampshire:

> Things look very much like business here and we can look to getting to the
> front very soon. Everyone is anxious to go – doubtless the time will come
> when we shall be anxious to return. There will be a great reunion when we do
> get back and in spite of all procostications [*sic*] I think we shall 'Carry on' in
> much the same old way. The world will be, generally speaking, much more
> broadminded which will be conducive to a general betterment of conditions.

Reginald went with his unit on active service in France and on 13 October
1916 at Courcelette was wounded in his right wrist but remained on duty. On 10
November, he received a shrapnel wound to his right thigh and a bullet wound
to his forearm. Consequently, Reginald was hospitalised first in Rouen then
Bristol. At the end of January 1917, after home leave with his family, he was passed
fit for active service. Reginald George Smith was promoted Lieutenant on 7
April 1917 (a note on his file shows he was subsequently made Acting Captain).
Between 9 and 12 April 1917, he saw action in and survived the murderous Battle
of Vimy Ridge but was killed in action during the Battle of Arras on 5 May
1917, aged 33. His Captain wrote that he had: 'just been recommended for his
captaincy, and a better officer it would be impossible to find'.

The 1905 portrait of Reginald concluded: 'He will if fates are kind and let
him walk in the paths the gods have placed before him, spend his life unfettered
faithful to the brook, the uplands and the woods: and free "to wonder the quiet
fields along" or "listen to the team-horse jangling", pleasure unto his soul, that
ever comes with a gentle freshness.' Alas, the fates were not kind, but the final
assessment of this remarkable undergraduate sums him up perfectly: 'And that
you know his character full, well I will tell you one thing further: he is an Honest
Cod.'

Reginald George Smith was buried at
Villers Station Cemetery, Villers-Au-Bois,
Pas de Calais, France. He is commemorated
on the Roll of Honour in St Leonard's
Church Tortworth and on a memorial cross
in the churchyard. There is a Canadian officer
file available online at www.central.bac-lac.
gc.ca/.item/?op=pdf&app=CEF&id=
B9093-S055.

The grave of Captain Reginald George Smith.

1904

DYER, **Harry Frank**, **2nd Lieutenant** (1886–1917), 1/6th Battalion Duke of Wellington's (West Riding) Regiment.

Harry Dyer was born in Bridgnorth, Shropshire on 25 June 1886, the son of the Reverend William John and Emma Dyer née Ward, of New Barnet, Hertfordshire. Unusual for a Corpus man, his father was a Baptist minister.

The 1891 and 1901 censuses have the family living at Bridgnorth, Shropshire. He attended Bridgnorth Grammar School (now Bridgnorth Endowed School), matriculated into Corpus in 1904 to read the Mathematical Tripos and graduated with a BA on 17 June 1907. At Corpus, he was a Mawson Scholar (First Senior Optime, 1907) and a book Prizeman. He was also a member of the Boat Club and coxed the winning crew in the 1905 trial eight; he also coxed the Corpus second eight (which was coached by Ronald Wilson – see below) in the 1906 May bumps.

In 1908, Harry became a junior mathematics master at Cardiff High School for Boys (now part of the comprehensive Cardiff High School) and whilst at the school played cricket for the XI. In 1911, he was sharing lodgings at Roath, Cardiff with fellow master, Owen Jardine Hobbs (a graduate of Merton College, Oxford, later Sub-Lieutenant RNVR. He was killed in action in 1916). Harry remained at the High School for six years until, in May 1914, he became mathematics master at Giggleswick School, Yorkshire. At Giggleswick, in the words of the headmaster: 'by his keen and conscientious discharge of his duties, his thorough understanding of boys, and his affection for them, his delightful sense of humour, and his high standard of life, he made himself a home in the hearts of all in the School'. He was also an officer in the Giggleswick OTC. In the spring of 1916, despite previous rejections because of poor eyesight, Harry was commissioned in the Duke of Wellington's (West Riding) Regiment and went to France in November that year.

On 8 September 1917, the *Bridgnorth Journal* published an obituary from which the following is extracted:

> We have to report the death of Second Lieut H F Dyer, of the Duke of Wellington's West Riding Regiment, second son of Reverend W J and Mrs Dyer, late of Bridgnorth, now residing at New Barnet, Herts.

Mr Dyer died on August 28th, at No. 7 Stationary Hospital, Boulogne, from wounds received in action on August 8th. He had laid the guiding tape for his men, preparatory to a raid, and was returning to the trench when he was severely wounded in the upper part of the right arm by a bullet at short range. The artery was severed and the bone smashed, but at first it was hoped the arm would be saved. However, amputation became necessary about a fortnight later, and though the operation so far was successful, loss of blood and extreme weakness disabled him from throwing off the septic poison in his system, and this was the cause of his death.

His mother and father were with him at the end, having crossed over to see him ten days before, when he was reported to be dangerously ill, and their visit was of much comfort to him. He was buried in Boulogne Cemetery, in the plot given by France for British officers and men, the last resting-place of so many who already have made the supreme sacrifice for their country and its cause.

After his death, his Commanding Officer wrote of him as: 'one of my best Officers, and the Captain of his Company gave unstinting testimony to his loyalty and courage, his quiet cheeriness, and the esteem in which he was held by the men under his command, his sterling worth and character, marking him out for future distinction if his life had been spared.' Harry Dyer is buried at Boulogne Eastern Cemetery, Pas de Calais, France. The personal inscription on his gravestone reads: 'I thank my God on all my remembrance of you from death unto life' (Philippians 1:3). He is commemorated on the Bridgnorth and Bridgnorth Grammar School war memorials. TNA have an officer file WO 374/21544 and a medal card WO 372/6/135429. See also: Stephen Barber, *Guiseley Terriers: A Small Part in The Great War – A History of the 1/6th Battalion, Duke of Wellington's (West Riding) Regiment* (2018).

OKE, Robert William Leslie, Captain (1884–1915), 3rd Battalion (attached to the 6th) (Princess Charlotte of Wales's) Royal Berkshire Regiment.

Robert Oke was born on 12 February 1884 in Gypsy Hill, Upper Norwood, London, one of five children and the only son of Alfred William Oke (1860–1944) a solicitor and Catherine Coldcall née Unwin (1867–1935). The family produced several prominent figures in Southampton where Robert's father was in practice; Robert's great grandfather had been mayor, a magistrate, and a merchant in that city. Robert was educated first at Highfield School, Southampton, then at Sherborne, and finally at Rugby. In 1902, he came up to

Cambridge, matriculating into Gonville and Caius College as a pensioner. He remained in residence for just one term and went down suffering rheumatic fever. In 1904, he returned, transferring to Corpus. During his time at the College, he studied both the Natural Sciences and the Historical Triposes. He was a friend and contemporary of Llewelyn Powys and, doing little by way of work, the two enjoyed their years at the College. He was a member and later Secretary of the Honest Cods (a College drinking society created by Powys) and the Chess Club. He played rugby for the College, of which *The Benedict* (Michaelmas Term 1906) said he was: 'The heaviest man in the team, uses his strength very well, and seldom misses his man. Rather slow but played splendidly against Oriel.' In 1906, he was awarded a Boxing Half Blue, representing the University in the heavy-weight division. In that same year, he was gazetted as 2nd Lieutenant in the University Volunteer Rifle Corps. *The Benedict* published an article about Robert which in its usual whimsical manner said of him:

> He is a man of many parts: he is a weight putter as well as a boxer; he has played cricket, where he fields with characteristic agility at point; he plays golf and tennis, and has rowed in the Scratch Fours ... He is fond of dogs, and has a nice terrier, which he often exercises by riding with it on his bicycle around Grantchester.

It goes on:

> [He is] very burly, very genial, you will know him as he comes into the court by his natty little moustache and his 'hullo guv'nor. How's the world treating you?' If he is training for a boxing match, avoid him; he spends his time practising knockout blows! If his smile, his cheery greeting and well-cut clothes have not fascinated you, you will be knocked all of a heap by his wealth of curly hair.

Robert graduated in June 1907 (MA 1912). After Corpus, he became a medical student first at the Hartley University College (now part of Southampton University) and subsequently at the London Hospital; the 1911 census describes him as a medical student living at 32 Denmark Villas, Hove with his parents and two of his sisters. In these immediate post-Corpus years, he also travelled in Canada and South America.

In 1912, Robert married Marjorie de Landulph née Sprye (b.1888); there do not appear to have been any children, nor does he appear to have completed his medical studies.

Nine months before the outbreak of war, Robert joined the 3rd Reserve Battalion Royal Berkshire Regiment and was promoted Lieutenant in December 1914. He arrived at the front just after the first Battle of Ypres and took part in the famous 1914 Christmas Truce. On 1 March 1915, Robert was invalided home with gastric flu and jaundice. Promoted Captain, he re-joined his regiment in July 1915. Thereafter, he remained on active service until he was killed in action. At the time, he was taking part in a secondary action: 'to capture about 1200 yards of the German front line system … thereby both shortening and strengthening the British position'. The attack had been prefaced by a four-day bombardment and the history of the 8th Division records:

> Three companies of 2nd Battalion Royal Berkshire Regiment attacked through the centre. One company was picked up in a searchlight and came under fire while forming up. The attack was also successful in capturing the front line, as was the effort of two companies of the 2nd Battalion Lincolnshire Regiment on the left. The one problem was a 200-yard section of trench between the Rifle Brigade and Berkshire companies that remained in German hands. It was linked to a communication trench through which the Germans could funnel forward counterattack troops. The Berkshires were ordered back when they came under heavy pressure. They did not reach the German lines and the centre gave way under the German assault.

His school obituary states that Robert: 'was leading his Company into action when he received a bullet wound in the shoulder, but still went on till he was killed'.

The *Reading Mercury* has an account of his death:

> in attacking the German trenches at dawn and taking them, Captain Oke was hit three times and his orderly was wounded whilst trying to dress his wounds. His colonel wrote of him 'He fell like the gallant soldier he was, leading his men, many of whom also fell with him … I do not know how to replace him. He had so much influence with the men. They fought splendidly for the rest of the day and showed a fine example.' A brother Officer wrote: 'We shall all miss dear old Oke more than any other Officer in the Battalion, and we have lost many. There was not a shadow of doubt about it, nobody disputed it, he was the best Company Commander in the Battalion. I tried many times to get into his Company and serve under him, but I was never lucky enough to get it.'

This echoes his *Benedict* profile, which asserts: 'He is an excellent fellow, good company and one of the best of good sorts.'

Robert Oke was killed in action on 25 September 1915 at Bois Grenier, Armentières, France aged 31 and has no known grave. He is commemorated on the Ploegstreet Memorial, Hainault, Belgium and at All Saints Church, Hove, East Sussex. Robert's name also appears on the Gonville and Caius war memorial and on the family tomb in Southampton.

An Oke family photo album is preserved in the College Archives. TNA have an officer file 339/9492 and a medal card WO 372/15/47787.

Robert Oke album CCCC Archives

Robert Oke and his wife Marjorie, and Oke the countryman both *c.*1912.

WILSON, Ronald Edward, 2nd Lieutenant (1885–1916), Bombay Volunteer Rifles attached to the Volunteer Maxim Machine Gun Company.

Ronald Wilson was born in Saltburn, Yorkshire on 8 May 1885, the son of Samuel Robert Shaw an HM Inspector of Schools and Annie née Binns. He attended Heath Grammar School (now Crossley Heath School) Halifax until 1900, then King William's College, Isle of Man.

Ronald matriculated into Corpus in 1904 with an Entrance Scholarship to read the Mathematical Tripos; he was later a College Prizeman. As a finalist, he changed subjects to the Mechanical Sciences with a view to training as a civil engineer. He was a member of several College societies and clubs including the Gravediggers, the Chess Club, the Rugby Club, and the Boat Club. He rowed at three in the 1905 Lent boat, bumping every day and rising from 22nd to 18th (for an account of this, see Reginald George Smith above). In 1906, Ronald and Reginald coached the second Lent boat and with Arthur Gillibrand (m.1904) won the Rowlandson pairs. That same year he rowed at two in the Corpus first May eight. On the first day, they bumped Pembroke II. On the second, they bumped Clare I, and on the third, Sidney. This made them the sandwich boat and they rowed over twice. As a result, Ronald won oars in both the Lent and May races and the crew went on to compete at Henley that year. *The Benedict* (Michaelmas Term 1906) said of his rowing: '[He] rowed hard throughout; should learn to control his slide better; held it out well.' The same edition remarked of his rugby prowess: 'A keen and plucky forward, fair

tackler and very useful in defence and saving forward rushes. Has been known to kick with his left foot but should still practise it.' In 1907, he stroked the second Lent boat and was also a member of the Henley boat; *The Benedict* (Michaelmas Term 1907) said of his rowing: 'A hard worker and backed up stroke well, should get his hands out quicker, is light at finish of stroke.' Ronald graduated in June 1907.

The Institution of Civil Engineers and King William's College, Isle of Man have online obituaries from which the following has been derived. Ronald Wilson was elected an Associate Member of the Institution of Civil Engineers on 3 December 1912. That same year, after gaining practical experience at the Royal Small Arms Factory, Enfield and serving with the North East Railway, both in the Dock and on the permanent-way staff, Ronald was appointed an assistant engineer with the Bombay Port Trust. On the outbreak of war, he joined the Bombay Volunteer Rifles as a Private, later promoted to Sergeant. He received a commission in December 1915. Ronald's regiment served in the East Africa theatre of operations. In a letter held at King William's College, Isle of Man he wrote:

> In September I heard of the formation of the Volunteer Maxim Gun Company (in Bombay [now Mumbai]) so enlisted as a Private. We had four guns each double manned (18 men) and the men were drawn from all over India. Bombay supplied the crew for one gun.
>
>
>
> Indian Volunteers Maxim Gun Company East Africa
>
> Four days later we embarked on a small steamer [the MT *Bandra*] of some 2,000 tons. We were hopelessly overcrowded and we lived like pigs – and ate food fit for them too. This on a voyage across the Equator! After a fortnight we arrived at Mombasa in British East Africa, and next day one half of the company with some 350 Indian troops were put on a steamer, about the size of our LCC boats, to go down the coast.
>
> We towed three barges behind and as it was rough the tow ropes kept breaking; also it rained hard so we got little rest, and our voyage of thirty miles took us as many hours.
>
> We disembarked in the barge at 1 a.m. and were all on shore at 4.30 a.m. with our kit. Daylight showed us that we were in a swamp, so we marched through it to the Camp about a mile away. Here we found about 400 Native troops entrenched, so our half company was the only white unit there. We found quarters in a tin coolie shed.

This post was about halfway between Mombasa and the border and was the only force that barred the Germans advance on the latter place, hence its importance. It was in the middle of a rubber plantation and the grass was seven or eight feet high all-round the Camp.

We turned in early, dog-tired, but at 8 p.m. the general alarm went and we had to parade in full fighting kit. Nothing further happened so we slept – and slept well – in the open with our bayonets fixed. Next morning the expected attack developed and there was a very hot fire for about an hour, but the grass hid the enemy effectively within 100 yards of our trenches. Finally they departed and our men tried a bayonet charge but couldn't get up with them.

Our casualties were light being thirteen all told, but the Germans were hard hit for we found fifty dead and no end of equipment etc thrown away in their retreat. Probably they had 200 casualties as one allows a proportion of three to one. Unfortunately our force was in no condition to follow up effectually, for over half of it had only disembarked the day before, after being cooped up on board ship for over a fortnight, and having had no sleep for two or three nights.

After that we spent two months in the continuous moist, sticky heat of the coast. We had various camps but always found thick jungle and mangrove swamps everywhere. At night we could hear the hippos grunting in the swamps, but I never saw one. The only roads were jungle tracks and our transport was hundreds of porters carrying 40lbs. apiece. Horses and oxen cannot live there owing to the Tsetse fly. We had plagues of mosquitoes nightly and got fever, drank swamp water (our only source in most Camps) and got dysentery: sandflies bit us by day and ants devoured us all the time. In some Camps we had bees and wasps, and everywhere scorpions and snakes.

Our patrols were usually in touch but we had no general action for our game (being the weaker force) was a waiting one and the enemy didn't seem inclined to trouble us again after the previous nasty knock. Our sole satisfaction was that we sat on the only road they could follow, and Mombasa was safe.

At the end of two months we got our move and the day before only had three men of our original eighteen fit for duty. All the rest were down with something and most of them were in the base hospital.  We travelled up country and after three days reached the base Camp. The journey alone deserves a letter, but I have no space here to describe it. Suffice it that the game seen from the train was wonderful, our chief joy being zebras and giraffes.

At an altitude of about 5,500 feet we quickly began to recover our health. I had been one of the few lucky ones on the coast, but now I went down with fever and spent Christmas in Hospital. Still the rest did me good and I came out feeling quite fit. We all went mad when we arrived here and spent much money on hotel dinners, cinematographs and the like. You see we had been away from civilisation for nearly three months.

Halfway through January we got orders to move in two hours and were rushed down to the coast once more and embarked on a transport. This time we disembarked on the frontier and found quite a large force already assembled. The situation seemed most promising for the enemy's Camp was only three miles away, but nothing happened except outpost actions and frequent alarms. After three weeks of this the force was brought back to the original Camp up country and here we are still.

I got another go of fever a fortnight after our return and spent a week in Hospital, after which I was sent to a Convalescent Home run by Lady [Zellie] Colvile for the troops [Ronald Wilson was unconscious with enteric fever (typhoid) for a month and then went to Lady Colvile's Convalescent Home in Nairobi where he remained for some weeks]. Here I am at present and enjoying the change tremendously. After six months lack of decencies of life, one can thoroughly appreciate excellent food, beds and, last but not least, hot baths.

Of the original eighteen men in our section, two are dead, one has gone mad, and two more are to be invalided. With one exception the rest of us have all had fever or dysentery several times. I mention this to show that although we don't get a great deal of fighting and are not getting frostbite, yet we still have our little troubles and are having our share of discomforts.

An account of his death is contained in a letter written by a brother officer to a mutual friend in Bombay (known today as Mumbai) a copy of which is also held at King William's College:

I feel certain you would want to hear first-hand how poor old Wilson carried on to the time he met his death in the last big fight we had on the border.

Moving out to the attack at 12.30 pm under a most trying sun, we crossed about three miles unmolested and then quite suddenly a furore of machine guns and rifles opened. We soon had all eight guns up in the firing line, Wilson's two being on my left, and we spoke together several times. My sergeant after about an hour got it in the back by a sniper and had to retire; we kept on rushing forward for short distances, when [Captain F N] James came.

I hardly need say that Wilson on every occasion had shown the utmost gallantry and entire disregard of self under the most trying conditions, and, on the day he was hit, his men on several occasions begged him to get down, but he went on calmly surveying the horizon for targets, snipers all around him popping at him, and the Hun machine guns making the devil's own tattoo from front and flank. Meanwhile, the gap in the mess will remain unfilled – he was such a dear cheery fellow. The position was captured.

Ronald Wilson was killed in action during the Battle of Latema Nek (in present-day Tanzania) on 13 March 1916 aged 31 and buried at Taveta military cemetery, Kenya.

Following its extraordinary success on the river, the 1905 Corpus Lent boat celebrate winning blades. They bumped up nine places taking the Boat Club into the First Division.

The crew was: bow, G. N. Graburn (m.1903)*; 2, F E Hodder (m.1902)*; 3, R E Wilson (m.1904); 4, A G Dare (m.1902); 5, C C Evans (m.1903)*; 6, K M Kemp (m.1903)*; 7, T Batterby (m.1904); stroke, R G Smith (m.1902)*; cox, F L I Bridges (m.1904). Six out of the nine crew members are known to have served in the war and of these Reginald George Smith and Ronald Edward Wilson were killed in action and Godfrey Noel Graburn was wounded twice. Five of the crew (marked with *) were members of the Honest Cods drinking society and Robert Oke and Llewelyn Powys (Secretary and President) can be seen forming part of the bank party.

The Chess Club in Lent Term 1906.
Robert Oke and Ronald Wilson are standing next to each other, second row right end two, standing behind them is Llewelyn Powys.

1905

KNIGHT, Ernest Alexander, 2nd Lieutenant (1886–1917), 233rd Company Machine Gun Corps (Infantry).

Ernest Knight was born on 15 September 1886, the son of William Knight (1852–1936) a stone merchant and Elizabeth née Peters (1849–1920) in Brockley, London. He was baptised on 9 January 1890 at St Paul's, Deptford (his brother and sister Norman and Rhoda were baptised on the same day). He attended the City of London School as a scholar before matriculating into Corpus with a Classical Scholarship. As an undergraduate, Ernest was awarded many academic prizes; in 1906 it was a book prize, the following year he became a Mawson Scholar and was awarded a Classics Prize Cup. He also contributed to the intellectual and sporting life of the College and was a founder member of the College Classical Society; in 1907, he gave a paper entitled 'The Greek Games'. He was also a member of several other College societies and clubs and was Secretary of both the Chess Club and the Staunton Club (which really did play chess). An all-round sportsman, he was Secretary of the Football Club. Of his playing, *The Benedict* (Michaelmas Term 1906) said: 'Knight and Mainwaring [see below] have played well together on the left wing but the latter centres wildly'. As a member of the College hockey team, it said: 'Knight (right half) [is] a useful and hard working half, but one who must get out of the habit of running behind or alongside his man instead of trying to hook his stick or get the ball.' And as a rugby player he: 'has taken to wing-three kindly. Fields the ball well and has often saved by good kicking'. However, it was as a cricketer that he excelled, becoming Captain of the cricket XI. *The Benedict* (Easter Term 1906) said of his form: 'A good sound bat especially on the leg side, and a most useful slow bowler. New to the team but quite invaluable. Has just a tendency at times to underpitch his bowling.' His batting average was 24.72 and 20.6 in bowling. Ernest was cited in *Wisden Cricketers' Almanack* 1917 obituaries as a player with Bishop's Stortford Cricket Club.

Ernest graduated in June 1908 (MA 1912) and became a master at Bishop's Stortford College, where he taught Classics until 1916. Soon after war was declared, he was commissioned 2nd Lieutenant with the 233rd Company Machine Gun Corps (Infantry), which joined the 3rd Division in July 1917. Between 20 and 25 September 1917, it was in action during the Battle of the Menin Road Ridge, part of the third British general attack of the 3rd Battle of Ypres known as Passchendaele. It was during this action, on 24 September 1917, that Ernest was posted missing presumed killed in action, aged 31. His body was neither recovered nor identified and his name is included amongst 35,000 others on the Tyne Cot Memorial near Ieper (Ypres), West-Vlaanderen, Belgium. His father received £51.8s.4d in pay owing and was granted probate in London on 1 December 1917 with effects valued at £359.15s.3d. TNA have an officer file WO 339/126062 and a medal card WO 372/11/197006.

Bishop's Stortford College

In 1920, Ernest Knight's parents commissioned three pairs of carved oak doors that form part of the Bishop's Stortford College Memorial Hall. They memorialise Ernest's strong association with Corpus and to that end each is emblazoned with the symbol of Corpus Christi, the pelican feeding its young with blood from its breast. In 2012, the doors underwent restoration and now look as they did when the Hall was opened.

1906

JAMES, Eric Samuel Pennant Kingsbury, Captain (1887–1915), 6th (Reserve) Battalion (attached to the 4th Battalion) King's Royal Rifle Corps.

Eric James was born on 4 September 1887, the only son of Sarah née Pook and Edward Lewis, a science master of Clapham, London.

Educated at Manor House School (now part of the Eaton House group of schools), Clapham and between 1901 and 1906 at St Paul's School where he was a Foundation Scholar, Eric matriculated into Corpus in 1906 with an Open Exhibition worth £20 (for two years) to read the Classical Tripos. He was also a John Stock Exhibitioner and during his time at the College the recipient of book prizes. He took Second Class Honours in the Classical Tripos, graduating in 1909 (MA 1914).

During his time at Corpus, Eric was a founder member, Secretary, and then President of the College Literary Society. He was also a member of the Chess Club. He proved an excellent oarsman, became Second Boat Captain and rowed in the 1909 Henley boat; he was also a member of the Thames Rowing Club. Of his rowing, *The Benedict* (Lent Term 1908) said he was: 'A very keen worker.' The Michaelmas Term 1909 edition reviewing the May and Henley boats in which he rowed at bow said: '[He] took some time to adapt himself to bow side, but eventually settled down and rowed a good blade'. He was known as a good rifle shot and took the Army School of Musketry course at Hythe. He visited the continent every year, was a good linguist, and after Corpus spent time studying at the University of Paris. In 1910, he became an assistant master and housemaster at Oundle School and in 1913 an assistant master at Merchant Taylors' School, where he attracted considerable attention by the success of his original methods of teaching history.[13]

In 1910, Eric was commissioned 2nd Lieutenant in the OTC (Territorial Force) (unattached list), promoted to Lieutenant on 18 October 1912 and Captain on 15 January 1914. He served in the OTC at both Oundle and Merchant Taylors'. In 1914, he was promoted Captain in the 4th Battalion King's Royal Rifle Corps (80th Brigade, 27th Division) and on 20 September 1914, six weeks after the declaration of war, Eric was gazetted as a Captain attached to 6th

---

13. Unfortunately, details of these methods seem not to have survived.

(Reserve) Battalion Kings Royal Rifle Corps. He left for France on 6 January 1915, this time attached to the 4th Battalion.

Graham Seel of St Paul's School has written:

> Captain James was killed in the trenches immediately to the east of St Eloi, a small settlement south of Ypres. His Company was involved in desperate resistance, the enemy having taken The Mound – a pile of waste material produced by a brickworks on the south side of the village. An earthwork such as The Mound offered its possessor the advantage of height and, as such, was hotly contested.

He continues,

> The situation thus remained critical. In an effort to resist the enemy, energy was expended completing the breastworks to the east of St Eloi, and it was while working on these … that Captain James was killed on 17th March, presumably by a sniper's bullet – the 27th Division HQ war diary entry recording there was 'a good deal of rifle fire, particularly during [the] night'.[14]

The *Cambridge Review* had an appreciation, written by an unnamed friend and contemporary. It reads: 'Those of us who were contemporaries of him at Corpus will hear with a deep sense of loss of the death of James … After serving for a short time with the 6th Battalion of the 60th, he was gazetted Captain to the 4th Battalion, and went out to join them in January.'

Captain Hugo Watson, then temporarily in command of the 4th Battalion King's Royal Rifle Corps, wrote:

> He was shot in the head last night, about 11.45, while standing behind a breast-work, while superintending his men at work filling sandbags. He was killed instantly. We buried him to-day in the military cemetery at Dicemberkebusch, four miles from Ypres and 2½ miles from where he was killed … I cannot tell you what a great loss he is. I was Adjutant of the 6th KRRC [King's Royal Rifle Corps] till recently when I came out here … I know what splendid work he did at Sheerness and how Colonel Brownlow depended on him. I was with him last Sunday, when we had a very nasty time; he was very cool and did admirably.

Lieutenant Colonel Brownlow, commanding the 6th Battalion, wrote: 'He did excellent work for me down here [at Sheerness], and I heard he was doing real[ly] well in France; I can only tell you your son will be very much missed in the regiment. He was most popular and looked up to by everybody and was a very smart and efficient soldier.' The 4th Battalion King's Royal Rifle Corps was

---

14. Research by Graham Seel, history master at St Paul's School, and communicated to the present author. Obituary *The Pauline*, Vol. XXIII, No. 217, June 1915.

specially mentioned in Sir John (now Lord) French's Despatch of 5 April 1915, for: 'a very gallant attack on the enemy's trenches on 2 March'.

Eric James was buried at Dickebusch (Dikkebus), new military cemetery, West-Vlaanderen, Belgium. The personal inscription on his gravestone reads 'May The Lord Of His Mercy Grant To Him Peace And Rest Amen'. His name appears on the St Paul's School and the Thames Rowing Club war memorials. TNA have an officer file WO 339/26598 and a medal card WO 372/10/192699.

MAINWARING, Cyril Lyttleton, Lieutenant (1887–1919), Royal Garrison Artillery, 422nd Siege Battery.

Cyril Mainwaring was born on 19 October 1887 in Kensington, London, the son of Alexander John Mainwaring, a newspaper correspondent and Emma née Horsepool. He was educated at the Perse School, Cambridge (he is not listed on either the Perse School Roll of Honour or war memorial, perhaps because his death occurred after the Armistice).

Cyril matriculated into Corpus in 1906 with an Entrance Scholarship of £40. He was both a Classical Scholar and the holder of a Goldsmith Exhibition and received awards of books. During his time at the College, he was a chapel clerk and helped form the Classical Society of which he was was first Secretary and then President. He is recorded as reading a paper 'The Homeric Question'. Cyril was a member of the Boat Club and at 10 stone 4 pounds rowed at seven in the Lent 1908 Second Boat. His sporting interests extended to cricket and rugby. He graduated with Second Class Honours in the 1909 Classical Tripos and subsequently became a Classics master at Oundle School, where he was also commissioned 2nd Lieutenant of the OTC.

According to an obituary in the March 1919 edition of *The Whitgiftian*, he was appointed an assistant master at Whitgift Grammar School in September 1910, again teaching Classics, and remained at the school until March 1917. It was said of him:

> Most of his contemporaries would associate him with the OTC or with the Latin Crusade; but his activities were by no means confined to these. He was a good athlete, and essentially a good all-round man. The key to character was a clear-headed rationalism; he invariably reasoned rationally, and then acted deliberately. One is almost tempted to regard him as an incarnation of the Scientific Spirit.

'Darcy's' [probably a nickname] meticulous primness was often amusing, as illustrated by the careful precision with which he lay flat close to the pavement when the Beech Avenue bomb (which he detested) nearly caught him walking along Fell Road; or the elaborate – and highly successful – preparations for the Easter camp of 1916 [of this Camp, the June 1916 *Whitgiftian* notes 'The weather was not exceptionally fine, the nights being cold and the days rainy; this no doubt was the cause of the colds from which few escaped, but which were valiantly combated by numerous doses of quinine. Capt Mainwaring was laid up with one for three days, and it was even feared that he might have been unable to resume command']. He always knew his own mind; and whatever he undertook – whether it was laying a gun or drawing up a memorandum, or slamming at bridge, he accomplished with the greatest of efficiency. Because he was always perfectly honest with himself, he could afford to be honest with others; one felt that he could be reliable and could be trusted to the hilt. But all this seems prosaically cold-blooded; if he was blessed with a first-class brain, he was also a delightful friend – and his saucy wit was softened by inexhaustible humour.

Cyril Mainwaring was the author, with Walter Lionel Paine (a graduate of Sidney Sussex who also taught Classics at Whitgift and was killed in action at Gallipoli in 1915) and Miss E Ryle, of *Decem Fábulae Pueris Puellísque Agendae: A Companion Volume of Plays* (1912); *Primus Annus* (1912) and *Secondus Annus* (1917). *Primus Annus* remains in print and provides a text for the direct method of teaching Latin. See www.gutenberg.org/ebooks/author/48972. Furthermore, after his death, the Secretary of the Association for the Reform of Latin Teaching said of him: 'We have lost one, who was not only one of our most brilliant leaders, but who had also endeared himself to us all by his charm and personality.'

According to the *Whitgift Grammar School Book of Remembrance, 1914–1919*, he remained active in the Whitgift OTC, reaching the rank of Acting Captain and second in command; he was also Adjutant to the local volunteers. In the summer of 1915, following on from his completion of a Musketry course, he was appointed divisional instructor in musketry at Ripon. In the spring of 1917, Cyril joined the Royal Garrison Artillery and in September 1917 went to Egypt where, as part of 422nd Siege Battery, he took part in Allenby's advance into Palestine, after which he was invalided to Alexandria.

According to *The Whitgiftian*, he returned to his family home on 7 February 1919 and was immediately demobilised. He was due to marry at Easter. Unfortunately,

> his party had taken six weeks over the journey, suffering much hardship, and losing five men enroute. He arrived with the 'flu' already on him, and this developed into bronchial pneumonia. At the end of a week, he appeared to have weathered the crisis; but his constitution had been damaged by malaria and other Eastern ailments and his heart gave out.

Cyril Mainwaring died at a nursing home in Croydon on 17 February 1919 and was buried at Croydon (Mitcham Road) Cemetery, London. His Commanding Officer wrote of him: 'He was a great acquisition to the mess, being always full of spirits and having a fund of information on all topics of conversation. It is a great pity that a man who had such a career in front of him should be cut off in his prime.' His *Whitgiftian* obituary concluded affectionately: 'many will remember the man with admiration, and in more than one heart "Cyril" will never be forgotten'. His name is recorded on the Corpus war memorial, but out of alphabetical sequence and tagged on at the end. Current research shows it was added in December 1932. Why his name was not included in the original war memorial listing has been lost to history. TNA have an officer file WO 374/45640.

1907

LAING, Alexander Torrance Reverend Captain (1889–1916), 13th Battalion Northumberland Fusiliers.

Alexander Laing was born at Burton, Northumberland on 21 October 1889, the son of Jacobina Christie Watt née Torrance and the late James Laing, a farmer of Mizen Head, Bamburgh, Northumberland.

Alexander was educated at Pocklington School near York and matriculated into Corpus in 1907 to read the Mathematical Tripos. The former Master Stuart Laing, a descendant of Alexander, has written of him:

My father's family farmed in the Scottish borders; but his father and uncle departed from the farming tradition. My grandfather studied medicine in Edinburgh, and became a doctor; and his brother, my great uncle, Alexander Torrance Laing, came to Corpus in 1907, where he took a first in mathematics [in 1907 he held an exhibition, and the following year became a scholar]. We don't know why he came south for study; he must have been unusually intellectual in a farming family.

During his time at the College, Alexander was a member of the Boat Club and at 9 stone 4 pounds rowed in the 1907 trial eight and bow in the 1909 Lent Second Boat. He was also a member of the Theological Society and read a paper entitled 'Extension of the Church' during Michaelmas Term 1909 and was President of a College archaeological society called the Cobwebs. He graduated with a BA in 1910 (MA 1914), began to train for the ministry, and was ordained a deacon. Stuart Laing said of this, 'I have in my bookshelves his Greek New Testament, given to him (and signed) by Cosmo Lang, then Archbishop of York.' In 1911, he was appointed a schoolmaster at Exeter School.

Alexander was Acting Captain when he died on 24 July 1916, from wounds received whilst leading his men into action near Fricourt during the Somme Offensive. Stuart Laing provides an account of Alexander's death.

> The story of his death as a young man is quickly told; I haven't seen it written down, but it's well enshrined in family oral tradition. My grandfather and great uncle Alec were both in the Northumberland Fusiliers. In July 1916, my grand-father had had a long day tending the wounded in his field hospital tent, and said to his orderly, 'That's enough for today; we can't take in any more wounded.' The orderly looked at those waiting outside, and said, 'I think you'll see this one, sir.' It was Alec, with severe abdominal wounds, I assume common in that conflict, where machine-gun fire raked across lines of advancing men. Alec died of his wounds very shortly afterwards. His name is on the Memorial in the College Chapel, and there is a fine brass plaque in his memory in Bamburgh Church, reporting that 'he was mortally wounded while leading his men in action … and died 24 July 1916. A brave soldier of Christ.'

He is also remembered on Bamburgh Castle war memorial and on the Agnes Stuart Dove Laing Monument in St Aidan's Churchyard, Bamburgh. Alexander Torrance Laing died of his wounds on 24 July 1916 aged 27 and is buried in St Sever Cemetery, Rouen, France. TNA have an officer file WO 339/36997.

Stuart Laing

As a Corpus undergraduate, Alexander Torrance Laing was the winner of two Bishop Green silver cups. They were awarded for his outstanding success in Tripos. One is inscribed 'Literatum Praemium 1908' and the other 'Alexander Torrance Laing Philosophiae Praemium 1909'.

The grave of Alexander Torrance Laing.

MARRIOTT, John Francis Laycock, 2nd Lieutenant (1889–1915),
7th Battalion Duke of Cornwall's Light Infantry.

John Francis Laycock Marriott was born on 29 March 1889 in Plymouth, Devon, the son of the Reverend George Herbert Marriott (1832–1918) (Trinity College, Dublin, m.1857) and his second wife Angeline Elizabeth née Berry (1846–1910) of Anglo-Irish descent. His father was vicar of Charles Parish Church, Plymouth.

John was educated at Plymouth Technical School and matriculated into Corpus in 1907. During his time at the College, he was a member of the Boat Club and at 10 stone 4 pounds rowed at two in the Michaelmas 1909 races and at seven in the May 1910 Second Boat. He read the Mechanical Sciences Tripos, graduating with a BA in June 1910. The 1911 census has him as a single man living in Gloucester and an engineering pupil at Fielding and Plate Ltd, makers of gas engines.

Two of his brothers were Corpus graduates, the Reverend Herbert (1868–1943) (m.1886) and the Reverend Edward Augustin (1874–1942) (m.1892). Both are believed to have served as Chaplains to the Forces between 1910 and 1922, though neither is listed in *The War List*, but see the entry for Herbert in the appendix.

John Francis Laycock Marriott died of spotted fever on 26 January 1915 aged 25 and was buried in Aldershot military cemetery. TNA have an officer file WO 339/18125 and a medal card WO 372/13/123188.

1908

CUNNINGTON, Edward Charles, Captain MRCS LRCP (1890–1918), 95th Field Ambulance Royal Army Medical Corps. Previously Regimental Medical Officer of the 12th Battalion York and Lancaster Regiment.

Edward Cunnington was born on 28 August 1890 in Devizes, Wiltshire. His parents were Edith Maud née Pegge and Benjamin Howard Cunnington, a wine merchant cum archaeologist of Devizes, Wiltshire. His mother (known professionally as Maud Cunnington OBE) was a distinguished archaeologist, famous for her work exploring the prehistoric archaeology of Salisbury Plain. His father became the curator of the Devizes Museum (known today as the Wiltshire Museum). His grandfather and uncle were both physicians (his uncle, Edward Vernon Pegge, was also a Welsh international rugby player). Like his parents, Edward was a keen archaeologist and a Fellow of the Cambrian Archaeological Society.

Educated at Reading School, Edward matriculated into Corpus in 1908. During his time at the College, he was a member of the Pious Pelicans and played rugby of which *The Benedict* (Michaelmas Term 1910) observed he was: 'A capable and efficient secretary, who had captained the team well throughout the season and has hardly done himself justice in consequence. Has a fair turn of speed and a good hand off. Excellent in passing back to his centre.' He took the Natural Sciences Tripos, graduating with a BA in 1911 and with an MB the following year. Thereafter, he did his medical training at St Bartholomew's Hospital, London; this he completed in 1915, becoming an MRCS and LRCP. He subsequently became a house physician and Medical Receiving Room Officer at the hospital. That same year, he obtained a commission in the RAMC and went to Egypt attached to the 95th Field Ambulance. On his return to Europe, he was appointed RMO to the 12th Battalion York and Lancaster Regiment with whom he served for two years in France. He was posted back to his original unit a few days before his death. At the time, Edward's father was a Captain in the Wiltshire Regiment on active service.

Dr Edward Cunnington was killed on 23 March 1918 when a shell hit an advanced dressing station near the front line where he was tending the wounded. He was 28 and is buried at Cabaret-Rouge British Cemetery, Souchez, Pas de Calais, France. His name appears on war memorials in St Bartholomew the Less, Archway, City of London (WMR 11641) and the Devizes and Roundway war memorial (WMR 24091). TNA have a medal card WO 372/5/129296.

LEEMING, Alfred Johnson, Captain (1889–1917), 6th Battalion (attached to the 1st Battalion) Royal Fusiliers (City of London Regiment). Mentioned in Despatches.

Alfred Leeming was born in Kent on 22 May 1889, the son of Henry Spencer Leeming the headmaster of Baring Road School (mixed), Lewisham and Fanny Leeming of Bognor, Sussex. At the time of his death, he was married to Hylda Elizabeth née Dewsnap. The marriage took place in Vancouver, British Columbia, Canada on 12 June 1915. Alfred was educated primarily at home, then for three years at Lucas Street Junior School, Deptford and Westward Ho! Between 1901 and 1908, having won a scholarship, he completed his education at Christ's Hospital, Sussex. At school, he was Senior Grecian (captain of the school) and captain of the cricket team. Alfred matriculated into Corpus in 1908 with an Entrance Scholarship and read the Mathematical Tripos. During his time at the College, he was a Prizeman and graduated with a BA in June 1911.

According to *Wisden Cricketers' Almanack* 'Obituaries for 1917' he was an outstanding Corpus and University cricketer and a Cricketing Blue; in 1911, he made twenty-five runs in the Varsity match. Alfred was also Captain of the College XI. *The Benedict* (Easter Term 1910) wrote of his skills: 'A promising bat with a very pleasant style. Can usually be relied upon to make some runs when needed, and at the same time proves a steady player at a crisis. Fields well and returns excellent.'

The Royal Bank of Canada website Roll of Honour says of him:

> Alfred joined the London branch of the Royal Bank of Canada on 1st September 1912, but later transferred to the Vancouver, British Columbia, Robson Street branch. On the outbreak of war, he tried to volunteer in Canada, but was rejected. In June 1915, the newly married Alfred and his wife sailed for Liverpool on the SS *Arabic* and on 22nd July 1915 obtained a commission with the 6th Battalion Royal Fusiliers (City of London Regiment) a training unit.

In May 1916, Alfred Leeming went to France with the 1st Battalion and saw action during the Somme Campaign at Delville Wood and Guillemont. He twice led raids into German trenches and was Mentioned in Despatches.

In April 1917, his battalion was in action at Vimy Ridge and Messine Ridge. The following month, Alfred was home on special leave, sadly missing his mother's funeral by four days. He was killed by a sniper's bullet on 31 July 1917, during the first day of the 3rd Battle of Ypres, known as Passchendaele, aged 28. Three weeks later, on 21 August 1917, his son Kenneth Johnson Leeming (1917–1983) was born. An internet account explains what happened:

> The 26th Battalion were fighting in heavy rain at Battle Wood on that day and lost 160 killed, wounded and missing. To their right was the 24th Division in which

were the 1st and 12th Battalions [Royal Fusiliers], both of whom suffered heavy casualties. They advanced towards Shrewsbury Wood but were held up at the German trench between Clonmel Copse and Shrewsbury Wood. Lieutenant Wilfred Flack and his men in the 1st Battalion rushed a machine-gun and knocked it out with a rifle grenade. When C Company reached the trench their officer, Captain Leeming was killed near Bodmin Copse. The worst of the fire was coming from Lower Star Post and it caused the Battalion on their right to swerve, and this resulted in a corresponding swerve of the right-hand company.

A post-war Royal Fusiliers history adds the following: 'This part of the line was then consolidated. C Company, under Captain Leeming, reached the trench on the south-western face of Bodmin Copse, and here he was killed. The German  snipers were very active, and C Company was deprived of an efficient leader.'

Alfred Leeming is buried at Bedford House Cemetery, West Vlaanderen, Belgium. The personal inscription on his gravestone reads 'Sleep in thy perfect peace o son of England W.S.L.' (derived from Isaiah 26:3). He is remembered on the Westward Ho! Church First World War Memorial Board and Brass Plate honouring old boys of the Junior School. TNA have a medal card WO 372/12/50752. He is also remembered on the Royal Bank of Canada website.

1909

CONINGHAM, William Francis Meyrick, 2nd Lieutenant (1888–1920), Royal Army Service Corps (Mechanical Transport).

William Francis Meyrick Coningham (known as Meyrick) was born in Brighton, the son of William John Capper (m.1864, Trinity Hall) and Harriette Ann Coningham née Claxton. In the 1891 census, his father described himself as being of independent means. Meyrick's grandfather William Coningham (m.1832, Trinity) was MP for Brighton between 1857 and 1864. He was educated at Rostellan House School, Brighton before matriculating into Worcester College, Oxford from where, in 1909, he came to Corpus. The 1911 census has him as a single man living at home with his widowed mother and sister.

On 4 April 1920, Meyrick became just one of thousands of unrecorded casualties of war; he took his own life. A *Chelmsford Chronicle* news report of 9 April 1920 records

Officer's sad death at Stebbing. On Easter Sunday morning Mr William Francis Meyrick Coningham aged 32, a discharged officer of the Mechanical Transport, was found shot in the head with a revolver bullet at Finistere Farm, Stebbing, Essex, which he had taken a few months ago. Dr Pearce, Great Bardfield, was summoned, but the injured man died the same night. He had suffered from shell shock and neurasthenia, due to his Army service. The deceased officer leaves a widow and two young children.

At the inquest on Wednesday, the widow stated that on Easter morning her husband got up early and lit the fire. She left at a quarter to eight to attend service at the church. When she came home she asked her little boy to find his father. He ran to the back of the house and returned to say. 'I heard a noise, and think it must be daddy.' On going to the back door witness found her husband lying the foot of the back staircase, and thought he had fallen down the stairs, she lifted him up, and saw a revolver lying near. Her husband was unconscious and did not recognise her. He was invalided out of the army, and had been depressed many times. He had not been altogether happy at the farm. They had not been very well off, but his mother was behind him, and he was not worried by any financial matters. He always said however, 'that he would not be able to do anything'. A verdict of Suicide during temporary insanity was returned, and the Coroner (Dr Harrison) expressed sympathy with the widow.

His wife, Sylvia Clare Granville née Allsop, later married Harry Sydney Radford. Meyrick left two small children William Donald Meyrick (1916–1942) (later Captain, 2nd Battalion Duke of Wellington's (West Riding) Regiment, who was killed in early 1942 during the opening phase of the Burmah campaign) and Audrey Sylvia (1918–2009) who had a distinguished wartime career in the WRNS and later married Major David John Hugh Roche.

Meyrick's wartime service was recorded on the war memorial of the now demolished All Souls Church, Eastern Road, Brighton (the memorial is now held by St Mary's Church, Kemptown, Brighton), In 2023 his name was added to the College war memorial. TNA have an officer file WO 374/15008 and a medal card WO 372/4/224171.

War memorial, All Souls Church, Brighton. Meyrick's name is in the left-hand column.

HARSTON, Frank Northey, Brigade-Major, MC (1890–1918), 11th Infantry Brigade East Lancashire Regiment. General Staff, 3rd Grade Headquarters, 4th Division. Formerly 9th Battalion Leicestershire Regiment.

Frank Northey Harston was born in Blatchinworth, Rochdale, Lancashire (now part of Greater Manchester) on 24 May 1890, the second of three sons of John Edwin HM Inspector of Factories (though described in the 1891 census as an architectural clerk) and Bessie Anne Northey née Plucknett of Olton, Warwickshire. Their youngest son died in infancy; however, the two surviving children, Frank and his elder brother Thomas Brunyee Harston (1888–1951), who saw wartime service as a Captain in The King's Regiment (Liverpool) and was a solicitor), were educated at Highfield Preparatory School, Liphook, Southampton then at Eastbourne College. At both, Frank was head of the school and played for the cricket XI and the rugby XV. According to the Eastbourne College website, 'Edward Carleton Arnold, headmaster of Eastbourne College between 1924 and 1929, said of Harston: "He was a pocket Hercules. Many a truculent opponent recoiled with the undisguised look of one who has caught a tartar when chopped by him at the commencement of a spectacular run."'

Frank matriculated into Corpus in 1909 to read the Classical Tripos, became a scholar, and was awarded several prize cups for his Tripos results; he graduated with First Class Honours. During his time at the College, he was a member of several societies and clubs including the Chess Club, the Pious Pelicans, the Classical Society, the Gravediggers, and the Cobwebs. At a Lent 1910 meeting of the last, he read a paper entitled 'The equivalent of the newspaper in ancient Rome', in the following term gave a paper to the Classical Society entitled 'The atomic theory of Lucretius', and in 1911 a paper entitled 'Cimon' about the 5th century BCE Athenian statesman and general. As an undergraduate, Frank was also an outstanding sportsman. He was a member of both the Boat and Rugby Clubs. He rowed in a trial eight (Michaelmas 1909) and at five in the 1910 second May boat. In 1911, he joined the Boat Club Committee, was elected Second Boat Captain in 1912 and rowed in the First Boat in both the Lent and May bumps. *The Benedict* said he was: 'A very hard worker who keeps his mind on his work. Has good body form.' That same year, Frank was elected Captain of rugby. His skills at the game were noted in *The Benedict* (Michaelmas Term 1910) as: 'A good dashing forward. Excellent in the loose: good dribbler and tackler works hard in the scrum.' In the Michaelmas Term 1911 edition, it added: 'Quite the best of a good pack of forwards. Very quick in the loose and works like a horse. As Captain has shown great energy and discrimination.'

A *Benedict* (Easter Term 1912) profile, published just before he graduated, noted: 'Both on the river and on the Footer field he has rendered conspicuous service to the College, and his keenness has been much appreciated.' It continued: 'In spite of numerous other attractions he has worked hard at those subjects which have interested him since childhood, with the result that we have great pleasure in congratulating him on securing a First Class in the Classical Tripos.' It concluded: 'Our best wishes go with "Chops".'

After he graduated in June 1912, he was appointed an assistant master first at Clifton (1912–13) and then at Radley (1914). At the outbreak of war, Frank joined the Public Schools Brigade and in October 1914 was gazetted Temporary 2nd Lieutenant. He was posted to the 9th (Service) Battalion Leicestershire Regiment and went to France in July 1915 as Captain and Adjutant. In January 1916, he was appointed to the General Staff of a Division and was given a regular commission with the East Lancashire Regiment. In February 1917, he was promoted and appointed Brigade-Major of the 11th Infantry Brigade, in which capacity he served until his death. Frank was twice Mentioned in Despatches and in May 1917 awarded the Military Cross. *The London Gazette* citation reads: 'He rendered most valuable service as Brigade-Major during the advance. When a gap occurred, he proceeded at great risk of capture and under continuous fire to rectify matters before daylight. He set a magnificent example throughout.'

Frank Harston was killed in action on 22 April 1918, aged 28. A Brigade Commander, under whom Harston served for nine months wrote:

> The news [of his death] has grieved me more than I can tell you, for I not only know what his death must mean to the Brigade, but I feel that it has deprived me of a very close personal friend … I am grateful for having been brought into such close touch with his charming personality. His attitude towards his work and life generally was splendid, and his keenness and contempt for danger the admiration of the brigade. He had a great capacity for work, and would, I feel sure, have gone far in the army, had he survived the war, while his bright nature and readiness to help others made him beloved by us all.

A contemporary at Eastbourne College paid tribute to him:

> The modern battlefield has proved a strange school of poets, and the love of nature was never more intimate and more real, than in this nightmare of destruction and rampant mechanism. There were two men here, whom we knew well, richly endowed with that quality – not a rare one, perhaps, but often disguised –

the love of Earth: I mean Frank Harston and his friend Lance Vidal [a keen Morris dancer and a fellow member of staff at Radley – another was the composer and fellow Morris dancer George Butterworth]. The official notice of his death, in our last number, reveals nothing of the man: I can, at least, say something of my own knowledge of him as a friend.

Both these men as we knew them were sane, sterling, generous souls, devoid of affectation and vanity. Such men are not as they had never been; something endures in the consciousness of everyone who associated with them.

When nearly every incident of the past is forgotten, a few luminous scenes remain, clear in the memory, like sunlight striking on a distant hill. I remember fishing with Harston, near Bablockhithe [*sic*, Bablock Hythe, near Oxford], one afternoon in summer. He was a gay and delightful companion, as he was, I imagine, punctilious and strict in form: for he did nothing by halves. Last April, he wrote to me expressing the wish that we should one day go fishing together again; and his letter recalled the whole scene most vividly, – the mown grass lying in swathes by the stream, the conversation we had sitting in the inn-garden, and the ride home in the dusk.

Personally, I shall always remember him and Vidal as men who loved earth and the sun, and who, full of the joy of living, were not afraid to enter the enchanted *Woods of Westermain*, [by George Meredith] – the mystery in nature. In Memoriam Frank Harston.

Frank Harston is buried at the Gonnehem British Cemetery, Pas de Calais, France. The personal inscription on his gravestone is a line from Robert Browning's 1861 dramatic monologue *Prospice*: 'The journey is done and the summit attained and the barriers fall.' He is also commemorated on St Margaret's Church, Olton, Solihull, Warwickshire war memorial. TNA have an officer file WO 339/20209 and a medal card WO 372/9/59054.

NELSON, Ernest Bertram, 2nd Lieutenant (1890–1916), Indian Army Reserve of Officers, attached to the Indian Infantry, 1st Battalion 8th Gurkha Rifles.

Ernest Nelson attended The King's School, Canterbury and this biography is derived from its Roll of Honour. Ernest was born in Kensington on 30 November 1890, the younger son of Sydney Herbert Nelson a sawmill engineer and Matilda Constance née Smart of Canterbury. Ernest was educated first at the Cliff House School, Southbourne then, between 1904 and 1909, at The King's School, Canterbury. In 1905, he was awarded a junior scholarship and then in 1908 a senior scholarship. On leaving school, Ernest matriculated into Wadham College, Oxford as an exhibitioner and then, on the award of a Parker Exhibition (later becoming a scholar), to Corpus.

During his time at the College, he was a member of the Corpus Classical Society and in the Michaelmas Term 1910 gave a paper entitled 'Classical Greek Mythology and Modern Greek Folk-lore'. He was also a member of the OTC, the Chess Club, the Gravediggers, the Strawberries, and the Boat Club. He rowed at bow in the 1910 second May boat and stroked the 1911 Lent boat. Of the latter, *The Benedict* (Lent Term 1911) noted he tried hard but was: 'Of a too excitable disposition for a stroke. Did much better on the last days of the races than the first.' In the 1911 May races, Ernest rowed at two and at bow in the 1912 Lent boat. In 1911, he took a 3rd in Part I of the Classical Tripos graduating with Third Class Honours in the 1912 Historical Tripos.

In 1913, he went to work for Baring Brothers Bank in London from where he was posted to India to work for the Bank of Bengal in Calcutta (now Kolkata). Also, that year he enlisted in the Calcutta Light Horse. On 8 January 1915, he

was commissioned a 2nd Lieutenant in the India Army Reserve of Officers attached to the Queen Victoria's Own Corps of Guides, the 33rd Punjabis, and later to the 2nd Battalion, 8th Gurkha Rifles. He was promoted to Lieutenant on 8 January 1916 and saw active service on the Indian Frontier as well as in France and Mesopotamia, where he took part in the capture of Baghdad and the attempts to raise the siege of Kut Al Amara. During this time, he was attached to the 1st Battalion 8th Gurkha Rifles and became Adjutant.

In the evening of 13 March 1917, the 400-strong Gurkha force was ordered to attack enemy positions along both sides of the railway line at Mushada. The next morning, they assembled five miles from their objective and at 8.00 am moved

forward. After a two-mile advance, they stopped to receive final orders, after which they crossed to the west side of the railway line under a culvert and were in position for the assault at 3.00 pm. The 2nd Battalion Black Watch were to attack on the right of the Brigade with their right flank on the railway line. The 9th Bhopal Infantry were to be in the centre with the 1/8th Gurkha Rifles on the left of the attack with their left flank protected by cavalry. Captain Bernard Abbott MC led the Gurkha left wing with Ernest Nelson leading the right wing. At 3.20 pm, the advance began but after a half a mile came under 'light and poorly aimed' shrapnel fire. When 2,000 yards from their objective, the enemy machine guns opened fire from a strongly held hill on the right of the attack. At 6.20 pm, the artillery fired a barrage on

the hill and the Gurkhas rushed forward and carried the position with the enemy retreating without putting up any resistance. Both Captain Abbott and Ernest Nelson were wounded during this attack. At 7.00 pm, the advance continued and the railway junction at Mushada fell at midnight at the point of the bayonet with the enemy falling back in disarray.

The following day, 15 March 1916, the battalion learned that Ernest Nelson had died of his wounds at a field hospital, aged 26. He has no known grave but is commemorated on the Basra Memorial, Iraq.

The 1912 Corpus Lent boat bow four.
Bow, Ernest Bertram Nelson; 2, John Selwyn (Captain of Boats 1912); 3, George Charles Henry Culley and 4, Frank Northey Harston. Nelson and Harston were both killed in the war and Selwyn (1893–1959) was wounded. Culley (1893–1982) was badly injured in a plane crash but survived. He saw service in the RAF during the Second World War and died aged 88 in 1982.

READ, Reverend Eric Oswald (1888–1918), Chaplain 4th Class Royal Army Chaplains Department, attached to the 5th Battalion Dorsetshire Regiment.

Eric Read was born in Thetford, Norfolk on 28 July 1888, the son of George Odden a solicitor and his wife Dora Read née Simpson, and at the time of his death was married to Alice Read of Canterbury.

He attended Thetford Grammar School and matriculated into Corpus in 1909, graduating in June 1912 (MA 1917). During his time at the College, he was a member of the Chess Club.

In early 1918, after ordination and prior to his becoming a Chaplain to the Forces, he had been a curate first in Retford and then Alfreton, Derbyshire. His RACD card shows details of an interview held on 11 December 1917 and gives his address as The Vicarage, 23 Crassy Road, Alfreton, Derbyshire. The card also reveals he had defective vision and goes on 'Will go anywhere, do anything.' The card describes him as a 'tall, bright, manly fellow'.

On 3 October 1918, six weeks before the Armistice, Eric Read was killed near Epinoy, in the Pas de Calais, aged 30. At the time of his death, he was ministering to the wounded in a small dug-out when it was hit by a shell. A 5th Battalion Dorsetshire Regiment website has the following: 'in late September and October 1918 the 5th Dorsets played a part in the final rapid advances that led to the Armistice. They achieved particular success in a fiercely opposed attack north-west of Cambrai, which cost relatively few lives although enemy shelling killed their Colonel, Padre and Medical Officer.' After his death, his Commanding Officer wrote to his wife:

> We, the battalion, have lost a very brave and true friend. His conduct throughout the action was admirable, and his total disregard for danger was an example to all. I visited him attending to the wounded during the action and was filled with admiration for his splendid work. A shell hit the dressing station, and his death was instantaneous. I can only say that I and the whole battalion have lost a very true and courageous friend who will never be forgotten.

Eric was buried at Chapel Corner Cemetery, Sauchy-Lestree, Pas de Calais. The personal inscription on his grave reads, 'He that loseth his life for my sake shall find it.' (Matthew 10:39). His life is commemorated on the Alfreton, Derbyshire war memorial and on a memorial stone at Lincoln Cathedral Hostel. His wife Alice died in 1923 aged 37 and her gravestone at St Ann's Church, Ings, South Lakeland, Cumbria memorialises Eric in the following terms: 'In loving memory of Alice Read died Jan 5, 1923 aged 37. Also of her husband Eric Oswald Read MA Chaplain to the Forces Killed Oct 3, 1918 whilst ministering to the wounded at Epinay near Cambrai and buried there aged 31. Reunited.' TNA have an officer file WO 374/56488 and a medal card WO 372/16/5029.

1910

BOWER, Charles Francis (Frank), Captain (1891–1917), 16th (Service) Battalion Sherwood Foresters (Chatsworth Rifles), Notts and Derby Regiment.

Charles Frank Bower was born in Norwich on 27 July 1891, the youngest son of James Garton and Helen Brooke Bower née Rhodes. The family lived at Earlham House, Norwich.

Educated at King Edward VI Grammar School, Norwich he matriculated into Corpus with a Parker Scholarship to read the Historical Tripos and graduated with a BA on 17 June 1913. During his time as an undergraduate, he played association football for the College. The *Eastern Daily Press* on 20 September 1917 published a report of his death from which the following is derived.

After graduation, he remained at the Cambridge Engineering School till Christmas 1913, when he returned to Norwich and joined the staff of the Norfolk Ironworks (Messrs Barnards Ltd), of which his father was chairman and managing director. In June 1915, he entered an officers' training school and was gazetted to a commission and almost immediately proceeded to France. Captain Bower was a brilliant student with unusual gifts in the way of engineering. Outside of his professional work he was best known by reason of his interest in the Boy Scout movement. He was one of the pioneers of it in Norwich. At the time of his death, he was still holding office as Master of the 1st Norwich Boy Scouts, of whom his father is president.

The 13 September 2017 edition of the *Norwich Evening News* noted: 'Charles Bower ... was the first Scout Master of the First Norwich Scout Troop. He is remembered with gratitude by all members of the First Norwich Sea Scout

Group [known as Captain Bowers' Own].'

On 1 April 1916, Charles arrived in France with his Battalion; that year, it took part in an attack near Richebourg l'Avoue and the fighting on the Ancre. He also took part in the Battle of Thiepval Ridge and, in October and November 1916, its continuation, the Battle of the Ancre Heights, and finally later in November 1916, the Battle of the Ancre.

In 1917, his Battalion took part in the 3rd Battle of Ypres, known as Passchendaele and saw action during the Battles of Pilkem Ridge and Langemarck. On 13 September 1917, Charles was killed in the aftermath of these engagements; he was 26. An account of his final engagement with the enemy appears in Roy Francis Truscott, *A Short History of the 16th Battalion, the Sherwood Foresters, Chatsworth Rifles* (privately published, 1928). In it, he writes of the Battalion moving into the Shrewsbury Forest Sector:

> This sector was on the left of the scene of our exploits at Klein Zillebeke, and, like its neighbour, was in a hopelessly broken up and devastated state. There were no trenches, and the line of pillboxes ran through a battered wood of shattered trees whose stark and gaunt trunks made sentry duty at night an eerie pastime, as arboreal figures were easily taken by the imaginative for enemy patrols. Communications trenches were not in the picture, and the passage to the front was affected by a double row of duckboards, forming an elongated viaduct over water-filled shell-holes, the edges of which formed the bastion of the bridge.
>
> We were in a position which afforded little or no security, and in these conditions were subjected to persistent and comprehensive shelling. Captain C F Bower, one of our original officers, a very gallant and conscientious soldier, was killed.

The final cost of this front-line duty was the deaths of two officers (including Bower) and two other ranks, with two officers and eight other ranks wounded and four other ranks missing.

Captain Charles Frank Bower is buried in La Clytte military cemetery, Belgium. The personal inscription on his gravestone reads: 'And his servants shall serve him and they shall see his face. Revelations 22.3–4'. TNA have an officer file WO 339/44436.

CLARKE, John [Jack] Percy Dalzell, 2nd Lieutenant (1891–1915), Royal Fusiliers attached to the 10th (Service) Battalion Worcestershire Regiment.

Jack Clarke was born on 28 November 1891 in Norwich, the son of the Reverend Percy Carmichael Clarke and Emma Anne née Piper of Thorley Wash, Bishop's Stortford, Hertfordshire. He was educated at St Edmund's School, Canterbury and although matriculating into Corpus in 1910 does not appear to have graduated. In November 1914, he was gazetted 2nd Lieutenant with the Royal Fusiliers but later attached to the 10th (Service) Battalion the Worcestershire Regiment. Jack died in St George's Hospital, Middlesex of injuries incurred in a riding accident on 21 February 1915, aged 23. The incident was reported in the *Marylebone Mercury* on 27 February 1915:

> Second Lieutenant J P D Clarke of the 10th Worcester Regiment, has been fatally injured in a riding accident in Piccadilly. He was going towards Hyde Park when he lost control of his horse. The animal tried to leap a road repairers' barrier, threw its rider against a van and kicked him on the head. He died in hospital on Sunday. A verdict of accidental death was returned at the inquest.

Jack Clarke was buried at Brookwood Civilian Cemetery. TNA have an officer file WO 339/23658.

DUCKWORTH, Walter Clarence, 2nd Lieutenant (1889–1918), 1st Battalion Welch Regiment, attached to the 1st Battalion King's Shropshire Light Infantry.

Walter Duckworth was born in Southport, Lancashire (now part of Merseyside) on 3 August 1889, the youngest son of Elizabeth Duckworth née Hilton of Birkdale, Lancashire and the late Egerton Duckworth, a stockbroker of Southport and Blackburn. At the time of his death, Walter was married to Marjorie Duckworth of Conyers Avenue, Southport, the daughter of an Anglican clergyman.

He was educated at Queen Elizabeth's Grammar School, Blackburn, came up to Cambridge in 1909 and matriculated into Selwyn College. At the start of his second year, he migrated to Corpus where he read the Medieval and Modern Languages Tripos, became a College Prizeman, and served as a sub-librarian. In 1912, he graduated with Third Class Honours.

He joined the armed forces in April 1917, enlisting as a Private in the 28th Battalion London Regiment but on 27 November 1917 was commissioned 2nd Lieutenant with the Welch Regiment. A local newspaper has the following 1918 report: 'He married Marjorie née Halstead on 9th February 1918. He initially went to work in Bombay [now Mumbai] India, but the work and the climate were unsuitable, and he returned to England and became an assistant master at Kirkham Grammar School. Joining the army in April 1917, he went to France last April [1918] and saw much action.' His Battalion was a combat unit throughout the German Spring Offensive, Operation Michael. On 8 August 1918, after desperate fighting, the German advance was halted in front of Amiens. Thereafter, it was in retreat. On 8 October 1918, the first day of the Second Battle of Cambrai and just over a month before the Armistice, Walter was killed in action, aged 29. His Commanding Officer wrote of him: 'He died splendidly, leading his men in an attack of the greatest value. His death is the greatest blow to the Battalion and his many friends.' Walter Duckworth is buried in Ramicourt British Cemetery, Aisne, France, and is commemorated on the Queen Elizabeth's Grammar School, Blackburn war memorial and the Selwyn College war memorial. TNA have an officer file WO 339/118451 and a medal card WO 372/6/101973.

Shaw, Robert, Captain (1892–1917), 1/7th Battalion The King's Regiment (Liverpool) (Territorial Force).

Robert Shaw was born in Bury, Lancashire (now part of Greater Manchester) on 14 August 1892 and baptised in the Parish Church of St Mary the Virgin, Bury. His parents were Robert (described in the Corpus Admissions Book as a 'Gentleman', in the baptismal register as a 'butcher', and in the 1911 census as 'private income') and Annie Shaw née Birtwhistle, of Ainsdale, Lancashire. In February 1917, Robert married Margaret Phyllis née Bell (after her husband's death she remarried, becoming Mrs Dod of 4 Buckingham Ave, Sefton Park, Liverpool).

Between 1906 and 1909, Robert attended Shrewsbury School, then matriculated into Corpus where he read the Economics Tripos. During his time at the College, Robert was a member of the Boat Club and rowed (weighing 12 stone 10 pounds) in the first Lent and May boats of 1911 and 1912. Of his skills, *The Benedict* (Lent Term 1911) noted: 'Has improved considerably during the term. Has a neat but very slow recovery, which produces a bad bucket with a fast stroke.' In 1913, the same journal observed: '[he] should learn to row himself clean out as he does not do anything like enough work. Could become a very useful heavy-weight.' Robert also played College football and as a centre half it was said of him: 'he played consistently well and always marked his man. His coming in from left-half to centre made all the difference, and he was useful both in attack and defence.' Robert graduated in June 1913 and was subsequently articled to a Liverpool-based firm of chartered accountants.

In December 1913, Robert was commissioned with the 1/7th Battalion The King's Regiment (Liverpool) (Territorial Force) and served as a Captain. He was mobilised on the outbreak of war and went to France in the spring of 1915, and again in December of that same year. Robert was back home in May 1916 on sick leave, returning to the front in December of that year.

The regimental war diary for period 20 to 25 September 1917 details the part he played in operations during the murderous 3rd Battle of Ypres, known as Passchendaele. On 18 September, his unit moved up to the front, which was little more than a line of shell holes and disused trenches in front of the Pommern Redoubt. The line of attack was due east and along the bank of the Zonnebeke. The following day, known as Y day, was spent preparing for operations. Z day operations began in the early hours of 20 September. According to the war diary and a regimental history, conditions for the attack were terrible. It was noted: 'No Man's Land was a mass of shell holes full of water and viscous mud which clung to the boots of the attackers.' Operations continued for five days during which the Battalion endured shelling and vicious hand-to-hand fighting. The objectives (such as they were) appear to have been taken, but casualties were high. Overall, the Battalion suffered 242 casualties of whom sixty-one were killed or died of wounds, including five officers. Among them was Captain Robert Shaw, who was killed on 20 September 1917 during the initial attack, aged 25.

A local press report notes: 'Captain Shaw was well known in Southport, and the sad news of his death will be received with the deepest regret.' His Commanding Officer wrote to his wife: 'It is with the very deepest regret that I have to inform you that your husband was killed in action on twentieth inst whilst leading his Company. All ranks state how splendidly he did both before and during the action and I trust that the knowledge of this may be some little comfort to you.'

Robert was buried in Dochy Farm New British Cemetery, West Vaarlanden, Belgium. TNA have an officer file WO 374/61720.

G C H Culley album

Robert Shaw rowed in Corpus boats between 1911 and 1913.

1911

CHURCHWARD, Hubert Alan, 2nd Lieutenant (1891–1917), 2nd County of London Yeomanry (Westminster Dragoons); attached to the 9 Squadron Royal Flying Corps.

Hubert Churchward was born on 25 November 1891 in Aldershot, the son of the Reverend Marcus Wellesley Churchward CBE and Mary Ella née Woodall of Clapham, London.

He was educated privately and matriculated into Corpus in 1911 to read the Economics Tripos. During his time at the College, he was a member of the Chess Club and graduated in June 1914. He had hoped to train for the ministry and to that end gained a testimonial from the College. However, in September 1914, Hubert enlisted in the 2nd Battalion County of London Yeomanry, having formerly served in the West Kent Yeomanry and the King Edward's Horse. In October 1914, he attained the rank of Sergeant and on 20 May 1915 was commissioned in the regiment. In 1915, he served at Gallipoli, but subsequently retrained as a pilot in the RFC. Hubert went to France with No. 9 Squadron, Royal Flying Corps on 24 July 1917 and three weeks later, on 16 August 1917, he was killed in action (shot down during a photo reconnaissance mission), aged 25.

In a 31 August 1917 letter to his father, who was serving as a London-based Assistant Chaplain-General, the Commanding Officer of No. 9 Squadron wrote:

> I cannot hold out any hope as to his fate. He went out on the 16th with 2nd Lt Ward as his observer on artillery observation about midday. About an hour later he rang me up on the phone from another aerodrome saying that his engine had given trouble and that he would go up as soon as it was put right. He left at about 3 pm. And about 5 pm another observer saw a RE8 go down out of control the other side. He thought it had been hit by anti-aircraft fire. I can find out nothing further. I am very much afraid it looks as if he had been killed instantaneously or stunned by a splinter and had gone down out of control, falling from 5,000 feet about. I am afraid there is very little hope…

Having no known grave, Lieutenant Hubert Alan Churchward's name is commemorated on the Arras Flying Services Memorial, Pas de Calais, France. TNA have an officer file WO 374/13711.

His brother, the Reverend Basil Churchward (m.1908) was an Army Chaplain. He too saw active service and survived the war; see appendix.

KEATING, George Henry, Lieutenant (1893–1918), 2/1st Battalion Cambridgeshire Regiment. George was an instructor in explosives (bombing officer) and formerly Private 16th Public Schools Battalion Middlesex Regiment.

George Keating was born in Edinburgh on 13 June 1893, the son of Mary Ellen née Bruce and Canon John Fitz Stephen Keating DD (m.1873) of Northwich, Cheshire; his father had previously been the College Chaplain and a precentor. During a long career, he had also held the posts of Pantonian Professor and, between 1887 and 1903, Principal at the Theological College, Edinburgh; further, between 1910 and his death the following year, he was rector at the College living of All Saints' Parish Church, Landbeach.

Before matriculating into Corpus, George was educated at Cargilfield Preparatory School, Edinburgh, then the Perse School, Cambridge, and finally at Glenalmond College, Scotland.

During his time at the College, he was a sizar and a member of several societies including the Corpus Classical Society, the Gravediggers, the Pious Pelicans, and the Strawberries. In 1912, he played cricket for the College and was a noted tennis player. On the outbreak of war, George left the College without completing his degree or graduating.

In September 1914, he enlisted as a Private in the Public Schools Battalion the Middlesex Regiment and the following year was commissioned 2nd Lieutenant in the Cambridgeshire Regiment. Before going to the front, he trained as a bombing instructor and gained his certificate as divisional instructor.

In September 1918, after a period of home service with his battalion, George was posted to France. His unit formed part of the 12th (Eastern) Division (comprising the 7th Battalion Norfolk Regiment and 9th Battalion Essex Regiment and 1st Battalion Cambridgeshire Regiment), George Keating took part in a large-scale attack on an outpost section of the Hindenburg Line (the heavily fortified German main defensive line) in an action known as the Battle of Epehy. The Cambridgeshires were tasked with clearing the ruined village of Epehy, which lay just in front of the line. However, the German defenders had turned it into a fortress with countless bunkers, fortified cellars, and a rabbit warren of trenches and tunnels.

George Keating was killed on 18 September 1918, during the initial attack, aged 25. By the time the village was finally taken, the Cambridgeshires had reported nearly fifty officers and men killed, together with more than 180 wounded and eight missing. According to an online account: 'among the casualties were a number of the most experienced officers and NCOs in the Battalion – men it would be nearly impossible to replace'.

George Keating is buried at Epehy Wood Farm Cemetery, Epehy, Somme, France. The personal inscription of his gravestone reads: 'Son of Reverend J. F. Keating D. D. *Fortis et fidelis amor dei omnia vincit*' ('Brave and faithful love of God conquers all' (derived from Virgil, Eclogues 10)). Although his name does not appear on the Perse School war memorial, it is included on its Roll of Honour. His name does, however, appear on both the Cargilfield Preparatory School and Glenalmond College War Memorials. TNA have an officer file WO 374/38851 and a medal card WO 372/11/104049.

Corpus Christi College Cricket XI 1912.
All but two members of the team are known to have served in the armed forces during the war.
A H Webb and G H Keating were both killed in action.

MACINTOSH, Henry Maitland, Captain (1892–1918), 1/8th (Argyllshire) Battalion Princess Louise's (Argyll and Sutherland Highlanders).

Henry Macintosh was born on 10 June 1892 in Kelso, Roxburgh, Scotland, the second son of the Reverend Dr William and Annie née Stewart Macintosh of Kinross, Scotland. He was educated at Glenalmond College, where he was an all-round athlete, notably as a short-distance runner and became the first boy to win the athletics challenge cup three years in succession.

Henry matriculated into Corpus as a sizar in 1911 to read the Historical Tripos and was awarded a Spencer

Scholarship the following year. During his time at the College, he was a member of the Chess Club and had the extraordinary distinction of being both a Rugby and an Athletics Blue. He was, in the former, described as: 'a fine rugby wing three quarter and played for the Cambridge XV'. *The Letter of the Corpus Association*, No. 1 (July 1914) reported he played in the winning 1913 Varsity match (Cambridge won 33–3). He also played rugby for London Scottish. Henry represented the University at the Queen's Club in 1912, 1913, and 1914, winning the hundred yards in the last two years and being President during the last pre-war Cambridge University sports.

As a field athlete, Henry experienced both success and failure. Of the latter, in 1912 at the Cambridge University sports he lost in the 100 yards to Trinity College undergraduate and fellow Olympian Duncan Macmillan (1890–1963). He also lost in the match against Oxford and finished last in his 100 yards heat at the AAA Championships; he did not run in the 220 yards. In 1912, he participated in the Stockholm Summer Olympic Games where, despite a poor domestic season, he won a gold medal as the second leg of the men's 4 × 100 metres relay. This remarkable achievement makes Henry the only Olympic gold medallist Corpus has so far produced. He and his relay team won despite finishing second to the United States in the semi-final. The United States team was later disqualified for a baton-passing fault, the German team made same mistake in the final.

In 1913, Mackintosh became Captain of the Cambridge University Athletics Club and went on to win the 100 yards against Oxford. His vastly improved form continued when he won the Scottish 100 yards title before equalling the British record of 9.8 seconds in Vienna. In 1914, he again won the 100 yards against Oxford and for a time he held the 100 yards championship in Scotland and England.

By the time of his graduation, the College had become immensely proud of Henry Macintosh's achievements, which were lauded in *The Letter of the Corpus Association*, No. 1 (July 1914). It reads:

> The President of the CUAC, Mr Macintosh, is a tower of strength in the College, particularly so far as athletics is concerned. His performances at the Olympic Games and in the Oxford and Cambridge match are familiar to Corpus men. He inaugurated the annual athletic contest against Exeter College, Oxford. In the first we won a match of nine events by five events to four.

Henry Macintosh graduated in June 1914 and had just begun a career as a District Officer with the Colonial Service in South Africa when war broke out. He immediately returned to Scotland, where he obtained a commission with the 1/8th (Argyllshire) Battalion Princess Louise's (Argyll and Sutherland

Highlanders). In May 1915, after a period of training, his Battalion landed in France as part of the 152nd Brigade, 51st Highland Division. It was immediately committed to the Battle of Festubert and then the Second Action of Givenchy.

The following year, the Battalion was again in action, this time at High Wood during the Somme Campaign and later in the year at the Battle of the Ancre. In 1917, the Battalion took part in both Battles of the Scarpe, the capture and defence of Roeux, and, during the 3rd Battle of Ypres, known as Passchendaele, the Battles of Pilkem Ridge and Menin Road Ridge. During the November 1917 Cambrai offensive, it took part in the capture of Bourlon Wood.

Henry remained on active service in France and Flanders until his death on 26 July 1918 at a casualty clearing station of wounds received during the 2nd

Battle of the Somme. He was aged 26. After his death, he was described by friends and colleagues as displaying the same keenness and thoroughness in his military work as he did in his earlier life and was extremely popular with his men and his fellow-officers.

Henry Maitland Macintosh is buried in Senlis National Cemetery, Senlis, France. At the time of his death, his two brothers were prisoners of war in Germany. His parents were living at St John's Rectory, Alloa, Clackmannanshire, Scotland. His name appears on the Glenalmond College war memorial. TNA have an officer file WO 339/32544 and a medal card WO 372/13/10671.

WEBB, Arthur Henry, 2nd Lieutenant (1891–1917), 4th Battalion (attached to the 8th Battalion) the Buffs (East Kent Regiment) (Territorial Force).

Arthur Webb was born on 18 December 1891 at Dairy House Farm, Manningtree, Wix, Tendring, Essex, the son of Sarah Emily Webb née Taylor and Arthur Webb, a farmer. Arthur and his younger brother George were educated at Colchester Royal Grammar School (Arthur between 1903 and 1911). During his school years, he captained the cricket and football teams and awarded colours in cricket, football, and shooting. In August 1910, he was selected to play cricket for Essex Public Schools. He took part in the debating society, cadets, and school

plays and eventually became senior prefect and school captain.

Arthur matriculated into Corpus in 1911 with a Hewitt Scholarship to read the Medieval and Modern Languages Tripos. To develop his language skills, he spent his College vacations in France and Germany, and in May 1914 was awarded a College grant of £30. During his time at Corpus, he was a member of both the Boat Club and the Chess Club. He was also first Secretary then Captain of Cricket. It was said of him: 'He was devoted to all games, a good shot and a good horseman.' In addition to engaging fully in the academic and social life of the College, he joined the Cambridge University OTC. Arthur graduated on 23 June 1913 with First Class Honours in the Medieval and Modern Languages Tripos. In 1914, he became a house tutor and master of languages at Clifton College, Bristol.

When war broke out, Arthur tried unsuccessfully to get a commission but failed the medical examination on three occasions because of a serious pre-existing knee injury. However, in January 1916, he was accepted into the Army Reserves. Mobilised on 25 April, Arthur returned to Cambridge and with the support of both his OTC unit and Edmund Pearce, the Master of Corpus, obtained a commission in the Buffs (East Kent Regiment). On 3 August 1916, he went for officer training with No. 9 Officer Cadet Battalion at Gailes Camp, Ayrshire, Scotland and was commissioned 2nd Lieutenant on 23 November 1916, gazetted 8 December. His skills as a linguist led to the offer of a post at General HQ but he rejected it, preferring instead to take his chances in the trenches.

In June 1917, in the aftermath of the Battle of Messines, the 8th Battalion took over front-line trenches near a Bluff known as Hill 60 and were tasked with capturing high ground to the east. It turned out the high ground was artificial, created by spoil dumped during the cutting of a nearby canal. At this point in the war, the area witnessed savage hand-to-hand fighting involving the Buffs. After the fighting, the spoilbank was renamed and marked 'Buffs Bank' on later trench maps and it was mentioned in the Buffs' regimental history.

On 23 June 1917, the 8th Battalion's war diary reported that, from Dickes-busch:

> they moved off by platoons to relieve 3rd Battalion Rifle Brigade NW of Battle Wood … Owing to heavy shelling of Shrapnel Corner, the route was changed at the last minute, and we moved via Chester Farm … Two Companies went somewhat astray at this point and, of these B Company lost 2nd Lieutenant Webb, and had two men wounded (our only casualties).

In a letter to his family, Major P. Vaughan wrote:

Never have I known an officer held in more universal esteem both by officers and men. This was the natural result of his conduct, which at all times was governed by the very highest sense of duty and which led his Commanding Officer to have the greatest confidence in him. At the time of his death, he was leading his men into action, when he was hit by a piece of shell and killed instantly.

Arthur Webb was killed in action at Hill 60 on 24 June 1917, aged 25. He was buried where he fell and has no known grave. He is commemorated on the Ypres (Menin Gate) Memorial. TNA have an officer file WO 374/72649 and a medal card WO 372/21/54647. He is also commemorated with a memorial in St Mary's Church, Wix, Tendring.

CCCC Chess Club serial

During his time at Corpus, Arthur Webb was a member of the Chess Club. In this picture, he is on the left standing next to his friend Hubert Churchward (see above).

CCCC Chess Club serial

The Chess Club October 1913.
Of the eleven undergraduates in this photograph, four were killed in the war. They were A H Webb, H A Churchward, M J G Whittam, and H M Macintosh (the only ever Corpus Olympic gold medallist). E D and A F Yencken were Australian brothers and although both experienced military service they survived the war. During the Second World War, Arthur Yencken (seated third right between H M Macintosh and G C H Culley) was Minister at the British Embassy in Madrid, Spain. In May 1944, he died when the plane in which he was traveling crashed.

1912

BROWNLEE, Wilfred Methven, 2nd Lieutenant (1890–1914), 3rd (Special Reserve) Battalion Dorsetshire Regiment.

Wilfred Brownlee was born on 18 April 1890 in Barton Regis, Gloucestershire, the son of William Methven Brownlee a wine merchant and writer (he was the author of a biography of cricketer W G Grace) and Edith Marian née Wilford. His sister was Gladys Methven Brownlee, who became a Bristol portrait photographer and his younger brother was Leigh Dunlop Brownlee (1882–1955), an Oxford Cricketing and Golfing Blue and county cricketer. He later became a journalist and editor of the *Daily Mirror*.

Wilfred was educated at Wilson's Grammar School, Camberwell and Clifton College where, between 1906 and 1909, he was a member of the cricket XI and in 1909 its captain. He also played for the Public Schools XI against MCC and took eight wickets for sixty-one. He went on to play first-class cricket as an amateur for Gloucestershire. The 1915 edition of *Wisden Cricketers' Almanack* has an obituary. It reads:

> At Clifton he showed very good all-round cricket. In 1908 he headed the batting averages with 23.57, and took most wickets (49), and in 1909, when captain, averaged 32.54 with the bat and headed the bowling with 34 wickets for 15.02 runs each. On his first appearance for Gloucestershire – against Worcestershire, at Worcester, in 1909 – he played an innings of 64, and if he had been able to play in first-class matches at all regularly, he would no doubt have developed into an excellent cricketer. In the second innings of the match with Essex at Cheltenham in 1909 he scored 49 not out, and in partnership with Langdon (38 not out) scored 91 without loss of a wicket in twenty-five minutes: the innings was then declared closed, but Gloucestershire were unable to snatch a victory.

The obituary concluded its cricketing assessment: 'Brownlee was a free hitting batsman, a fast-medium paced bowler who could make the ball swerve and a brilliant fieldsman.' His prowess as a cricketer was such that when he came up to Corpus, it was reported that: 'Clifton were weakened by the going down of the admirable all-round cricketer, Mr W M Brownlee.' He also played racquets and in his final year at Clifton won the challenge cup. During his time at Corpus, he played hockey as well as cricket. Of this, *The Benedict* (Lent Term 1913) said of him: 'A somewhat "fidgety" forward, with a horrible habit of always trying to pick up the ball with his stick. Latterly, has much improved in combination, and is a goodish shot. Has been very useful in getting back to help the backs.' He was also a member of the Strawberries.

Wilfred Brownlee left the College on the outbreak of war and never graduated. He enlisted as a Private in the 6th Battalion Gloucestershire Regiment but was immediately commissioned 2nd Lieutenant in the 3rd (Special Reserve) Battalion Dorsetshire Regiment. Within days, the Battalion was posted for training at Wyke Regis, Dorset, where living conditions were described as 'initially sparse'. His unit's first wartime role was to guard local railways, waterworks, and other sites of strategic importance. However, the Battalion quickly became a vehicle for equipping and training men prior to sending them on active service. Unfortunately, soon after his arrival at the camp, Wilfred contracted meningitis and pneumonia and on 12 October 1914 died in a military hospital, aged 24. The local military establishment followed his coffin, draped in the Union Flag and decorated with a full-length floral cross, to the railway station where a salute was fired over his body. In their book *For Club, King and Country*, Martin and Teresa Davis wrote of Wilfred Brownlee: 'His death would typify that of many others who had been plucked from the relative comfort of a home environment and thrust into the harsh and demanding one of the British Army as it prepared its young men for what would be the unimaginable rigours and hardships of the battlefield.'[15]

After his death, it was said of Wilfred that his greatest challenges in life were to be his future direction. A Corpus contemporary wrote: 'should he be captain of the England cricket team or, perhaps, Prime Minister?' A brother officer later said: 'he might equally have played either role, or possibly both, with distinction.'

The Times said of him: 'all the gifts of the Gods were his, among them tireless energy, intellect, Grecian good looks, a fundamental kindness and charity, (and) a Christian soul beyond his years'. Wilfred Brownlee was buried alongside his father at Bristol (Arnos Vale) Cemetery. The army had offered full military honours, but this was declined by the family who requested a quiet and simple service. TNA have an officer file at WO 339/10822.

---

15. Martin and Teresa Davis, *For Club, King and Country: The Story of the Gloucestershire County Cricketers and the Gloucestershire Rugby Club Players as Soldiers of Gloucestershire in the Great War 1914–1918* (2014). See also Nigel McCrery, *Final Wicket: Test and First-Class Cricketers Killed in the Great War* (2015), and Roger Gibbons, *In Memoriam, Gloucestershire County Cricketers Killed in the Great War* (2015).

DAVIES, Trevor Arthur Manning, Lieutenant (1893–1916), 4th North Midland (Howitzer) Brigade, Royal Field Artillery (Territorial Force) attached to the 1/5th

Battalion Sherwood Foresters (Nottingham-shire and Derbyshire Regiment).

Trevor Davies was born on 6 April 1893 in Walsall, Warwickshire, the son of Arthur Manning Davies and Ada Rose née Jennings of Llandudno, Caernarvonshire (now Clwyd). His father described himself as a colliery agents' manager in the 1901 census; he subsequently established a wholesale coal business. In the 1911 census, the family, which included a second son Horace (aged 16), lived at Handsworth.

During the academic year 1908–09, Trevor attended the King Edward's School, Birmingham, where he was a Foundation Scholar. The next academic year saw him transfer to Clifton College, Bristol as a boarder. During his time at Clifton, he was a member of Barff's House, and in 1911, he played for the House XV. The following year, he was made head of house. In 1912, Trevor matriculated into Corpus where he was Senior Classical Scholar, held a Manners Scholarship (with his Clifton contemporary Frank Terrell, see below) and awarded the Latin Declamation Cup two years in a row. Trevor was also a member of the OTC.

When war was declared, he had completed two years of his degree course and like so many of his cohort, he left the College to join the armed forces and did not graduate. On 29 August 1914, Trevor Davies was gazetted 2nd Lieutenant in the 4th North Midland (Howitzer) Brigade, Royal Field Artillery (Territorial Force). In 1915, it reformed as the 139th Brigade, 46th North Midland Division and became the first Territorial Force Division to land in France, serving initially in the Ypres Salient. Trevor Davies arrived in theatre on 24 February 1915, at which point he was promoted to Lieutenant. On 12 May, he was in action at

Hooge. He also took part in the October 1915 attack on the Hohenzollern Redoubt. Over the New Year of 1916, his unit was briefly in Egypt before returning to France.

The beginning of the Somme Campaign on 1 July 1916 saw Trevor's unit (the 1/5th Battalion Sherwood Foresters) form part of a diversionary attack on Gommecourt, eight miles to the north of Albert. The attack aimed to draw German troops away from the main British offensive and at the same time take the Gommecourt Salient. Trevor's role was as a liaison officer between the artillery and infantry. Unfortunately, as with so many Forward

Observation Officers, he was killed relaying infor-
mation back to his guns. He was aged 23. In a final
letter to his parents, sent on the morning of 1 July
1916, Trevor wrote: 'I am starting in 20 minutes.
Thank you so much for all you have done for me,
and all you have had to put up [with] from me;
I am sorry. My love to you all. Trevor.'

When the battlefield was cleared, his body was
buried in Gommecourt No. 1 Cemetery. However,
after the war, his remains were reinterred in
Gommecourt extended British No. 2 Cemetery, Pas de Calais, France. Probate
on Trevor's estate was granted to his father and valued at £187.

There is some confusion about Trevor's memorial as he is mistakenly
recorded being commemorated at both Arras and Thiepval. Furthermore, the
King Edward's School service record mistakenly states he was killed at Ypres. In
the event, neither is correct; all the evidence shows he was killed on the Somme.
His life is commemorated on tablets in the Memorial Chapel of Holy Trinity
Church, Llandudno. In addition, two large wooden candlesticks, still in use,
were presented to this church in Trevor's memory. TNA have an officer file
WO 374/18429 and a medal card WO 372/5/197424.

TERRELL, Frank William, Lieutenant (1893–1916), 8th (Service) Battalion
Gloucestershire Regiment, attached to the 3rd Battalion Worcestershire Regiment.

Frank Terrell was born on 15 March 1893
in Hankow (Hankou), China, the only son
of missionaries William Girdlestone and
Gertrude Ann Lucy Terrell. His father died in
1897 at Hiao Kan, Hankow. At the time, he and
his family were serving as missionaries with
the Church Missionary Society, Bristol. The
Terrell family owned a Bristol-based business
manufacturing wire and rope, which was the
largest of its kind in the south-west. Frank's
grandfather was a Bristol-based physician
William Lucy MRCS LRCP. On the death
of his father, Frank, aged 3, returned to
Britain; his mother and elder sister, however,
continued their missionary work.

Frank was educated at Blackheath School for the sons of missionaries,
Eltham College, and finally at Clifton College, where he was both a scholar and
a member of the OTC. In 1912, he matriculated into Corpus to read the Classical
Tripos as the holder of a Manners Scholarship, as did his Clifton contemporary
Trevor Davies (see above). He intended to follow his father's calling and after

graduation undertake missionary work in China. Unfortunately, war intervened and he never completed his degree nor did he graduate. Instead, Frank volunteered for foreign service with the Bristol OTC and later transferred to the Cambridge OTC where, on 27 November 1914, he was gazetted 2nd Lieutenant with the Gloucestershire Regiment; he was promoted Lieutenant on 17 March 1915. He served with the BEF in France and Flanders between July 1915 and March 1916, when he was wounded at Neuve Chapelle and invalided back to Bristol. Frank returned to France in July 1916, attached to the 3rd Battalion Worcestershire Regiment.

On 3 September 1916, during the Somme Offensive, Frank Terrell was killed during an attack on German trenches near Thiepval, aged 22. Writing to Frank's family, his Commanding Officer said: 'We all miss Terrell very much. He was always smiling and cheerful. He was killed while gallantly leading his men on the early morning of 3 Sept.' The officer commanding his company at Seaford, East Sussex said of him: 'Indeed, he was one of the finest of officers that one could possibly meet, and both the men of the company and myself count it as a pleasure and benefit that we should have had the opportunity of working with him to further our great common end.'

Frank Terrell had been a member of the Highbury Congregational Church, Cotham, Bristol (now Cotham Parish Church), and on the Sunday following his death the minister, the Reverend H Arnold Thomas, spoke of him. His remarks were included in an appreciation which was published in the *Western Daily Mail* on 11 September 1916:

> He was (he said) in a peculiar sense a child of that church, both his father and grandfather having been members of the congregation, and many who were present had known him from his earliest childhood. He had been well named 'Frank', for he was specially characterised by the qualities indicated by the word. He was so fresh, so outspoken, so bright and fearless, so full of boyish energy and fun. They knew what his history had been, how when his father died in China, twenty years ago, he was brought as a child of three years old to this country to be educated, how he was sent first to the missionary school at Blackheath, then to Clifton College, where he won an Entrance Scholarship, and afterwards proceeded to Corpus Christi College, Cambridge, where also he won an Entrance Scholarship. Boyish as he was in manner, he had remarkable intellectual gifts. He had a natural gift for music, and Dr Davis had told him (Mr Thomas) that he had displayed a rare talent for mathematics. Mathematics had a rare fascination for him, and so absorbed his mind that he could not sleep, and he was recommended to give up the study and turn to classics. This he did and made such progress that he was able to gain a scholarship for Cambridge. They knew, too, how it had been his hope to carry on his father's work as a

missionary, and that it was in his view of this purpose that the 'David Thomas' Scholarship had been awarded to him. He intended if his life should be spared, to complete his education at Mansfield College, Oxford. He was a man of very sincere and simple piety. Perplexed, as most open-minded people are likely to be perplexed, he was fighting his way through these troubles, and had come to trust in God and the future with a steadfast faith. His Chaplain (Captain Weir) has written that Frank and he had recently agreed to pray for each other, and Captain Weir was especially to pray that Frank's courage might not fail him when he entered into action last Sunday. He was one of those heroic and sensitive souls that are afraid of being afraid, but the men of his regiment bear witness that he was distinguished for his daring, and he certainly showed no fear when the critical moment came. He valued their prayers greatly, and last Sunday morning, when he had to go into that 'hell' at the battle front, he was rejoicing in the thought that it was their Communion Sunday and that they were meeting in fellowship with one another, and with him. It was all very sad and very tragic, and they could not think without profoundest sympathy of the mother and sister in China, but they must hope that the sacrifices of these noble young men would not be in vain, and that the country and the church would be enriched and purified by the consecration of those who had thus laid down their lives.

At the close of the service, the congregation stood while the organist played the Dead March from *Saul*.

Frank William Terrell was buried at Heath Cemetery, Harbonnières, Somme, France. The personal inscription on his gravestone reads *Resurgam* ('I shall rise again'). He is remembered on the Eltham College and Clifton College war memorials. TNA have an officer file WO 339/1581 and a medal card WO 372/19/192556.

WHITTAM, Matthew John Goldsborough, Lieutenant (1893–1915), 8th (Service) Battalion Duke of Wellington's (West Riding) Regiment.

According to a newspaper death notice, Matthew was born on 24 September 1893 in Ryde, Isle of Wight, the only son of the Reverend William Goldsborough Whittam and Florence Lucy née Pierce, of Kelvedon, Essex; his father had been headmaster at the Isle of Wight College, Ryde. He was educated first at Reading School and then, between 1908 and 1912, at St Paul's. According to *The Pauline* (October 1915) obituary: 'He had taken a prominent part in the life of the School. He was a member of the Gymnasium VIII, obtained his 1st XV colours, and was on the committee of his club (A).' Matthew was elected to a Pauline Exhibition at Corpus, matriculating

in 1912 and had completed his second year when war broke out. During this time at Corpus, he was a member of the Chess Club and showed great promise as an athlete. On the declaration of war, Matthew, like many of his cohort, left the College for the armed forces and did not graduate.

In September 1914, he was gazetted to the 8th (Service) Battalion Duke of Wellington's (West Riding) Regiment. Raised at Halifax in August 1914, the Battalion was part of Kitchener's First New Army and an element of 34th Brigade (subsequently 32nd Brigade), 11th (Northern) Division. In February 1915, he was promoted Lieutenant and in July, following training, Matthew Whittam and the 8th Battalion sailed from Liverpool via Mudros to Gallipoli, landing at Lala Baba, near Suvla Bay on 6 and 7 August. On 10 August, he was part of the attack by British forces on the nearby Scimitar Hill attempting to clear it of Ottoman units who were preventing the Allies getting off the Suvla Bay beach head. Unfortunately, this attack failed and saw the decimation of the Division as a fighting unit. It was on 11 August, during the Battle of Scimitar Hill, that Matthew was wounded and died, aged 21. He is buried at Lancashire Landing Cemetery, Gallipoli and his headstone bears the inscription 'Beloved son of W. G. and F. L. Whittam "True Till Death"'. *The Pauline* obituary noted: 'His kindly and modest nature made him a general favourite, and his loss is greatly mourned by those who were associated with him at St. Paul's.'

His name was added to the Praelector's Book as matriculating 22 October 1912. TNA have an officer file WO 339/12260.

1913

BUDGEN, Robert Gordon, Lieutenant (1894–1915), 5th (Service) Battalion King's Shropshire Light Infantry.

Robert Gordon Budgen was born in Bishopwearside, Sunderland on 5 March 1894, the son of the Reverend William Budgen (m.1888) and Elizabeth Esther née Scott. Known as Gordon, he was the second son and third of ten children, five boys and five girls. Between 1897 and 1903, he lived in Stafford and, between 1903 and 1913 (when he came to Corpus), at Newport, Shropshire, where his father was rector of St Nicholas' Parish Church.

Prior to coming to Corpus, he was educated at Adams Grammar School, Newport, Shropshire.

During his time at the College, Gordon was a member of the Boat Club and rowed at four in the 1914 second Lent boat, which bumped up three places. On the outbreak of war, he left the College to join the armed forces and never completed his degree or graduated.

Gordon was commissioned 2nd Lieutenant in the 5th (Service) Battalion King's Shropshire Light Infantry and after training at Aldershot and Chiddingfold landed in Belgium on 20 May 1915. Arnold Mathews (see below) also joined this Battalion, which formed part of the 42nd Brigade in the 14th (Light) Division. The Battalion saw action during the final days of the 2nd Battle of Ypres (which witnessed the destruction of most of the town and the first use of poison gas by German forces).

In a highly ironic 9 July 1915 letter from Ypres to his sister, he wrote referencing the chaotic scenes in the ruins of the town and the German use of gas in the recent attack:

> We are in dugouts built in the town walls of a certain city and the certain city lies before us with only a few policemen in it. Our dugouts are really extraordinarily comfortable, I for instance have a beautiful mattress to lie on, a chair, a foot stool, a table, a lamp, an unlimited supply of crockery and the secret of where there is an unlimited supply of coal, what more does anybody want? We even have gas laid on (by the Germans). Today I have been amusing myself by building a messing dugout. In a lordly way I got a fatigue party of 20 men and then realised I was an architect and had to superintend things generally, I knew nothing about building. The house lacks its roof but hasn't fallen down to date: it has had to be propped up however. It has two doorways (both looted) set askew and the walls bulge; the men gave me such encouragement and told me that everything would be alright when it had settled but I am afraid the whole caboose will settle in a different sense.

Six weeks later, on 24 August 1915, Robert Gordon Budgen was killed in action on the Ypres Salient, aged 21. Although it is uncertain, it probably occurred in the aftermath of the Battle of Hooge during which the Battalion was attacked by the Germans with the first use of flamethrowers.

A descendant has observed:

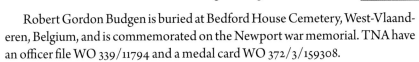

> One of our Aunts described Uncle Gordon's death as having 'torn the heart out of the family', but this was only the beginning of the catastrophe, which overtook Granny Budgen and her family. During the 2nd World War, Gordon's brothers Bob and Roger were both killed, as was Bill Budgen MC, the only son of another brother Air Commodore Douglas Budgen.

Robert Gordon Budgen is buried at Bedford House Cemetery, West-Vlaanderen, Belgium, and is commemorated on the Newport war memorial. TNA have an officer file WO 339/11794 and a medal card WO 372/3/159308.

CROSSE, Robert Grant, Lieutenant (1894–1916), 7th Battalion The Queen's Own (Royal West Kent Regiment).

Robert Crosse was born in Canterbury on 15 June 1894, the second son of the Reverend Canon Thomas George and Fanny Marie (née Nelson) Crosse of Ickham Rectory, Canterbury. His father was vicar of Faversham.

He was educated at Faversham Grammar School (now Queen Elizabeth's Grammar School), and between 1908 and 1913, at The King's School, Canterbury, where he was a day boy. According to its Roll of Honour, in 1909, he gained a junior scholarship and in 1912, a senior scholarship. He played for the 2nd XV rugby team in the academic year 1912 to 1913 and awarded colours in 1912. He rowed for the Second Boat in 1913 and awarded rowing colours that year. He was appointed a house monitor in September 1911 and a school monitor the following year. He was a member of the OTC from 1909 and appointed Quartermaster Sergeant in September 1912. He passed the practical paper for Certificate A in February 1914 and received hunting and military riding instruction at Canterbury Barracks.

On leaving King's in 1913, Robert matriculated into Corpus as a Parker Exhibitioner. He was a member of the Boat Club and rowed in a trial eight in the Michaelmas Term. He never graduated and left the College on the outbreak of war.

Robert obtained a commission in the Special Reserve of Officers for the infantry on 7 August 1914 (three days after war was declared) in an application supported by the Reverend Charles Robert Loraine McDowall, headmaster of The King's School, Canterbury and commissioned 2nd Lieutenant in The Queen's Own (Royal West Kent Regiment) on 1 November 1914. He was promoted to Lieutenant on 13 March 1915 and went to France that summer.

The circumstances of his death are as follows: on the evening of 12 July 1916, at the height of the Somme Offensive, his battalion took up positions in the southern end of Trones Wood. Its objective was to clear the remaining enemy positions in the woods in preparation for a major attack planned for 14 July. The woods were full of the shattered trees and enemy strong points and as the orders arrived late in the day on 13 July, there was little time to prepare. At 7 pm, after a three-hour bombardment, the attack began. The support companies lost

heavily due to a German counter barrage, but the Battalion made good progress. By 7.30 pm, B Company had reached a light railway that ran through the wood; however, German troops filtered back behind them reoccupying a strong point to their rear. A mixed group under Captain Holland dug themselves in along the

railway line but were unsupported and under almost constant attack mainly from their rear. Meanwhile, nothing had been heard of C Company. Captain Anstruther went forward to find a mixed group of about 150 men from various companies whose own officers had either been killed or wounded. He reorganised them, placing 100 men and six Lewis machine guns along the eastern edge of the wood, taking the rest forward. By midnight, there were some 250 Royal West Kents in Trones Wood. Captain Holland's party were still isolated, hard pressed and subject to counterattacks. Captain Anstruther, in a similar position, successfully fought off the attacks, declining assistance from the Middlesex Regiment who offered two platoons as reinforcements. At daylight, the attacks intensified, and ammunition ran low, but the 12th Battalion Middlesex Regiment and 6th Battalion Northampton Regiment rushed the woods linked up with the

two groups of West Kents and drove out the Germans. The surviving enemy troops were shot down by the group on the eastern side of the woods with their Lewis guns. Casualties were heavy; Lieutenants Skinner and 2nd Lieutenants Cathcart, File, Forsyth and Saveall were all killed or died of wounds with 28 other ranks killed, 23 missing and 174 wounded. Robert Crosse was badly wounded and evacuated to 28 Field Ambulance. The following day, 14 July 1916, he died aged 22.

An interview with Private 1899 George Gillian, 9 Platoon, C Company, 7th Battalion The Queen's Own (Royal West Kent Regiment) on 17 July 1916 revealed: 'Informant states that on July 13th, 1916, at about 7 pm at Trones Wood. "I saw Mr Cross [*sic*] killed by a shell. He was a few yards from me and died in a few minutes. His body was left in the trench when we retired, I was wounded about 15 minutes after that."'

Robert's brother, Captain Thomas Latymer Crosse BA (who was born in 1889, educated at St Lawrence College, Ramsgate and read the Classical Tripos at Gonville & Caius (m.1908)), 7th Battalion Border Regiment, was killed in action on 3 July 1916, also during the Somme Offensive, at Fricourt, eleven days before his brother. They are commemorated by a brass plaque in St Mary of Charity Church, Faversham, Kent, where their father was vicar. It reads:

> In loving memory of THOMAS LATYMER CROSSE, B.A. Captain 7th Bn.
> The Border Regiment killed in action at Fricourt July 3rd, 1916 aged 27 years.
> Also of ROBERT GRANT CROSSE Lieut. 7th Bn. Royal West Kent Regiment
> died of wounds at Trones Wood July 14th 1916 aged 22 years sons of the Vicar of
> Faversham and Mrs CROSSE 'In the Lord I put my trust' (Psalms 31:1).

Both are commemorated on The King's School, Canterbury war memorial; Mrs Crosse gave a donation to the school in memory of Robert. This was to be used by the Boat Club or for Hodgson's Hall. The *Cantuarian* reported that an adjustable invalid couch had been bought for the sanatorium.

Robert Crosse is buried at Peronne Cemetery, Maricourt, Somme, France. The personal inscription on his headstone reads 'Not my will but thine be done R.I.P.' (Luke 22.42). TNA have an officer file WO 339/20835 and a medal card WO 372/5/105269.

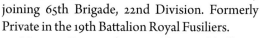

DAY, Norman Leslie, 2nd Lieutenant (1894–1916), 'C' Company 14th (Service) Battalion The King's Regiment (Liverpool), part of Kitchener's Third New Army

joining 65th Brigade, 22nd Division. Formerly Private in the 19th Battalion Royal Fusiliers.

Norman Day was born in Olton, Solihull on 3 June 1894, the only son and eldest child of William Henry, a commercial traveller in varnishes and colours and his wife Emily Louisa. The family lived in Crouch Hill, London and Norman had two younger sisters Theodora Gwendolyn (1897– 1991) and Eileen Christina (b.1902).

Between 1910 and 1912, Norman was educated at Southgate County School, Palmers Green, London, where he was a prefect and prize winner. In 1911, he passed the London University Matriculation 'with Distinction in Mechanics, Electricity and Magnetism' and the following year was awarded a Special Prize 'by Vote to the Prefects who in Work, Sport, and Public Spirit set the Best Example'.

He matriculated into Corpus in 1913 on a three-year Open Scholarship of £40 a year for the study of Science and Mathematics and a three-year Senior County Scholarship of £50 a year. During his time at the College, he read the Natural Sciences Tripos. Norman was also a member of the Boat Club and rowed at two in the 1914 second Lent boat, bumping up three places. Like so many of his cohorts, he left the College on the outbreak of war and never graduated.

He enlisted as a Private in the 19th Battalion Royal Fusiliers, but quickly obtained a commission with The King's Regiment (Liverpool). Norman Day's regiment formed part of the 22nd Division, one of six created for the Third New Army. It moved to France in early September 1915 and then a month later to Salonika (now Thessaloniki). In December 1915, during the Retreat from Serbia, Norman saw action against Bulgarian forces and in August 1916 at the Battle of

Horseshoe Hill. On 14 September 1916, he was killed in action during the Battle of Machukovo and has no known grave. He is commemorated on the Doiran war memorial, near the Doiran military cemetery, Greece. TNA have a medal card WO 372/5/225015.

L to r: Robert Crosse, Norman Leslie Day and Sidney Leslie Roy Sharp: this photograph shows them as part of the bank party on the Cam during the 1914 Lent bumps.

DEVEREUX, Humphrey William, Lieutenant (1894–1916), 1/5th Battalion South Staffordshire Regiment (Territorial Force).

Humphrey William Devereux was born in Scarning, Dereham, Norfolk on 3 June 1894, the elder son of Walter de Laci Devereux (1864–1959) and Blanche Isabel née Johnstone (1867–1949) of Great Shelford, Cambridge-shire and formerly of Middlewood, St Saviour's, Jersey, CI. He was educated at Victoria College, Jersey and its Roll of Honour has the following:

He entered College in 1905 and was with us for more than five years. From here he went to the Perse School, Cambridge and later obtained an Open Classical Scholarship at Corpus Christi College, Cambridge.

From the age of thirteen he was a member of the Cadet Corps and OTC and went to camp every year. He was in his second year at Cambridge when war broke out, and he obtained a commission in the 1/5th Battalion, The South Staffordshire Regiment (T) under his old Commanding Officer, Lieutenant Colonel Raymer.

A note on a Great Shelford history website has the following information:

Walter Devereux, the brothers' father, was the West Cambridgeshire Conservative agent, while his own father had been a rear-admiral in the navy… When war broke out Walter devoted himself to the war effort, while his three sons all served in the forces – Humphrey William, Edmund Bourchier and Robert de Bohun Devereux MBE (1897–1981). Humphrey's younger brother, Flight Lieutenant (Lieutenant RN) Edmund Bourchier Devereux (1895–1917), (educated at Victoria College and Dartmouth Naval College) was killed on 27th November 1917, aged 22, when the RN Airship P2 was lost at sea off the Orkney Islands.

The youngest, Robert, survived the war and served in the Second World War attaining the rank of Lieutenant Colonel in the Royal Scots.

During the war, his parents lived in Great Shelford, though at the time of Humphrey's death his father was working with the YMCA huts in France; both sons are commemorated on the Great Shelford village war memorial.

At the Battle of Loos in October 1915, Humphrey Devereux was wounded during the attack on the Hohenzollern Redoubt. He was repatriated and in January 1916, after a period of recovery, returned to his Battalion. In April 1916, after home service, he returned to the front. On 26 June 1916, just before the opening phase of the Somme Campaign, he was killed by a shell whilst serving in the trenches. After his death, his Colonel wrote: 'He was my best subaltern, and in a few weeks would have been recommended for promotion to Captain. His loss is a great grief to all who served with him. I wish to heaven I had more like him. His fearless resolution was an inspiration to his men.' His Company commander said:

> It is impossible to tell you how much he will be missed by the whole battalion, particularly by those of us, and they are now very few, who were privileged to be in close contact with him since the regiment came to France. He has been in my company since he joined and has earned the love and admiration of all.

Humphrey Devereux is buried in Humbercamps Communal Cemetery Extension, Pas de Calais, France. His headstone bears the inscription; *Memento Pueruli Illius Quem Cognovisti Atque Tantopere Amavisti* ('In memory of that boy whom you knew and loved so much'). TNA have an officer file WO 374/19399 and a medal card WO 372/6/11131.

LEWIS, Arthur Milton, Acting Captain (1894–1919) 1st Battalion 52nd Sikhs (Frontier Force), Indian Army Reserve of Officers. Formerly Lieutenant, 9th  (Service) Battalion Devonshire Regiment and previously Private, Public Schools Battalion Royal Fusiliers.

Arthur Lewis was born on 14 November 1894, the son of the Reverend Walter A Lewis MA (1851–1947), rector of St Gregory's Church, Goodleigh, Devon and Annie Phoebe Campbell née Briggs (d.1934). Arthur and his younger brother John Walter (1896–1916) were educated first at Bath College and then, between 1907 and 1913, at King William's College, Isle of Man. Arthur was a sixth form praepositor, had rugby XV colours, captained his house in running, was captain of the fire brigade, a Lance Corporal in the OTC and swam the Grand Test four years in a row.[16]

In October 1913, Arthur matriculated into Corpus with the intention of taking his degree prior to training for the Anglican priesthood. During his time at the College, he was a member of the Boat Club and rowed bow in the 1914 first Lent boat and in the May boat. He was also a member of the University OTC. Arthur was about to start his second year when war was declared and he, like many others, left his studies for the armed forces.

He enlisted as a Private in the Public Schools Battalion Royal Fusiliers and on 7 December 1914 was commissioned 2nd Lieutenant in the 9th Battalion Devonshire Regiment. He went with his Battalion to France in October 1915 and took part in the Battle of Loos. He was wounded on 1 July 1916, the first day of the Somme Campaign and Mentioned in Despatches. Of this he wrote:

> My luck still follows me. I was in the casualty list for the third time today, with another soft wound. A Boche machine-gunner legged me in front of Mametz wood on the morning of July 1st. We were one of the first divisions to go over the top, and I feel no small pride that GHQ sent a special aide-de-camp to congratulate our brigade after the attack.

Unfortunately, the true cost of this war quickly caught up with Arthur as, on 15 July 1916, his younger brother 2nd Lieutenant John Walter Lewis, 8th Battalion Devonshire Regiment, but attached to the 9th to be with his brother, died of wounds received the previous day. He was aged 20.

On 7 September 1916, Arthur was promoted Lieutenant and on 23 March 1917, selected as an Indian Army probationer attached to the 1st Battalion 52nd Sikh (Frontier Force). His Battalion was posted to Mesopotamia (present-day

---

16. This refers to its annual open water half-mile swim in Derbyhaven Bay, which usually takes place in late June, depending on tides and weather conditions. Around thirty pupils and staff take part each year. It is compulsory for all other students to watch the swim.

Iraq), arriving in November 1917. In November 1918, his unit entered Mosul to accept the surrender of Ottoman forces. He was subsequently Mentioned in Despatches 'for services rendered as advanced guard commander in the advance from Samara to Mosul'.

The war in Mesopotamia dragged on after the Ottoman surrender and in July 1919, during an Ottoman inspired insurgency, his Battalion advanced into Kurdistan. At the same time, he was given the rank of Acting Captain. On 8 August 1919, Arthur was amongst those killed in action in a mountainous region at Mazurkha Gorge near Amadiya (close to the present-day Iraq-Turkish border). His column was ambushed and decimated by a band of Kurds under the leadership of Rashid Beg. An online website has the following account of the action: 'The 52nd Sikhs moved to Mosul on 5th November 1918 where they remained until late July 1919 when they marched to Suwara in Central Kurdistan.' A further account has the following:

> On 8th August Major J D Shepherd, Royal Engineers, led a column consisting of one section of sappers and miners; one section of 34th Mountain Battery; 'B' Company 52nd Sikhs (Dogras and Pathans) and a Medical Detachment up into the gorge; this force was too weak to picquet the heights on either side. The local Kurdish insurgent leader Rashid Beg was waiting for the column with his followers. The two leading platoons of 'B' Company were shot down by large numbers of Kurds firing from the front and both flanks. Major Shepherd and 'B' Company Commander Captain A M Lewis were killed, as were Lieutenant B W P Dodds MC, Indian Army Reserve of Officers attached to the battery, and Jemadar Abdulla of 'B' Company. Confusion reigned and the gunners were unable to bring their guns into action as many of the men and mules were shot down.

An obituary in the King William's College journal *The Barrovian* (March 1920), quotes from a letter written by his Commanding Officer to Arthur's parents: 'There was no officer more loved and respected by British and Indian ranks than he was. His company would do anything for him, and they have to a large extent gone too … I have seldom met such a character, never a harsh word to say about anyone, a perfect temper and great control of his men.'

On 11 September 1919, a service was held in his memory at St Gregory's Church, Goodleigh. The local press reported the union flag being draped on the altar frontal with Arthur's sword beneath it. He is commemorated on the Goodleigh, Devon war memorial and by a stained-glass window in St Gregory's Church. His name also appears on the King William's College, Isle of Man Roll of Honour (as does that of his brother) and on the Bath College war memorial in Bath Abbey.

Arthur Lewis died aged 24. He has no known grave but is commemorated on the Basra Memorial, Iraq. There is one further memorial and that is contained in the personal inscription forming part of his brother's gravestone which reads: 'A/Capt A. M. Lewis Devonshire Regiment and 52nd Sikh Regt. Age 24 killed in Mesopotamia Aug. 1919'; thus, the two brothers are forever linked in death. In 2023 his name was added to the College war memorial. TNA have an officer file WO 339/2644 and a medal card WO 372/12/73030.

Stained-glass window commemorating Arthur Milton Lewis at St Gregory's Church, Goodleigh, Devon.

LOCKHART, Norman Douglas Stewart Bruce, Lieutenant (1894–1915), 7th Battalion Seaforth Highlanders, 9th Highland Division (the Commonwealth War Graves Commission database has his name as Norman Douglas Stewart Bruce-Lockhart).

Norman Lockhart was born on 28 November 1894 in Beith, Scotland, the fourth son of Florence (1864–1928) née McGregor and Robert Bruce Lockhart (1858–1950) who was, from 1906 to 1927, headmaster of Eagle House School, Sandhurst, Berkshire. In all, Norman had six siblings. His elder brother was Sir Robert Hamilton Bruce Lockhart (1887–1970), a journalist, author, diplomat and spy, and another was John Bruce Lockhart (1889–1956), a double Blue at Cambridge, a Scottish rugby international and later headmaster of Sedbergh School. His father's family were from Broughty Ferry and Beith, Scotland. They were well known in Scottish rugby circles and in education; his father being founding rector of Waid Academy, Anstruther, Fife, Scotland. According to the Eagle House Roll of Honour, Norman was educated by his father until he was 14. It goes on:

> At Eagle House he was Head of the School in work, as well as Head Prefect and Captain of Games, and was particularly noted for his skill as a 'stand-off-half'. He was very good all round in work, especially in Classics and French: in the latter he took a leading part in the school's French plays. On entering Marlborough [where he was a student between 1908 and 1912], he took a high place and did well in work and football. He was a School Prefect, Head of his House (Preshute), a Member of the Race Committee and he was in the rugby XV for two years [and an NCO in the OTC]. Finally, he took up Modern Languages and, after residence in Germany and France, entered Corpus Christi College, Cambridge in October 1913, and read for the Modern Languages Tripos.

During the single year he spent at Corpus, Norman revealed himself as both a talented student and athlete. He played College rugby and was selected to play in the University Freshman Varsity match. He was also an outstanding freshman talent of the Boat Club (he did so well at these sports that it was suggested he might be elected Secretary of both clubs). According to the Corpus Boat Club minute book, he rowed at five in both the Lent and May boats of 1914; his weight is recorded at 12 stone 1 pound. Unfortunately, according to the Eagle House obituary: 'he broke down in the May Races'. *The Letter of the Corpus Association,*

No. I (July 1914) has an enigmatic reference to the incident: 'In the Mays we were dogged by bad luck. One of the crew had a heart attack in the middle of the race on the first night.' The Boat Club minute book has its own laconic entry: 'Wednesday June 10th, Bumped by Queens' kept well away at the start but were caught by Morley's Holt. '5' petered out, and the doctor will not allow him to row again.' The next entry in the minute book is an account of the General Meeting on 13 June, at which Norman was elected to the committee. At the end of the academic year, he travelled to France but returned, though still not fully recovered, when war broke out.

The Eagle House obituary continues:

However, he came home to volunteer, and joined the 7th Battalion Seaforth Highlanders, 9th Highland Division, at Aldershot on 26th September 1914. After undergoing training, he went to France on 10th May 1915, not long after which he was promoted Lieutenant. He had a short leave from 13th to twentieth September, which he spent at Eagle House. As part of the Battle of Loos, his regiment was given the place of honour to lead the attack on the Hohenzollern Redoubt on the morning of 25th September. Kitchener's famous First Division did not belie its reputation and advanced far into the enemy's lines, but early in the advance a shot struck Norman Lockhart as he mounted a German parapet, and the school magazine reported: 'as he fell, he murmured, "Go on, boys!" and was dead.'

An online account of this action notes:

Within an hour, 7th Seaforth Highlanders had negotiated the southern part of the Hohenzollern Redoubt and captured all its objectives. However, this came at a high price. In consolidating the captured trenches, 7th Seaforths were 'exposed to a murderous fire from the enemy's guns', and 'the behaviour of the men was worthy of the very highest praise'.

The Eagle House obituary goes on:

He was much loved and honoured in his School, his College and his Battalion, and he loved them all with a very strong affection. His Captain, on the eve of the battle, in his last letter to his wife, wrote, 'Bruce is back, I am thankful to say: he is my greatest stand-by.' No-one needs a better epitaph than that, but Captain Kerr Clark often spoke of his subaltern's 'wonderful reliability and grasp of his work', while the following perhaps sums up most concisely the testimony from other brother officers. 'He was loved and admired by his men and by the whole Company and to his brother officers he was a friend in a thousand. As an officer he was one of the very best, and by far the most relied on by the senior officers – he is such a loss to us all.' Many tributes were paid to his lovable nature and high qualities, and perhaps the school magazine may be allowed to quote one in full, because it comes from a very able man who met him in an ordinary business way and had no prejudice of school, college or relationship to influence his words. Mr E S Quiggin [the British linguist Dr Edmund Crosby Quiggin], Fellow of Gonville and Caius College, wrote to the headmaster: 'My name is doubtless entirely strange to you, but I cannot refrain from writing to express the great sorrow I felt on reading of your son's death yesterday. During his residence at Cambridge, he worked under me and I was extremely fond of him. He was one of our very best type of undergraduates, excelling both in work and play, and exercising a very wholesome influence on his fellows. I had hoped that a brilliant future lay before him. England can ill spare such men as your son, as even in times of peace they are too few. You have the consolation, such as it is, that he died the noblest of deaths. One can only hope that England will prove herself worthy of such sacrifices.' What he was to his father and mother, to his brothers and sister, words fail to tell. By a strange coincidence, Norman Lockhart was killed in action on Saturday 25th September, exactly one year after he joined the Regiment.

He has no known grave and is commemorated both at Loos Memorial, Pas de Calais, France, at the Malvern Wells Parish Council chapel and in the Eagle House chapel. Norman Lockhart was 20 years old. TNA have an officer file WO 339/24360.

Eagle House roll of Honour

Lieutenant Norman Lockhart with his father:
probably taken on his last home leave in September 1915.

G C H Culley album

Corpus Christi College First Lent Boat, 1914.

Back row (l to r): 3, C A Looseley (m.1911); 5, D V Bernard (m.1913); 4, E G Collins (m.1913); bow, A M Lewis (m.1913); 2, M V T J La Brooy (m.1913); 6, J T Hall (m.1912); Seated (l to r): 7, J T Smith (m.1912); coach, G L Churchill (Brasenose College, Oxford); coach, J Selwyn (m.1911); stroke, G C H Culley (m.1911); coach, R Shaw (m.1910); cox, H E Churchill (m.1912). Five of the nine crew members are known to have seen war service and A M Lewis was killed in action in Mesopotamia in August 1919. Of the coaches, J Selwyn was wounded, G C H Culley was injured in a flying accident and Robert Shaw was killed.

G C H Culley album

Proudly sporting their new Corpus Boat Club blazers and three bumps,
the Lent Second Boat, 1914.

Back row (l to r): 3, B St J Boultbee (m.1913); 7, N L Day (m.1913); 2, R G Budgen (m.1913);
4, N D S B Lockhart (m.1913); 5, L J Hooley (m.1913). Front row (l to r): bow, G I Kirkcaldy
(m.1913); coach, G C H Culley (m.1911), coach, J Selwyn (m.1911); stroke, R G Christie (m.1913);
6, F N Holt (m.1912) and cox, S L R Sharp (m.1909), cox. All but one of this crew are known
to have undertaken war service and three, N L Day, R G Budgen and N D S B Lockhart,
were killed and L J Hooley was wounded, losing a hand. G C H Culley was injured in a flying
accident and J Selwyn was wounded. In 1919, L J Hooley, R G Christie, F N Holt and
G C H Culley returned to the College to complete their degrees and Christie, Holt and Culley
became key figures in the re-establishment of the Boat Club.

MACKAY, Claude Lysaght, 2nd Lieutenant (1894–1915), 5th Battalion Worcestershire Regiment (Special Reserve), attached to the 2nd Battalion Manchester Regiment.

Claude Mackay was born on 29 October 1894 in Rajkot, Kithiawar, India, the second son of Jane (Nina) Whitty of Clifton and the late Edward Vansittart Mackay (a former District Superintendent of the Indian Police).

He was educated at Clifton College, where he was a prominent member of the cricket XI and the winner of the challenge cup in the athletics sports. In the academic year 1912–13, he was a Lance Corporal in the OTC. Also in 1913, he won the Public Schools' heavy-weight boxing competition at Aldershot. An account of his victory appeared in *The Sportsman* (15 June 1915). In it, the reporter said he had never seen such an electrifying performance. He won a leaving scholarship to Cambridge and was awarded a Classical Exhibition at Corpus, matriculating in 1913. The following year, he received a College grant of £30. Whilst at the College, he again distinguished himself in athletics, coming third in the hurdles in the Freshman's Sports. *The Letter of the Corpus Association*, No. 1 (July 1914) reported Claude playing in the 1914 Freshman versus Oxford University cricket match and the Freshmen versus the London Scottish Athletic Club. He also played cricket for Gloucestershire. After his death, the *Wisden Cricketers' Almanack* obituary asserted: 'he would undoubtedly have made a name for himself had he been able to devote himself to first-class cricket'.[17]

On the day war was declared, Claude was taking part in an Old Cliftonians' cricket tour. However, before the end of that day he had completed an application for a commission. Claude never returned to or graduated from Corpus. On 15 August 1914, he was gazetted to the 5th Battalion Worcestershire Regiment (Special Reserve) and on 1 January 1915 joined the British Expeditionary Force in France and Flanders. He obtained a regular commission into the regiment on 14 February 1915 and was then posted to the 2nd Battalion Manchester Regiment.

Following a period of home leave recovering from influenza, he returned to active duty and a posting to the 2nd Battalion Manchester Regiment. On 28 May 1915, a few days after the murderous 2nd Battle of Ypres had ended, at Zillebeke, to the south of the city, Claude was wounded whilst commanding a Company (a great responsibility for so young an officer) and died in the military hospital at Boulogne on 7 June 1915, aged 21.

17. Roger Gibbons, *In Memoriam, Gloucestershire County Cricketers Killed in the Great War* (2015).

Among the many letters speaking of him, one from the Sergeant of his platoon says:

> I do not think he will ever be forgotten. There was no braver officer; he always did his duty, and more than his duty, staying out when on patrol duties close to the enemy trenches; and when our trenches were being shelled he was always near at hand, bandaging up the wounded and cheering the men on and sometimes, when we would all be wet through and in thoroughly dismal conditions, up he would come with cigarettes, and then he would receive the smiling thanks of the men, nothing like a cigarette to put a smile on our faces! He was very popular with us all, always doing what was in his power to make things as pleasant as possible for us under very trying conditions.

He is buried in Boulogne Eastern Cemetery, Pas de Calais, France. The personal inscription on his gravestone reads 'Son of Edward & Nina Vansittart Mackay Love, Joy, Peace'. TNA have an officer file WO 339/17082.

MATHEWS, Arnold, Lieutenant (1894–1915), 14th (Reserve) Battalion Cheshire Regiment. Mentioned in Despatches.

Arnold Mathews was born on 7 August 1894 in Nantwich, Cheshire, the only son of Dr Frank Edward Mathews and Lizzie Ethel née Guest of Nantwich, Cheshire.

Prior to his matriculation into Corpus, he attended first Nantwich and Acton Grammar School (now part of the mixed comprehensive Malbank School and Sixth Form College) and then, between 1908 and 1913, Shrewsbury School.

He matriculated into Corpus in 1913 as a Foundation Scholar to read the Classical Tripos. During his time at the College, he proved a prominent long-distance runner, taking part in the 1914 University Freshman's Sports in which he came third in the three miles. He left the College on the outbreak of war and never graduated.

Arnold first enlisted in 'D' Company, 5th (Service) Battalion King's Shropshire Light Infantry (the same Battalion as Robert Gordon Budgen). On 20 October 1914, he was commissioned 2nd Lieutenant in the 14th (Reserve) Battalion Cheshire Regiment and promoted Lieutenant in December 1914. He served first on the Western Front then in Mesopotamia, taking part in the attempt to relieve the besieged city of Kut Al Amara. He was mentioned in General Sir Percy Lake's Despatches for gallant and distinguished service in the field.

On 9 April 1915, Arnold Mathews was wounded in the head at Sanna-i-yat and died at Orah on the Tigris on 14 April 1915, aged 21. A brother officer wrote: 'It would do your heart good if you could hear how his platoon sergeant and his men speak of Arnold. The whole regiment feels his loss.'

He has no known grave. Arnold is commemorated on the Basra Memorial, Iraq. There is also a memorial to him in St Mary's Church, Nantwich. It reads: 'In memory of Arnold Mathews beloved and only son of Frank and Ethel Mathews of this parish. Scholar of Corpus Christi College, Cambridge and Lieutenant, Cheshire Regiment who gave his life for his country. He was fatally wounded at Sanna-i-yat on the Tigris April 9th and died on April 14th, 1916. He was Mentioned in Despatches for gallant and distinguished service in the field.' TNA have a medal card WO 372/13/168039.

SANDFORD, Clement Richard Folliott, Captain, MC (1893–1917), 5th Battalion King's Own Yorkshire Light Infantry (Territorial Force).

According to a Doncaster Minster website, Clement Richard Folliott Sandford (known as Richard) was born on 23 November 1893 in Sheffield, the younger son of the Venerable Folliott George Sandford (1861–1945) archdeacon of Doncaster (m.1880) and Rosamond Mary née Blakelock. He was educated at Doncaster Grammar School and Repton School, where he was a member of the OTC. He matriculated into Corpus in October 1913. During the year he spent at the College he competed as a bantamweight in the University boxing trials and represented his College in the Mile Race against Exeter College, Oxford. It was his intention to join the ministry after graduation, but instead with the coming of war he left the College and never graduated.

Clement already held a pre-war commission in the Doncaster Territorials and was in training with his Battalion when war broke out. He was commissioned 2nd Lieutenant in the 5th Battalion King's Own Yorkshire Light Infantry and embarked for France in April 1915. In December 1915, he was wounded in the arm and invalided home suffering from blood poisoning. Richard was awarded the Military Cross in June 1916 for throwing a box of blazing gun cotton out of the trench after the bomb store in which it was stored had been hit by a shell. He was promoted Captain in October 1916.

Richard Sandford was shot and killed by a German sniper on 22 February 1917 in the aftermath of the German retreat to the Hindenburg Line (known as Operation Alberich). At the time, he was in the line opposite Serre on the Somme, his Battalion being engaged in patrol work. They were advancing across devastated, booby-trapped ground and in constant contact with the German rear guard. Richard was leading his men across open ground under cover of fog. Unfortunately, the fog lifted and the Germans opened fire. He was shot after ensuring all his men had safely returned to their trench and into cover. He was later described as: 'being very popular with his brother officers and with his men. He was absolutely fearless, and on many occasions won high commendation from his Commanding Officers'.

At the time of his death Clement Richard Sandford was 23 years old. He was buried at Cambrin military cemetery, Pas de Calais, France. His estate was valued at £228.19s.1d. TNA have an officer file WO 374/60297.

WYNNE, Edward Ernest, Captain (1895–1917), 1/5th Battalion Leicestershire Regiment (Territorial Force). Formerly, Private 11th (Public Schools) Battalion Royal Fusiliers.

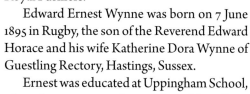

Edward Ernest Wynne was born on 7 June 1895 in Rugby, the son of the Reverend Edward Horace and his wife Katherine Dora Wynne of Guestling Rectory, Hastings, Sussex.

Ernest was educated at Uppingham School, where he was a member of the cricket, fives, rugby football and hockey teams and captained the first two. He matriculated into Corpus in 1913 but left on the outbreak of war after completing his first year and never graduated. According to *The Letter of the Corpus Association*, No. 1 (July 1914), he played in the Freshman Varsity match and trialled for the University hockey and association football teams. During his time as an undergraduate, he made seven appearances for Leicester RFC's 1st XV and scored one try; he also played for Rosslyn Park RFC. He additionally played cricket for Leicester Ivanhoe and made one appearance for Leicestershire 2nd XI.

On 20 August 1914, he enlisted as a Private in 11th (Public School) Battalion Royal Fusiliers and was commissioned 2nd Lieutenant two days later with the 5th Battalion Leicestershire Regiment. He served with the 1/5th Battalion, entering France on 18 July 1915. Promoted Lieutenant in October 1915, in December he was wounded and gassed.

On 1 June 1916, Edward Wynne was promoted Captain and killed in action seven days later, aged 21. A surviving account of the action notes he was Company Commander during an attack at Riaumont Hill:

> [He] led 'B' Company from their trenches and advanced towards the 'L-shaped' building. They had hardly started before their ranks were swept from end to end with machine gun fire from the houses to their left and front. Capt Wynne and 2nd Lieut R B Farrer were killed, 2nd Lieut W I Nelson was wounded, and the company had no officers left.

A brother officer wrote: 'I defy anyone to find one more fitted than Ernest to be the original of Donald Hawkey's *Beloved Hope.*' Ernest Wynne was buried at Bully-Grenay Communal Cemetery, British Extension, France. The personal inscription on his gravestone reads 'A very gallant gentleman'.[18] There is a memorial to him in St Laurence Guestling Church, Hastings (where his father was rector), and his name is on the First World War memorial at Uppingham School. TNA have an officer file WO 374/77393 and a medal card WO 372/22/105274.

---

18. The inscription is taken from the title of John Charles Dollman's 1913 painting of Captain Lawrence Edward Grace (Titus) Oates walking out of the tent into the blizzard and to his death on Captain Scott's return journey from the South Pole in 1912.

G C H Culley album

Corpus Christi College May boat 1914.

Cox, H E Churchill (m.1912); stroke, G C H Culley (m.1911); 7, J T Smith (m.1912); 6, A A Payne, (m.1909); 5, N D S B Lockhart (m.1913); 4, E G W Collins, (m.1913); 3, D V Bernard, (m.1913); 2, J T Hall (m.1912) and bow, A M Lewis (m.1913).

1914

BARNES, John Edward Templeman, 2nd Lieutenant (Acting Captain) (1895–1917), 7th (Service) Battalion Gloucestershire Regiment.

John Barnes was born on 26 August 1895, the second surviving son of Edward Daniel a solicitor and his wife Lily Evelyn Barnes of Holmefield, Godalming, Surrey.

He was educated first at Ridgeway School, Enfield and then, between 1907 and 1913, at Sherborne, where his father had been educated. His contemporary Dudley Stuart-Prince also won an Entrance Scholarship to Corpus, but like John never matriculated and never came to the College (see appendix). When John was in the sixth form, he was both a prefect and head of house. He was also a member of the Sherborne OTC (Colour-Sergeant) and shot at Bisley in 1912 and 1913.

In December 1913, John was admitted to Corpus with an Entrance Scholarship to read the Historical Tripos and should have matriculated in October 1914 but never did. However, his name appears in the Admissions Register. On 8 September 1914, John was commissioned with the 7th (Service) Battalion Gloucestershire Regiment, which became part of the 39th Brigade in the 13th (Western) Division. On 22 June 1915, after basic training, the Battalion left Bristol for the Gallipoli Campaign, sailing via Alexandria, Egypt to the British-held harbour and town of Mudros (Moudros), Greece. On 11 July 1915, John's battalion landed at Cape Helles on the southern tip of the Gallipoli peninsula and were immediately committed to battle. Then, in August 1915, they took part in the Battle of Chunuk Bair. The Gallipoli Campaign failed and on the night of 8/9 January 1916, the 7th Battalion was evacuated back to Mudros aboard HMS *Ermine* en route to Eygpt where, after a few weeks' service, the unit went to Mesopotamia, arriving in Basra on 27 February 1916. In April 1916, the Battalion took part in the attempted and ultimately failed relief of Kut Al Amara.

In the New Year of 1917, John took part in the offensive to capture Baghdad (which succeeded in March 1917). Advancing slowly up the River Tigris during the night of 2/3 February 1917, 39th Brigade (of which the 7th Battalion Gloucestershire Regiment was a part) encountered strong Turkish resistance. They were seeking to take the Hai Salient to establish positions close to the River Tigris. During this action, two platoons of 'C' Company suffered considerable casualties (three officers and sixteen other ranks killed, four officers and forty-four other ranks wounded). Unfortunately, among these losses was John Edward Templeman Barnes. He was aged 21. On learning of his death, H R King his housemaster at Sherborne wrote in his diary 'Death of Barnes, notified by his father, on Tigris Feb 3rd – the best boy I ever had and most affectionate.'

John Edward Templeman Barnes has no known grave but is commemorated on the Basra Memorial, Iraq. He is also commemorated on the Sherborne School war memorial and in a memorial window at St John the Baptist Church, Busbridge, Waverley, Surrey. His name is recorded in Bury's supplemental list as one of the scholars who never came into residence. TNA have an officer file WO 339/20849.

JOHN EDWARD TEMPLEMAN BARNES
Second-Lieutenant
GLOUCESTERSHIRE REGIMENT

Joined the Regiment in September 1914 and proceeded overseas with the 7th (Service) Battalion on 22nd June 1915.
Served at GALLIPOLI, in EGYPT and MESOPOTAMIA and attained the Acting rank of Captain.
Was KILLED IN ACTION against the Turks on 3rd February 1917 in MESOPOTAMIA during the British Advance after the fall of KUT.
Buried in the British Military Cemetery at the Headquarters of 39th Infantry Brigade XIII Division.
Aged 21½ years
He was in possession of 2 blue chevrons and gained the 1914/15 Star, British War Medal and Victory Medal.

· · ✠ · ·

Born at Winchmore Hill in Middlesex on 26th August 1895.
The Son of EDWARD DANIEL BARNES Esqre, Solicitor, and LILY EVELYN BARNES of Homefield, Summerhouse Road, Busbridge.
Educated at Sherborne School where he held the rank of Color-Sergeant in the O.T.C. and was a Member of the School VIII at Bisley in 1912/13.
A Scholar of Corpus Christi College, Cambridge in 1914 and a Member of the Cambridge University Officers Training Corps.
He was unmarried.

The entry for John Edward Templeman Barnes in the memorial book at St John the Baptist Church, Busbridge, Waverley, Surrey.

The life of John Edward Templeman Barnes is commemorated in a memorial window
at St John the Baptist Church, Busbridge, Waverley, Surrey by the noted ecclesiastical
stained-glass maker Archibald Keightley. The following is taken from a church history:
'In November 1918, a window was given in memory of two Shirburnians killed in action:
Percival Whately and John Templeman Barnes. The connection to Sherborne is represented by the figure of Aldhelm, first Bishop of Sherborne, and below him Sherborne
Abbey. The Figure of Godfrey [Geoffrey] de Bouillon, first King of Jerusalem, is shown
over a medallion of the city of Jerusalem. An interesting iconographical detail is the
crown of thorns on de Bouillon's helmet, which was designed to symbolise his refusal
to wear a gold crown when his Saviour's crown had been of thorns.'

GLEGG, Arthur Livingstone (Bury has Livingstone; military sources have Linningstone), 2nd Lieutenant (1896–1915), 6th (Reserve) Battalion (attached to the 9th (Service) Battalion) King's Royal Rifle Corps, 42nd Brigade part of the 14th (Light) Division.

Arthur Glegg was born in 1896 (mistakenly, the College Admissions Book says 1895) in Edinburgh, the younger son of Margaret and her husband Arthur Thomson Glegg (former advocate and Sheriffs' substitute of Lanarkshire) of 2 Lynn Gardens, Glasgow. His grandfather was J L Douie JP, of Moira, County Down, Ireland (now Northern Ireland).

He attended St Bees School and was nearly five years at Grindal House. He distinguished himself in the school athletics and for two seasons was a member of the rugby football XV and later captain. He also attended Kelvinside Academy, Glasgow.

According to the Admissions Book, Arthur matriculated into Corpus in October 1914 (though Bury mistakenly has 1915) with a sizarship. He never came into residence and in January 1915 was commissioned 2nd Lieutenant in the 6th

(Reserve) Battalion King's Royal Rifles later attached to the 9th Battalion. The Battalion landed in France on 20 May 1915 and took part in the action at Hooge during the 2nd Battle of Ypres. On 10 August 1915, soon after arriving at the front as part of the 9th Battalion, he was mortally wounded by a rifle grenade aged 19 (his brother 2nd Lieutenant Walter Scott Glegg, who was not a Corpus alumnus, of the same regiment was killed on 15 September 1916).

Arthur Glegg was buried in Cambrin Churchyard extension, Pas de Calais, France. The personal inscription on his gravestone joins the two brother and reads 'Also in memory of 2/Lieut. W. S. Glegg K.R.R.C. Faithful unto death', Revelation 2:10. Their names are recorded in the Glasgow Roll of Honour and on the Glasgow war memorial at St Mary's Episcopal Cathedral. TNA have a medal card WO 372/8/34044.[19]

---

19. See also www.everyoneremembered.org/profiles/soldier/170698.

GOOLDEN, Donald Charles, 2nd Lieutenant (1896–1916), 6th (Reserve) Battalion (attached to the 4th Battalion) City of London Regiment, Royal Fusiliers.

Formerly Private, 16th (Public Schools) Battalion Middlesex Regiment.

Donald was the younger son of Charles Joseph Goolden and his wife Isabel née Asmit of Earls Court, London. The 1911 census has him living at 47 Nevern Square, Earls Court with his widowed mother, elder brother Hugh Joseph (1893–1965) then aged 18 (m.1912, St John's), 10-year-old sister Barbara, grandfather, two aunts and three servants. Donald and his brother were both educated at Shrewsbury School, where in 1914, his final year, he was a praeposter (prefect) and head of house, as was his contemporary Denis Digges La Touche (see below).

Donald was due to matriculate into Corpus in October 1914 but he instead, on the outbreak of war, enlisted as a Private in the 16th (Public Schools) Battalion Middlesex Regiment.

In April 1915, he was commissioned 2nd Lieutenant with the City of London Regiment. After basic training, he saw service in France and Flanders and his Battalion (as part of the 56th Division) took part in the Somme Campaign. On the disastrous 1 July opening of that campaign, he was in combat at Gommecourt and later that same month at Delville Wood. H C O'Neill's *The Royal Fusiliers in the Great War* (2006) (pp. 129–30) explains how, on 14 August 1916, Donald was killed by an artillery shell as the 4th Battalion was moving into position to attack the village of Gullimont. O'Neill noted: 'The approach was across open country which the enemy had direct observation, and the Germans had concentrated a heavy volume of machine gun fire into the village.' Summing up his short life, the Shrewsbury School website comments: 'he had won the respect of all ranks' and *The Salopian* observed: 'he lived a good and happy life'. Post-war editions of *The Salopian* show that his brother Hugh Joseph Goolden, a barrister, perpetuated Donald's memory by placing an oak credence table in the Chapel at the School Mission (Shrewsbury House in Liverpool). It bears a brass tablet inscribed: 'In Memoriam Donald Charles Goolden' and the school motto *Intus si recte ne labora* ('Be not anxious if thy soul be upright'). He also established the Goolden medals, which are awarded annually by Shrewsbury School to the four boys who have made the highest individual scores for their respective houses. Although Donald was admitted to the College, he never matriculated nor did he come into residence and is not listed in Bury. His name does, however, appear in *The War List* but is not marked as being killed. In 2023 his name was added to the College war memorial. Donald was aged 21 when he was killed and is buried at the Peronne Road Cemetery, Maricourt, near Albert, Somme, France.

The personal inscription on his gravestone is *Vincit qui patitur* ('He conquers who endures': Persius). TNA have an officer file WO 339/68477 and a medal card WO 372/8/66707.

Shrewsbury School Archives

Shrewsbury School 1914 praeposters (prefects)

l to r: Denis Digges La Touche, N B Stones and Donald Charles Goolden. Denis and Donald were due to come up to Corpus when war broke out, but instead both joined the armed forces and were killed in action.

HILL, William Reginald, Lieutenant, MC and Bar (1896–1918), 4th Battalion (attached to the 12th) Durham Light Infantry. Formerly Private Public Schools Battalion Middlesex Regiment.

William Hill was born in Durham in 1896, the youngest son of William and Katharine Hill of Sunnycroft, Tamworth, Staffordshire and lived at Polesworth, Warwickshire. Between 1911 and 1914, he was a student at Oakham School, where he was both a prefect and a member of the Games Committee of Management. Academically, William was a high-flyer and won the Form 6 French prize, gained an Upper Certificate and Senior County Scholarship in the summer of 1913. The following year, these achievements were crowned with Higher Certificates at the Oxford and Cambridge Board Examination and an Open Exhibition at Corpus.

William was also a keen and enthusiastic all-round sportsman. Reports in the Oakham School magazine show a student growing in confidence, maturity and ability. For example, the summer 1914 cricket review describes him as: 'The most improved member of the team. He is a really good bat possessing a very powerful off-drive. At present, his defence is somewhat shaky and he must cultivate a cut. A much improved field, and useful change bowler at times.' In a similar vein, the rugby review for winter 1914 described him as: 'A powerful three-quarter who runs strongly and hands off with vigour. Takes and gives his passes well and tackles well. Kicks a very good length and with judgement.' William obtained rugby colours and, in the spring of 1914, came first in the place-kicking competition (rugby football). It was not all sport, that same spring he played Aeacus in Aristophanes *The Frogs*.

Although William Hill was admitted to Corpus with an Entrance Scholarship, he never matriculated or came into residence. Instead, as the Oakham School Archive website records: 'William left school prematurely to serve in the Durham Light Infantry.' He first enlisted as a Private in the Public Schools Battalion Middlesex Regiment and was subsequently commissioned 2nd Lieutenant in 4th Battalion (attached to the 12th) Durham Light Infantry; in addition, he saw service with the 8th Battalion. He served on the Western Front between 1915 and 1918 and his service was marked by the awards of an MC and Bar for his bravery and distinction; he was also wounded twice.

William Hill was awarded his first Military Cross on 16 August 1917. *The London Gazette* (8371) citation reads: 'For conspicuous gallantry and devotion to duty in entering a village and capturing four enemy officers aided by his Lewis gun section. His skilled leadership and energy were of the greatest value in consolidating the captured position and he continually displayed great fearlessness in encouraging his men under heavy shell fire.'

The citation of 20 September 1918 for the Bar reads:

> For conspicuous gallantry and devotion to duty during a raid. While the raiding party, who had secured a prisoner, were withdrawing under heavy machine-gun fire and bombing, this officer rushed forward and picked up one of his wounded men from the enemy wire, so that the enemy might not secure an identification. He had previously carried out several daring patrols and shown fine leadership.

On 27 May 1918 at the Craonne Plateau, Chemin des Dames on the first day of the 3rd Battle of the Aisne, whilst engaged in bloody hand-to-hand combat that decimated his Battalion, William was first gassed, then wounded and subsequently taken prisoner.

On 6 November 1918 (five days before the Armistice), William died of blood poisoning in a German prisoner of war camp at Stralsund, aged 22. He is buried in Berlin South-Western Cemetery, Brandenburg, Germany and his gravestone is inscribed 'He died for freedom and for honour'.

His elder brothers were Lieutenant Harold Belfit Hill (RAF pilot instructor) (1893–1918) who was killed in a flying accident and Lieutenant Arthur Moberly Hill (1895–1917) who was killed in action at the Battle of Arras. William Reginald Hill is commemorated at www.rutlandremembers.org/fallen/627/hill-lieutenant-william-reginald. William is also commemorated on the Oakham School war memorial, the Polesworth war memorial and the Dordon war memorial. His name is listed in Bury as one of the scholars who never came into residence. His name does not appear in the Admissions Register. TNA have an officer file WO 339/61219 and a medal card WO 372/9/194510.

The grave of Lieutenant William Hill MC and Bar at Berlin South-Western Cemetery, Brandenburg, Germany.

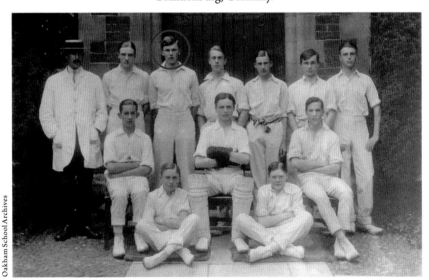

Oakham School cricket XI 1914: William Hill is ringed.

PIERSON, Leslie Dilworth, Lieutenant (1896–1916), 10th (Service) Battalion East Yorkshire Regiment, 'The Hull Commercials'.

Leslie Pierson was born in Hunslet, Yorkshire in 1896 the son of Sarah Maria Pierson of South Kensington, London and the Reverend William Birkbeck Pierson formerly of Rothwell Vicarage, Leeds.

The Kingston upon Hull online war memorial has the following information: 'Lieutenant Pierson was the only surviving son of William Birkbeck and Sarah Maria Pierson. He left Rugby school in 1914 intending to go up to Cambridge but the national situation intervened. He was commissioned into the 10th Battalion (1st Hull) in 1915 and went straight to Egypt before arriving in France and Flanders in February 1916.'

The Rugby School Roll of Honour adds:

In February 1916, his Battalion was transferred to the French Front, and he took part in the Battle of the Somme beginning on 1st July 1916. He also took part in the closing stages of the offensive and, in October 1916, he was reported missing in action. At the time he was officer in charge of a patrol of five reconnoitring the German wire in the Hebuterne Sector. The patrol made it through the wire and was within a few yards of the trench when they were fired on and bombed. They scattered, by pre-arrangement, into shell holes and, though the rest returned, Lieutenant Pierson was never heard of again. In 1918 he was officially assumed to have been killed on October 30th, 1916, aged 20. He was Mentioned in Despatches of January 4th, 1917, 'for excellent work in the trenches and for setting a fine example to his men by his bravery and courage on patrol and for obtaining valuable information whilst on patrol work.' A boy of shy, retiring and gentle disposition at School, he developed supreme courage during the War. His Captain said that 'no praise could be too high for his magnificent courage and unselfishness'.

The Kingston upon Hull online war memorial noted: 'As one of his men who was interviewed in hospital said,

If he had a fault, it was that he was too daring and constantly went out scouting alone and did valuable work in this way. There was great trouble among the men, when the news came that the most popular officer and NCO were missing together. He was very good to his men, his first thoughts were always for them and they would go anywhere with him.

His Captain made a statement that included

> from the letters written by men of his platoon I know they literally loved him …
> no praise could be too high for his magnificent courage and selflessness …
> With regard to the 'great trouble among the men' mentioned above – there was
> a rumour circulating at the time that the real reason for the patrols made by the
> Battalion that week were made with the aim of recovering the body of the son
> of someone with influence; merely rumour but I would like to know more.

He has no known grave and is commemorated on the Thiepval Memorial, Somme, France. He is not listed in Bury, nor does his name appear in the Admissions Register. TNA have an officer file WO 339/18943.

ROXBURGH, John Hewitt, Major, MC (1895–1918), 63rd Battalion Royal Naval Division, Machine Gun Corps (Infantry). Formerly 2nd Lieutenant 17th Battalion The King's Regiment (Liverpool). Mentioned in Despatches.

John Roxburgh was born at Liverpool in 1895, the son of Hugh Laughland Roxburgh (b.1866) a cotton merchant and his wife Ethel (b.1871) of Prenton, Birkenhead, Cheshire (now Merseyside) and grandson of George H Hewitt JP of Aigburth, Liverpool. According to the 1901 census, he lived with a sister Sylvia (b.1898) and a brother Caleb (b.1900). The census shows two aunts and three servants resident at the house. Educated first at Greenbank School and then Clifton College, where he was a member of the OTC and head of the School House Corps, he was awarded a Corpus Exhibition to read the Classical and Historical Triposes. Although admitted to the College, he never came into residence nor did he matriculate and instead on the outbreak of war went from school into the army. *The London Gazette*, 13 November 1914, shows him commissioned a Temporary 2nd Lieutenant on 1 September 1914 with The King's Regiment (Liverpool).

He was appointed Brigade Machine Gun Officer early in 1915 and gazetted Captain in the Machine Gun Corps on 14 January 1916. In July–August 1916, John Roxburgh took part in the Somme Campaign at Montauban, Trones Wood. He also saw action in 1917 at Guillemont during the 3rd Battle of Ypres, known as Passchendaele, was Mentioned in Despatches by Field Marshal Sir Douglas Haig and awarded the MC: 'for gallant and distinguished service in the field'. In April 1918, he was in action at Cambrai and between May and September 1918, when he was promoted to Major, was Commandant of the Machine Gun School at Camiers, training American troops and attached to the 63rd Naval Division.

On 12 October 1918, the following article appeared in the *Liverpool Daily Post*:

Death of Major John H Roxburgh: The death in action is announced of Major John Hewitt Roxburgh MC, of the Machine Gun Corps … Major Roxburgh, who was 23 years of age, joined the Liverpool 'Pals' shortly after the outbreak of war and after receiving his training was commissioned second lieutenant. During his four years of military service, he has seen a great deal of fighting on the Western Front. He was looked upon as an officer of much promise and earned rapid promotion to the rank of Captain. Some time ago his services were rewarded by the bestowal of the Military Cross, and recently he was promoted to be Major. He was killed on the 2nd inst., while taking part in the present offensive.

After his death, his family received many tributes. His Commanding Officer wrote:

His death was very unfortunate and tragic, he having only returned to billets, from the burial of a brother officer, when our area was shelled, with the result that your son was instantaneously killed … He had only been with us a few weeks, during which time we had learned to love him, and we all miss him very much.

His Brigadier wrote:

He was one of the finest officers imaginable, and he will be a very real loss to the Army … In spite of his age he was grand, and clearly showed that he was a born leader of men. Over and over again I had reason to be very thankful that he was with us, and he was the most charming lad to deal with – always keen, clear-headed and brave to a fault. We were all devoted to him, and so were his men, who held him in the greatest admiration. I feel I have lost a very great friend.

A brother officer wrote: 'He was respected, admired, and loved by us all. … He was an extraordinarily clever fellow, and the way he ran his command, in view of his age and experience, was little short of marvellous. He was wonderful.'

John Roxburgh was killed in action on 2 October 1918 during the attack on the Hindenburg Line, aged 23. He was initially buried at Graincourt Cemetery, but subsequently reburied in Hermies Hill Cemetery, Pas de Calais, France. He is remembered on the war memorial at Clifton College, in St Stephen's Church, Prenton and the Prenton war memorial.[20] He is not listed in Bury nor does his name appear in the Admissions Register. TNA have an officer file WO 339/1955 and a medal card WO 372/17/111679.

The grave of Major John Hewitt Roxburgh MC
at Hermies Hill Cemetery, Pas de Calais, France.

20. See also www.liverpoolpals.com/soldier/?i=3154%2F-major-john-hewitt-roxburgh+%28mc%29.

SANKEY, William Mandeville (known as Mandeville), **Lieutenant,** MC (1895–1918), 2nd Battalion Monmouthshire Regiment. This was the same battalion as his friend and contemporary Lieutenant Alan Gledhill MC (m.1914); see appendix.

Mandeville Sankey was born in 1895 into a prominent Anglo-Irish and military family of Coolmore, Fethard, Co. Tipperary, Ireland. He was the son of Colonel Alfred Robert Mandeville Sankey (Royal Engineers) and his wife (who was his cousin) Ida Villiers née Sankey. Mandeville had a sister Marjorie who later in life became a well-known writer and illustrator of children's books. Tragedy befell the family when, in 1891, his mother died; it was reported she fell overboard from a ferry making the crossing to Ireland.

After Ida's death, Mandeville and Marjorie were sent to live with an aunt in Lympstone, Devon. Their father was subsequently posted to the Straits Settlements in the Strait of Malacca (today part of Malaysia). Between 1908 and 1914, Mandeville was educated at Haileybury College and in October 1914 matriculated into Corpus as a Foundation Scholar to read the Historical Tripos. At Corpus, he joined the Boat Club and rowed during the 1914 Michaelmas Term. He was also a member of the Chess Club, as was Alan Gledhill. His matriculation coincided with the early weeks of the war and like so many others of his cohort Mandeville joined the University OTC (Senior Division) remaining at Corpus to await his commission. On 29 April 1915, he was commissioned 2nd Lieutenant, 2nd Battalion Monmouthshire Regiment, a Welsh Territorial Battalion. He then left Corpus and never graduated.

In August 1915, Mandeville landed in France, where his unit was posted to the Somme theatre. Earlier in the year, the Monmouthshire Regiment had participated in the bloody 2nd Battle of Ypres and suffered losses so great that its battalions were amalgamated and sent to recover in reserve lines. During the winter of 1915, the 2nd Battalion was among several infantry units recruited from mining areas that were reconstituted as divisional pioneer battalions. As these were adept in the use of picks and shovels, it was argued, they could quickly entrench and speed up the consolidation of newly captured positions. Additionally, as they were also trained and organized as infantry, they were also available as a divisional reserve. At the end of April 1916, the 2nd Battalion was thus re-equipped and joined the 29th Division.

On the first day of the Battle of the Somme, 1 July 1916, the 2nd Battalion played a key role in the initial assault. The 29th Division attacked Beaumont Hamel, with Mandeville assisting the advancing troops as commander of the Battalion bombing party and its snipers. According to an account of the action, its task was to advance and remove blockages caused by German defenders. The account continued: 'At the start of the attack, "A" Company moved up to the front line along the Old Beaumont Hamel Road, the bombers, under Sankey proceeded to clear the way for Company platoons carrying bombs into Beaumont Hamel. Unfortunately, they were held up by machine-gun fire and by the end of the day, despite many attacks, the advance failed.' It is believed Mandeville's actions led to the award of an MC in the 1917 New Year's Honours.

By the end of July 1916, Mandeville had been wounded twice. The Battalion war diary entry at Mailly Wood on 14 July confirms his second wound, which was caused by shell splinters outside a billet at Mesnil. A subsequent medical board report confirms the severity of his injury. It reads: 'A shell splinter pierced his steel helmet and lodged in his skull causing a depressed fracture. The splinter was removed by operation on the 18.07.1916. He suffered paralysis of his right arm and right side of his face.' On 8 August 1916, Mandeville was evacuated and hospitalised in Southampton. It is not known if he was sufficiently recovered to receive his MC personally from the King at Buckingham Palace.

He subsequently undertook light home duties, gradually recuperating from his wounds. However, at the end of 1916 he was serving at Oswestry, Shropshire and attended an army medical board. The result was a questionable 'deemed fit for active service'. In early 1917, promoted to a full Lieutenant, he re-joined his battalion in the Ypres Salient. At the time, they were involved in major construction and maintenance work. This included the making and repairing of forward roads and the digging of trenches along a ridge, ironically named Belle Vue. Conditions were dreadful, as previously the ridge had been the site of fierce fighting and the human detritus of war was still being removed. The Battalion constructed a road from Gravenstafel to Belle Vue along ground pitted with shell holes. These roads were logistically critical, allowing wagons to transport *matériel* to forward positions. The work had to be undertaken at night as the unit operated under German shellfire. Each night, Mandeville and his unit marched four or five miles laden with rifles, ammunition, picks, shovels, and other heavy impedimenta before starting work. It was in these circumstances that William Mandeville Sankey was killed.

Unfortunately, the war diary does not note his death or the circumstances, but it is likely that he was struck by a German shell burst. It is known that he was wounded on 22 March 1918 and taken to No. 8 Corps Main Dressing Station near

Ypres and the following day he died from his wounds. He was buried in Ypres Reservoir Cemetery. The personal inscription on his gravestone reads: 'Rejoice because your names are written in heaven' (Luke 10:20). As a boy he often stayed in Charmouth, Dorset where his uncle the Reverend Spencer Simms was rector. He placed a memorial plaque to him in St Andrews Church. His name also appears on the Haileybury College war memorial. In 1922, his war medals were sent to his father who was living at Old Brompton, Kent. See also www.hertsatwar.co.uk/biographies/854660/william-mandeville-sankey. TNA have an officer file WO 374/60362.

1915

DIGGES LA TOUCHE, Denis, Captain (1895–1915), 8th (Service) Battalion Welch Regiment. Formerly 2nd Lieutenant King's Shropshire Light Infantry.

Denis Digges La Touche was born on 6 March 1895 in Kingstown (now Dún Laoghaire), Co. Dublin, Ireland, the son of Anna Frances née Handy and Thomas Henry Digges La Touche BA FGA FASB (1855–1938) (m.1876, St John's). Thomas was well known for his contributions to the Geological Survey of India. By the outbreak of war, he and the family had retired to 230 Hills Road, Cambridge. However, in the 1911 census, the family were still living in Kingstown. Present were Thomas Henry, aged 55, born in Stokesat, Shropshire and his wife, aged 45, who had been born in Co. Kilkenny,

Ireland. Married for nineteen years, the couple had five children, all of whom were alive. In residence on census day were Avice Gertrude, aged 18, born 23 March 1893 in Lahore, India; Denis, aged 16, born Co. Dublin; Edith Mary, aged 13, born 5 September 1897 in Mussoorie, Bengal India; and Lynette Nowelle, aged 7, born in Co. Dublin. There was another child, James Fleming Digges La Touche (1900–63) (m.1919), born in India. He was clearly not at home that day.

The Digges (sometimes known as Digues) La Touche family can be traced back to aristocratic roots in sixteenth-century France. David Digues La Touche was a Huguenot Protestant who in 1685, following the revocation of the Edict of Nantes, refused to renounce his faith and escaped persecution by leaving France for Holland. There he joined the army of William of Orange and fought at the Battle of the Boyne. Awarded lands seized from the indigenous Irish population, he subsequently settled in Dublin, where he established a weaving business. Because of his apparent honesty and integrity, fellow Huguenots trusted him with their surplus cash. Over time, this side of his business developed into a bank, becoming the leading private bank in Ireland. The bank's fortunes waned in the nineteenth century, and in 1870 it was taken over by the Munster Bank.

Denis was born in Dublin and educated first at Baymount Preparatory School and then Shrewsbury School (where he was a contemporary of Donald Charles Goolden, see above), where he was a keen runner and a school praepostor (prefect). In a 2014 online posting to mark the centenary of the outbreak of war, Shrewsbury School has an obituary from which the following is derived. He was Captain of the shooting VIII for three years, contributing greatly to the increase in the standard of shooting at the School, a Gentleman of the Runs and subsequently Huntsman and good cross-country runner. During his time at the school, he was a member of the OTC.

In January 1913, at the age of 17, Denis was elected to an Entrance Scholarship at Corpus and was also awarded an Oswald Smith Exhibition to read the Classical Tripos. However, he deferred entry for a year, then war broke out. He immediately enlisted as a Private in the 5th Battalion King's Shropshire Light Infantry and was subsequently commissioned 2nd Lieutenant. In February 1915, he transferred to the 8th (Service) Battalion Welch Regiment and promoted Captain. In the summer of 1915, Denis and his battalion sailed for the Dardanelles as part of the 40th

Brigade in the 13th (Western) Division, landing at ANZAC Cove Gallipoli in early August. He was killed in action on 8 August 1915 landing at Anavarta: he was initially reported missing after the attack on Chanok Bair. Although his body was found by an Officer of the East Lancashire Regiment, who was himself wounded while burying him, its location was subsequently lost.

An obituary in *The Salopian* remarks that he was: 'unselfish and unassuming in a marked degree, in spite of the distinctions gained in several fields, he won the affection of all with whom he came into contact; and with his simplicity of character was joined unswerving loyalty to the School and to the House – one of the best of Salopia's sons.'

His younger brother, James Fleming Digges La Touche, matriculated into Corpus in 1919. In a 1939 obituary of his father, the following was noted: 'La Touche's elder son whose childhood antics and early education 1895–1910 occupy many pages of the letters between Nancy and Tom, was killed in Turkey five years after La Touche retired.' Denis Digges La Touche was killed in action, aged 20. He has no known grave but is commemorated on the Helles Memorial, Gallipoli, Turkey. TNA have an officer file WO 339/21054.

He is not listed in Bury but does appear in both the Chapter Book and Admissions Book.

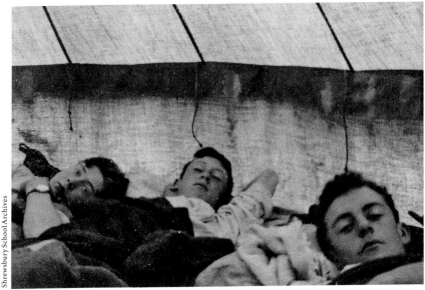

Denis Digges La Touche (middle) at the Shrewsbury School OTC camp.

LING, Leonard Simpson, 2nd Lieutenant (1893–1917), 3rd Battalion (attached to the 1st Battalion) Norfolk Regiment. Formerly Private 29771, South Staffordshire Regiment.

Leonard Ling was born on 3 August 1893 in Chelmsford, Essex the only son of Harry Ling a corn merchant and his wife Sarah Anne née Simpson of Seven Kings, Ilford, Essex. He also had a sister Bertha Ellen.

Educated at St John's College, Westcliffe on Sea, he matriculated into Corpus in October 1915 and briefly came into residence. Until that point, ill-health had kept him out of the armed forces. However, during his time at the College, his health improved to the point he was able to join the OTC. In 1916, he enlisted as a Private in the South Staffordshire Regiment and was quickly sent to train with No. 8 Officer Cadet Battalion. In August 1916, he was commissioned with the 3rd Battalion Norfolk Regiment.

On 23 April 1917, he was killed in action during the Battle of Arras when his detachment was held up on the wire at Avion, which the guns had failed to breech. He was 23 at the time of his death, has no known grave and is commemorated on the Arras Memorial, Pas de Calais, France. Leonard Simpson Ling is also commemorated on memorials at All Saints' Church, Goodmayes, Essex (brass plaque), Ilford War Memorial Gazette, St Clement's Church Memorial Panels, Ilford War Memorial Hall. TNA have an officer file WO 339/56194 and a medal card WO 372/12/97202.

ROBERTS, William Arthur, Lieutenant (1897–1917), 19th Battalion Royal Fusiliers, attached to the 30th Training Reserve Battalion, Dover, Kent.

William was born in 1897, the only son of William T and Ethel Roberts of Pimlico, London. Between 1910 and 1915, he was educated at St Paul's School where he was a contemporary of Lawrence Norris Gaskell (see below). In 1914, he was awarded an Open Exhibition to read the Classical Tripos at Corpus, but due to the war deferred matriculation and instead joined the armed forces. *The Pauline* (Vol. XXXV, No. 234, November 1917) has an obituary.

He was one of the best all-round athletes that the School has ever produced. He was Secretary of Cricket, obtained his First XV colours, was Captain of Fives for two years, won the Shepard Cup, and was Captain of A Club. He won an Open Exhibition at Corpus Christi College, Cambridge, in December 1914. At School he was remarkable for his coolness and steady nerve in games, and for his unfailing cheerfulness, which greatly endeared him to all who knew him. He [obtained a commission with the Royal Fusiliers,] went out to the front in May 1916, and was wounded in the following July, and returned home with his health and nerves absolutely shattered. After undergoing two operations he was placed in a Training Reserve Battalion at Dover and was one of several officers on the tram which was overturned in the fatal accident that occurred there in August of this year. He and another officer attempted to put the back brakes on, and in doing so he met his death. More than one, on hearing the details of the accident from the present writer, exclaimed at once, 'Just like Roberts, to think of other people before himself!'.

The accident claimed the lives of eleven people and many more were seriously injured. William Roberts died in hospital of a fractured skull on 20 August 1917. His funeral took place in Dover with full military honours and he was buried in Dover (St James's) cemetery.

William Robert's name does not appear in *The War List*, though it is included in the Bury appendix of exhibitioners and scholars who did not matriculate because of war service. In 2023 his name was added to the College war memorial.

THRING, Ashton Edward, 2nd Lieutenant (1896–1917), 'D' Battery, No. 1 Reserve Brigade Royal Field Artillery.

Ashton Thring was born on 14 June 1896 in Dunstable, the son of Lionel Charles Reginald Thring MA JP and his wife Jessie Margaret of The Grange, Ash, Martock, Somerset. His father had been the first headmaster of Dunstable Grammar School (now part of Manshead Church of England Academy) and his grandfather Edward Thring was a celebrated nineteenth-century British educator and headmaster of Uppingham School.

Ashton first attended the Dunstable Grammar School, then Haywards Heath and finally, during the academic year 1911 to 1912, Marlborough College (where his father had been educated). He was a keen sportsman and won the Hankey Gold Medal as the pupil who made the best use of his opportunities in life as a Dunstabolian.

Admitted to Corpus, Ashton was due to come up in October 1915 but instead, on the outbreak of war, he joined the Inns of Court OTC at Berkhampstead and soon after received his commission into the North Midland Royal Field Artillery.

He served in Dublin and took part in the suppression of the 1916 Easter Rising. It was during a posting to Ripon in North Yorkshire, at No. 1 Reserve Brigade Royal Field Artillery, that he succumbed to influenza, dying in the military hospital at Ripon of pneumonia on 9 February 1917, aged 20. He was buried with full military honours at Dunstable Cemetery, Bedfordshire. His name does not appear in Bury. TNA have an officer file WO 374/68695 and a medal card WO 372/20/24160.

The funeral of Ashton Edward Thring, 1917.

CCCC Chess Club serial

Chess Club, Lent Term 1915.
William Mandeville Sankey is standing back row right and Alan Gledhill is seated front row right.
Both served in the 2nd Battalion Monmouthshire Regiment. Sankey was killed in action, but
Gledhill survived to become a judge and academic lawyer.

1916

BLYTH, Alick Frederick, Lieutenant (1897–1917), Northern Cyclists Corps (attached to the 2/5th Battalion Gloucestershire Regiment), 19th Division.

Alick Frederick Blyth was born in the Punjab, India, the son of Margaret and Colonel Frederick Augustus Blyth (who served with the 10th Duke of Cambridge's Lancers (Hodson's Horse), Indian Army) of Kensington, London. Between 1910 and 1915, he was a student at Radley College where he was senior prefect, captain of cricket and Radley's first captain of rugby. In a note on the Radley website is the following:

Blyth had a career full of promise at Radley. Like Geoffrey Adams, whom he succeeded as Senior Prefect for one term, he combined a variety of gifts. In the years 1913 to 1915 he won the Gibbs, Heathcote and James Scholarships and in 1915 the Worsley Prize. In that year he was awarded a Classical Scholarship at Corpus Christi College, Cambridge.

The Radley website goes on:

He was in the Cricket Xl in 1915 and played a fine innings against Sherborne [according to *Wisden Cricketers' Almanack* he was a good bat and change bowler and had an average of 33 taking sixteen wickets]; and in the XV in 1914 and 1915 captaining it in the latter year. He was also a keen lover of literature and of nature, especially of birds, moths and butterflies. With these gifts and tastes he combined a character of unassuming gentleness, thoughtfulness, and charm, which gained him a multitude of friends.

Although admitted to the College, he deferred matriculation and never came into residence. Instead, on 14 December 1915, he was commissioned 2nd Lieutenant in the Northern Cyclists Corps, later attached to the 2/5th Battalion Gloucestershire Regiment, which was itself part of the 184th Brigade, 61st Division. In July 1917, Alick's Battalion moved to the Ypres Salient and on 22 August 1917, although untried, were committed to combat during the final stages

of the Battle of Langemarck. During this action, the 2/5th Gloucesters remained in close support behind the leading Battalions. However, the 184th Brigade made slow progress against the concrete pillboxes and machine-gun nests hidden in the Pond Farm buildings on their front. The 2/4th Oxfordshire and Buckinghamshire Light Infantry failed to take the Pond Farm strongpoint, but two platoons of 'D' Company, 2/5th Gloucesters and two platoons of 'C'

Company succeeded in killing or capturing the whole garrison, at heavy cost to themselves. That night, a German counterattack temporarily recaptured Pond Farm, but it was easily secured next morning. It was during this final phase of battle that Alick Blythe was killed in action on 23 August 1917, aged 20. His Company Commander wrote of him:

Our battalion was in support, but he was detailed for a special job in the line. There was a strong point called Pond Farm giving a lot of trouble. We had taken it once but had lost it and were going for it again. Both the D Company officers had been killed, and the remnants of the Company were going over with the attacking party without an officer. Blyth at once went to the Colonel in charge of the attack and insisted on taking this Company over, which he did. The place was captured, but he was sniped through the head. This place was held by Prussians and had before resisted seven attacks. Those who knew him are not surprised to hear that he died so gallantly, and that his Platoon was easily the best in the battalion.

The same officer adds that: 'he was nearly always ill, but would never go sick, but kept hanging on'.

He has no known grave and is commemorated on the Tyne Cot Memorial and on the war memorial in St Michael and All Angels Church, Eastbourne, East Sussex. His mother gave the flowers for the Radley Chapel 1919 Armistice Day service. See also www.radleyarchive.blog/2017/08/23/commemorating-the-fallen-of-ww1-146.

He is mentioned in Bury's supplemental list of scholars who never came into residence. TNA have a medal card WO 372/2/191781.

Alick Frederick Blyth, senior prefect Radley College, 1915–16.

COBHAM, Frederick George Brian, Lieutenant (1897–1918), 2nd/1st (Territorial Force) Battalion Cambridgeshire Regiment.

Frederick George Brian (known as Brian) Cobham was born at Gateshead-on-Tyne, County Durham (now Tyne and Wear) on 2 January 1897. At the time, his father, the Reverend George Henry Cobham (1866–1939) (m.1890), was curate at St Mary's Parish Church, Gateshead, married to Florence Barker née Chapman and Brian was their eldest son. In 1906, the family moved to Guisborough-in-Cleveland, Yorkshire, where his father became vicar at St Nicholas' Church (in 1919, he became rector of St Leonard's Church, Beeford, Driffield, Yorkshire). Brian's uncle, John Lawrence Cobham (1873–1960), was also a Corpus alumnus (m.1891) and an Anglican clergyman. During the Great War, he was a Chaplain to the Forces, though his service is not recorded by *The War List* (however, see appendix).

Between 1907 and 1910, Brian was educated at Aysgarth Preparatory School and from 1910 to 1915 at Repton. He was admitted to Corpus and would have come up in October 1916, probably to read Divinity prior to ordination. However, he deferred matriculation until the end of the war. Instead, on 6 August 1915, after leaving Repton, he was commissioned 2nd Lieutenant in the 2/1st Battalion Cambridgeshire Regiment. He trained as a Battalion signalling officer and promoted Lieutenant, with seniority from June 1916. Unusually, he worked with the regiment in Britain for nearly three years and did not leave for France until 20 April 1918, during the German Spring Offensive.

In August 1918, Brian Cobham, attached to the 38th Eastern Division (which included 1st (Territorial Force) Battalion Cambridgeshire Regiment), took part in the Battle of Amiens. This engagement marked the beginning of the 100 days offensive that led to the Armistice. Unfortunately, there are no surviving letters from the period of Brian's military service. The following is derived from the regimental history and the thoughts of one of his nephews.

At the start of August, the Battalion was in a fresh line near Ribemont expecting the enemy to attack. This occurred on 6 August when an allied forces' Brigade was driven out of some 800 yards of trenches in front of Morlancourt. An inevitable massive counterattack was planned for 8 August, with prominent involvement of the Cambridgeshires. Prior to the attack at 6.20 am that day, they experienced intense gas bombardment. The enemy were expecting and had prepared for a counterattack aimed at recapturing the lost trenches but did not expect an assault on an extended front.

For some time, the allied Brigade HQ were unsure how its troops had fared but, except for the Cambridgeshires, two advancing Corps and two other Companies had met their objectives. The Cambridgeshires:

> were lying in the open, short of the enemy position. Here they were being subjected to a hail of shrapnel and gas shells and the casualties were mounting up rapidly. The Padre, leading a gas-blinded soldier down to the aid-post, was met on arrival by the CO of the Ambulance: 'Your bloody Cambridgeshires came to this Division with a hell of a fighting reputation; they have let the Division down badly in their first show.' (Later, when the true circumstances became known, the CO apologised unreservedly.)

Meanwhile, two of the other Companies launched a surprise attack and the enemy was overcome with 316 wounded and unwounded in total. However, during that attack, the two Cambridgeshire Companies suffered severely: 186 men were wounded, of whom 141 were suffering from gas, thirteen men and two officers were killed (one being Brian Cobham). In short, the Battle of Amiens had been won, but at an incalculable price! That price did, however, result in the fulfilment of Field Marshal Sir Douglas Haig's aim of ending the war in 1918.

In a letter to his parents by Lieutenant R S Grose written the day after Brian was killed, he wrote:

> Your boy was in command of a platoon of 'A' Company, which was on the extreme right of the Battalion front. He gallantly led his platoon and must have outstripped his men because accompanied by his servant and runner he came suddenly upon an enemy machine-gun post. From two men, who have since seen the runner and servant, he was killed instantly – his two men being wounded. They were captured and kept in a dug out until 'C' Company coming up later on swept through the position, releasing them. They have both been sent back, so I have had no opportunity to question them personally.

In a second letter, written on 11 August to his father by the Methodist Chaplain, George F Walters, he said:

> It is with the deepest sorrow and sympathy I write to confirm the sad news that your son Lt Frederick George Brian Cobham 1/1st Cambridgeshire Regiment passed away during action near MORLANCOURT [Somme] on 8.8.18. I have lived with and intimately known your boy. He was white in soul and body. I do not think he ever uttered an unchaste word or did an ungenerous or unchristian act. And we shall greatly miss him. He went into action with his platoon on the morning of the 8th. He was absolutely successful taking his objectives, but was killed immediately afterwards. He was shot through the head and must have died instantly. We got his poor body down and buried it last evening [the 10th] in a quiet little cemetery (Military), just behind the French … Cemetery at RIBEMONT. The Church of England Chaplain to the Forces read the service. His personal kit is being sent on to you …

The brutality of the hand-to-hand fighting that claimed the life of Brian Cobham is revealed in a letter dated 7 September 1918 to Brian's father from his servant, Private F W Shallow:

> I was close to Lt Cobham when he fell, but whether he was wounded or not I cannot say, as I went down at almost the same time receiving a very bad wound in the leg and in front of my left shoulder. I am quite certain that my Officer [Brian Cobham] and one or two more went into the German trench after they fell, as while we laid [sic] there the Germans kept throwing bombs and firing at us and I heard Lieut Cobham call out to them to 'stop it', and then I heard one of the Germans call out 'well, come on in', and I am certain that they went in, but I could not get up myself and I did not intend to lift my head up for them to put a bullet through, so I laid [sic] there until a German fetched me in, and as soon as I got up, with the help of the German, I looked round to see if I could discover my Officer or any of our fellows, but I could not, so I am certain that your son went prisoner. I am informing you of this, because, when I showed them the German Officer at the 1st Field Hospital I got to, they told me that he had shot one of our officers, and I said that 'if he had, he had shot my Officer, Lt. Cobham' and I am sure Sir that that was how he met his death.

In 1919, after service in the Royal Field Artillery, Brian's cousin, John Oldcastle Cobham (1899–1987), matriculated into Corpus. His obituary appears in *The Letter of the Corpus Association*, No.66 (Michaelmas 1987), pp. 80–1. In 1927, his brother, John Hargreaves Ashworth Cobham (m.1927), came to the College (he too became an Anglican clergyman).

Brian Cobham was killed in action at Morlancourt, Somme on 8 August 1918, aged 21. He was buried in Ribemont Communal Cemetery Extension, Somme, France. The personal inscription on his gravestone reads 'I thank my God upon every remembrance of you' (Philippians 1:3). He is commemorated on the Repton School war memorial, the cross of which is inscribed *Adi audem dei et in honorem fratum qui morte obita salurem nobis sibi gloriam comparavere MCMXIV–XVIII* ('The glory of God and to the honour of our brothers who, by meeting their death, won safety for us and glory for themselves 1914–18'). He is not listed in Bury, nor does his name appear in the Admissions Register. TNA have an officer file WO 374/14469.

LIEUTENANT
F.G.B.COBHAM
CAMBRIDGESHIRE REGIMENT
8TH AUGUST 1918 AGE 21

STOKES, Louis Mander, 2nd Lieutenant (1897–1916), 2nd Battalion Royal Marine Light Infantry, Royal Naval Division.

Louis Stokes was born on 19 July 1897, one of four children and the only son of Sophia Emmeline née Mander and the Reverend Dr Henry Paine Stokes MA LLM LLD LittD. (m.1872), whose papers are held at the Cambridge University Library. His father was a noted writer, antiquarian and vicar of St Paul's Church, Cambridge. In 1917, he was appointed rector of Little Wilbraham and Honorary Canon at Ely Cathedral. He was, between 1912 and his death in 1931, an Honorary Fellow of the College. The family had a long association with the College and Henry's younger brother, also named Louis, matriculated in 1876.

Louis was educated first at St Faith's School, Cambridge and then, between 1911 and 1915, at Rugby School, where reports show he was a talented student. He also had the advantage of being good at games. As he grew up, Louis and his father were regular spectators at the nearby Fenners, the University cricket ground.

His clergyman father held decidedly pacifist views and after war was declared in 1914 Louis felt compelled to write to him justifying his wish to join the Rugby OTC. In the letter, he said: It would naturally be a regret to you if I were not to agree with you that war is wicked; but I do agree most thoroughly with you on that score.' However, the toll of war quickly hit home to Louis and in November 1915, just before he left Rugby, he wrote: 'Every week more boys I know are killed or wounded.'

Louis had planned to come up to Corpus in October 1916 and to this end, in early January 1916, he sat the Corpus scholarship examinations. Unfortunately, he was not successful, though he was accepted as a pensioner.

However, before January was out Louis was, like others of that putative 1916 cohort, commissioned and in uniform: in his case with the Royal Marine Light Infantry. After a few months of training, he was sent to France, arriving on 7 July 1916 during the Somme Offensive. He was thereafter quickly engaged in front line duties. Louis Stokes was killed in action at Beaumont-Hamel on 13 November 1916, aged 19. In his last letter home, he wrote: 'I wish I could tell you what we are doing, but I can't. However, I am having great fun, as I hope you are.'

After Louis's death, his Colonel wrote to his parents: 'He was a great favourite with his brother officers and his men. He died while doing his duty as a very brave and gallant gentleman.' His Adjutant said of him: 'I assisted him in his training. It did not take long to find out that he stood head and shoulders above the ruck, and that he was made of the stuff which makes leaders.' One of his Captains wrote: 'If I had had my own choice, I could never have chosen a braver or a finer Officer. He was always cheerful, always willing and always thinking of the comfort of others. He was wonderfully popular with his men.' And another Captain who was wounded in the same battle, writing from hospital a few days before he died, said: 'He was very brave and courageous, and, for that reason, I put him to lead my wave into action.'

Louis Mander Stokes was buried at Mailly Wood Cemetery, Mailly-Mailet, Somme, France. The personal inscription on his gravestone includes a reference to Psalm 23.1 'The Lord is my shepherd. I shall not want'.

The diaries and letters of Louis Mander Stokes, together with an account of his time at Rugby and the events leading up to his early death in the trenches of the Somme, were published in 1995 as *A Dear and Noble Boy: The Life and Letters of Louis Stokes 1897–1916*, edited by R A Barlow and H V Bowen (1995). His papers and other possessions, retained first by his parents then his sister, are now held in the Rugby School Archives.[21]

He is not listed in Bury, nor does his name appear in the Admissions Register. TNA have an officer file ADM 196/97/13.

Louis Stokes, bottom right, Royal Marine Light Infantry, Gosport 1916.

21. See also www.findinglouis1916.wordpress.com/about.

1917

BRAY, Frank, Flight Sub-Lieutenant (1898–1917), 8th (Naval) Squadron, Royal Naval Air Service.

According to the Commonwealth War Graves Commission website, Oundle School Roll of Honour and Walmer Airfield online memorial, Frank Bray was born on 22 October 1898. He was the eldest son of Marion and John William Bray, formerly of Scalby, Scarborough (the Commonwealth War Graves Commission website has his mother's address as Hambleton House, Roundhay Park Lane, Moortown, Leeds).

Frank was educated at Orleton Boys Preparatory School, Scarborough (now part of Hull College Group) and Oundle School. The Oundle School Roll of Honour records he entered School House in 1912 and left at Christmas 1916. During his time at the school, he was a prefect and a member of the sixth form. He was admitted to Corpus and would have come up in October 1917 but instead, in January 1917, joined the Royal Naval Air Service. He subsequently trained as a pilot and commissioned as a Sub-Lieutenant. On 16 April 1917 flying an Avro Biplane Frank Bray obtained his Flying Certificate at the Royal Naval Air Service Station, Redcar, Yorkshire (the previous day, also at RNASS Redcar, Frank Titcomb (see below) was killed in a flying accident). His officer file described him as: 'a very good pilot. Promising and keen officer.' On 18 June 1917, he was posted to France. Less than a month later, on 15 July 1917, he was flying in a patrol with several other machines and in an engagement with the enemy they lost a machine. Unfortunately, it was Frank Bray's aircraft, an 8th (Naval) Squadron Sopwith Camel (B3755). It was brought down in flames at Vimy on the German side of the lines. He was at first reported missing, but afterwards posted killed that day. His Squadron Commander wrote to his mother: 'His loss is deeply mourned by everybody in the squadron, with whom he was very popular. I know that I have lost a very good and extremely gallant officer.' He was 18 years and 9 months.

Frank Bray has no known grave and is commemorated on the Arras Flying Services Memorial, Faubourg-d'Amiens Cemetery, Arras, Pas de Calais, France. He appears on the Oundle School Roll of Honour. He is not listed in Bury, nor is his name in the Admissions Register. TNA have an officer and other files ADM 273/28/79, AIR 76/52/221 ADM 273/23/46 and ADM 273/4/79.

GASKELL, Lawrence Norris, 2nd Lieutenant (1898–1918), Royal Flying Corps and General List (1/7th Battalion Middlesex Regiment).

Lawrence Gaskell was born on 14 August 1898, the son of John (who was chief clerk at the Bow Street Police Court) and Sarah née Norris of Twickenham, Middlesex. He was a scholar of St Paul's School where, in 1916, he was captain of the school swimming and water polo teams. Lawrence was also a contemporary of William Arthur Roberts (see above). In December 1916, he was admitted to Corpus with an Entrance Exhibition to read the Classical Tripos and should have matriculated in October 1917. However, he never came into residence and instead on leaving school was commissioned into the armed forces. He quickly transferred to the RFC and trained as a pilot.

Lawrence Gaskell died on 1 March 1918 of wounds received from anti-aircraft fire two days earlier. According to an obituary in *The Pauline* (Vol. XXXVI, No. 238, April 1918), his Major wrote:

> He and his observer, Lieutenant Ritchie, were conducting a shoot on the enemy trench system and at about 1.15 p.m. their machine was struck by an enemy shell, which exploded and blew off a piece of the petrol tank. It also wounded your son in the thigh and the observer in the ankle. It set some part of the machine alight after a short space of time. They were about 2,000 feet up at the time, and with great pluck and presence of mind your son regained our lines and landed very well among shell holes about 2,500 yards from the front line. His machine immediately caught alight all over on landing. Your son managed to get out into a shell hole and thence to a trench. Both in piloting his machine to the ground and escaping from it while alight, he was very badly burnt. I wish to express my great sorrow at losing him from my squadron. He was all that could be desired as a pilot, and this last effort was a very noble and plucky one, and his observer undoubtedly owes his life to his pluck and tenacity. He was no trouble to me, and I trusted him implicitly, for he always did his job conscientiously and very well.

The Pauline obituary noted he had joined the RFC just a year earlier and was gazetted at the beginning of the previous October.

Lawrence is buried in Maroeuil British Cemetery, Pas de Calais, France. The personal inscription on his gravestone reads 'I have fought a good fight' (2 Timothy 4:7–8). At the time of his death, he was aged 19 years and 7 months. His observer, Lieutenant L McRichie, was wounded but survived. Lawrence Gaskell's name is recorded on the St Paul's School Roll of Honour. He is not listed in Bury. TNA have Army and RFC officer files WO 339/107373, AIR 79/626/67845 and AIR 76/178/20.

TITCOMB, Francis Holt Yates, Lieutenant (Probationary Flying Officer)
(1898–1917), Royal Naval Air Service.

Francis (known as Frank) Holt Yates Titcomb was born on 19 February 1898 at St Ives, Cornwall, the only son of William Holt Yates (1858–1930) and Jessie Ada née Morison Titcomb, of Clifton, Bristol. His paternal grandfather Jonathan Holt Titcomb (Peterhouse m.1837) had been the first Bishop of Rangoon, Burmah (now Yangon, Myanmar) and his maternal grandfather was John Morison, a shipowner. Frank had a sister, Mary Loveday Titcomb (b.1900), who later married a Clifton schoolfriend, Leonard Bampfield Cogan of Exeter. Frank's parents were both well-known professional artists.

During the years 1905 to 1909, the family lived in Düsseldorf, Germany, where Frank was educated at the Königliches Gymnasium. In 1909, they returned to England and settled in Bristol. Thereafter, until 1916, Frank was a student at Clifton College. Impressively, he quickly made the not inconsiderable transition from the German to the English public school system. He was also an exceptionally talented violinist and won the Junior Eisteddfod in Bristol. However, his main interest proved to be the new science of aeronautics.

In December 1916, Frank left Clifton College, having won an £80 Entrance Scholarship to read the Natural Sciences Tripos at Corpus (as did his exact Clifton contemporary Leslie Gilbert Laws (m.1919), who was awarded the same scholarship). He would have come up in October 1917, but instead opted to join the Royal Naval Air Service as a Probationary Flying Officer. After five weeks of basic training at Crystal Palace, he was posted to the Royal Naval Air Service Flying Training Airfield, Redcar, Yorkshire for flying instruction. Although he successfully completed his training, it was during his first solo flight, described in his officer file as 'an instructional flight', that he lost his life. According to an online obituary and another published source:

> On 15th April 1917 the pilot of this Maurice Farman Longhorn took off from Redcar for what was to be the pilot's first solo cross-country flight. The pilot became disorientated in some snow clouds whilst flying over the Moors and the aircraft crashed upside down at 12.05hrs between Egton Bridge and Goathland, it crashed on what is known locally as Dowson Garth, Castle Hill. Local people found the pilot in the wreckage and carried him on a farm gate to nearby High Burrows Farm where he died soon after. The aircraft was probably severely damaged by today's standards, but it was, in the main, recovered and rebuilt. An inquest returned a verdict of accidentally killed.

In 1929, John Kenneth Foster JP of Egton Manor arranged for a cross to be erected close to the crash site (see below). According to the Historic England website, the Memorial Cross was erected

> circa 750 metres south-west of Dowson Garth, Castle Hill, Egton Bridge, North Yorkshire, YO22 5AS. It is inscribed 'KF 1929'. It was built from local Egton stone by R. Harrison of Ashley House, Glaisdale and the cross itself was sculpted by J W Hill of Whitby. 'Swinsty Cross', as it is known, stands close to the spot where the Longhorn crashed. It is a copy of a cross found near Vittel, Vosges, France originally designed by Sir E L Lutyens ARA.

A painting entitled *Conservet Corpus Tuum et Animam Tuam* ('Preserve your body and soul', better known as 'The Soldiers Communion') by his father in 1915 was exhibited first at the Royal Academy and later in Liverpool (see below). It contains an image of Frank and now hangs in Clifton College Chapel, Bristol. At the time, the picture proved very popular and was reproduced first as a full-page illustration in the Christmas 1915 supplement to *The Graphic* and later lithographically in both black and white and coloured versions.

Francis Holt Yates Titcomb was killed on 15 April 1917 aged 19 years and 2 months. He was buried in the Brompton Cemetery, London with full naval honours. His life is commemorated on the Wickersley village war memorial, Rotherham, South Yorkshire (the Holt Yates family home was Wickersley Hall) and the Clifton College war memorial. TNA have an officer file ADM 273/12/147. He is not listed in Bury.

Memorial to Frank Titcomb erected on the crash site in North Yorkshire and his grave in Brompton Cemetery.

Clifton College Chapel

Detail from *Conservet Corpus Tuum et Animam Tuam* or
'The Soldiers Communion' by William Holt Yates Titcomb.
It features Frank Titcomb.
The original hangs in the chapel at Clifton College.

Clifton College Chapel

Conservet Corpus Tuum et Animam Tuam 'Preserve your body and soul', better known as 'The Soldiers Communion', by William Holt Yates Titcomb (1915). The picture now hangs in the chapel at Clifton College. The faces of the communicants are all Clifton boys: Frank Titcomb is kneeling second left. Only one soldier in this picture survived the war, he was Leonard Cogan (back row third left), who later married Frank's sister.

College Servant

CRACKNELL, Edwin George, Private 16641 (1890–1917), 11th (Cambridgeshire) Battalion the Suffolk Regiment.

Edwin George Cracknell was born at Feltwell, near Ely in 1890. However, the 1901 census has him, aged 11 and a scholar, living with his uncle and family at Hockwold cum Wilton, Norfolk. Although it is known he was working for the College on the outbreak of war, no records survive as to his occupation. The *Cambridge Independent Press* (20 November 1914) reported E G Cracknell (Littleport) had recently enlisted. He was a Private in the 11th (Cambridgeshire) Battalion the Suffolk Regiment, a unit established in Cambridge during August 1914 with the assistance of the Cambridge MP, Almeric Hugh Paget (later Lord Queenborough, an Honorary Fellow of Corpus). Edwin's Battalion landed at Boulogne in January 1916 as part of the 101st Brigade in the 34th Division. The Battalion took part in the Somme and Arras campaigns and in a doomed assault on a heavily fortified position near Roux. Edwin Cracknell was killed on 17 October 1917 during the 3rd Battle of Ypres known as Passchendaele, aged 27. He has no known grave and is commemorated on the Tyne Cot Memorial. His name appears on a University war memorial in St Botolphs Church, the Feltwell war memorial and it is also recorded on the Parish Church of St Mary, Feltwell memorial. He is further commemorated on the City of Cambridge war memorial in the Guildhall. In 2023 his name was added to the College war memorial.

The Feltwell War Memorial

Cambridge, Corpus Christi College, Old Court

CCCC Archives

Corpus Christi College Cambridge Old Court, *c.*1861: the earliest known
photographic image of the Old Court.

Appendix

A list of those members of Corpus Christi College, Cambridge who are known to have undertaken service in the British and Imperial armed forces during the years 1914 to 1919 compiled either by year of admission or matriculation.[22]

1866

ALFORD, Reverend Josiah George, VD (1847–1924), CF First Class, Royal Army Chaplains Department. Josiah was born in Doncaster, Yorkshire on 1 January 1847, the second son of Charles Richard Alford, Bishop of Victoria, Hong Kong and his wife Sarah Jacosha née Fleet. He was educated at King's College School, London and matriculated into Corpus in 1866. He graduated with a BA in 1869 (MA 1873) and was ordained priest in 1871. That same year, he married Catherine Mary née Leslie. One of their children, the Reverend Charles Symes Leslie Alford (1885–1963) (m.1903), also saw war service (see below). In 1880, after several appointments, he became vicar of St Nicholas' Church, Bristol and served as chaplain to the lord mayor, Sir Robert Symes. After 1895, he held several livings and served as chaplain to the Gloucestershire Volunteer Artillery. In later life, he was awarded a CBE, was a canon at Bristol Cathedral, and a noted composer of church music. During his war service, he was Mentioned in the Secretary of State's List twice.

---

22. The wartime College and University admissions and matriculations listings becomes unreliable after 1914. To ensure a more complete listing for these years, this appendix is based on admissions data rather than year of matriculation. As a result, it has been possible to include all those known to have been admitted to the College during the war years, including those who were killed or who (after war service) were able to take up their place following the Armistice. For the latter group, their entry includes the actual matriculation date. Names marked with an * denotes killed or died undertaking war service and whose biographies are to be found in the main text.

1871

*BURGESS, Duncan, Lieutenant Colonel (1850–1917), Royal Army Medical
Corps (Territorial Force). Officer in charge of the 3rd Northern General
Hospital. A College Fellow, he died from overwork on 17 January 1917.

1874

PALMER, Reverend Samuel, DSO MC (1854–1937), CF First Class, Royal
Army Chaplains Department and an Assistant Chaplain-General. Samuel was
the son of John Lowden and his wife Mary Palmer of Trinity Street, Cambridge.
He was educated at the Perse School and matriculated into Corpus in 1874. The
following year, he became a scholar. During his time at the College, he was an
Athletics Blue first in 1877 and again in 1878 (100 yards and hurdles). He graduated with a BA in 1877 and became a teacher. He is recorded in the 1901 census as
a married man with a son living in Bare, Morecombe, Lancashire. Although his
profession is given as a teacher, he was ordained a priest two years later. In the
1911 census, the family (now two children) were living in Wallasey, Cheshire.
During his war service with the RAMC he was awarded an MC; the citation
reads 'Although wounded, he rescued several wounded men with the greatest
courage. He has on many previous occasions displayed great courage.'

1879

COPEMAN, Sydney Arthur Monckton, Lieutenant Colone, KStJ FRS FRCP
(1862–1947), Royal Army Medical Corps, Sanitary Service 1st London Division
(Territorial Force Reserve). Sydney was born in Norwich, the son of Reverend
Arthur Charles Copeman. Educated at Norwich Grammar School, he was
admitted to Corpus as a pensioner in 1879 and made a scholar in 1880. Sydney
read the Natural Sciences Tripos, became a College Prizeman and graduated
with a BA in 1883 (MA 1886). He became MB in 1887, and in 1890 MD DPH and
FRCP. In 1898, he was made MRCS and LSA.

Between 1883 and 1891, Sydney was lecturer in physiology and demonstrator
of pathology at St Thomas' Hospital, London. In 1898, he was the Milroy
Lecturer at the Royal College of Physicians, London and between 1891 and 1919
lecturer on hygiene and public health at Westminster Medical School, London
(now part of Imperial College School of Medicine). Following that appointment,
issues relating to public health became the focus of his career and he became
Medical Inspector for the Local Government Board; and between 1919 and 1925,
he was Medical Officer to the newly formed Ministry of Health.

In 1903, Sydney Copeman was elected a Fellow of the Royal Society. He was, in addition, awarded the Cameron prize of the University of Edinburgh, the Buchanan gold medal of the Royal Society, the Fothergillian gold medal of the Medical Society of London, the Jenner medal of the Royal Society of Medicine, and the gold medal of the International Faculty of Science.

The greatest of his many contributions to medical science was the refinement of Edward Jenner's smallpox vaccine. He successfully developed mechanisms to stabilise it and by doing so made the vaccine safer. This innovation has enabled its continued widespread use, which in turn has led to the eradication of this disease. He saw war service as a Lieutenant Colonel in the Royal Army Medical Corps, Sanitary Service. In the post-war years, he was a member of the London County Council and Hampstead Borough Council, London. In 1899, he married Ethel Margaret nèe Boord and the couple had three children; his grandson was Peter William Monckton Copeman FRCS MRCP (1932–2018) (m.1950). In 1929, Sydney created the Copeman medal as an award in the gift of the College Executive Body: 'for marked achievement or promise in medical or biological sciences to members of the College of under ten years' standing from their BA degree; in exceptional circumstances, more especially for research involving long experience, the Executive Body have the power to waive this limitation'. It has not been awarded for several years. TNA have a medal card WO 372/5/19687.

Corpus Christi College, Chess Club 1879.

CCCC Chess Club serial

1881 Corpus Christi College Freshmen.
This is the earliest known matriculation photograph. It includes the ten 'Kaleidescopes'.[23]

1882

P E R O W N E , John Thomas Woolrych, Lieutenant Colonel, VD TD (1863–1954), Royal Field Artillery (Territorial Force). John was born in Lampeter, Cardiganshire (Ceredigion), Wales, the eldest son of Reverend John James Stewart Perowne. Educated at Haileybury, he matriculated into Corpus as a pensioner in 1882, became a scholar the following year, and graduated with a BA in 1885 (MA 1889). Also in 1889, he was commissioned Lieutenant in the 1st Volunteer Battalion Northamptonshire Regiment and in 1894, promoted Captain. A professional soldier, he served as a Lieutenant Colonel with the Royal Field Artillery during the First World War, was a King's Messenger between 1919 and 1921, and a Gold Staff Officer at the coronation of King George VI in 1937. In 1951, he was living at Falconer's House, St James's Court, St James's, London. He was married to Edith Marione née Browne (daughter of the Bishop of Worcester) and had two children. TNA have a medal card WO 372/15/203358.

R I N T O U L , David, Colonel (1862–1919), Clifton College OTC. David was born at Upper Cairnie, Perthshire, Scotland in 1862, the son of David Rintoul a farmer of Mains, Blebo, Cupar, Fife, Scotland. Between 1877 and 1881, David attended Madras College (now a comprehensive school), St Andrew's, Fife and then spent a year at Edinburgh University. He matriculated into Corpus as a pensioner in 1882 and became a scholar the following year. He read the Mathematical Tripos and was 14th Wrangler in 1885. He graduated with a BA (MA 1889) and was a College Fellow between 1888 and 1894. Between 1885 and 1919, he was a master and later head of physics at Clifton College and between 1904 and 1919, a housemaster. He wrote *An Introduction to Practical Physics for Use in Schools* (1898). David Rintoul was married and had two daughters and two sons, one of whom was killed at Ypres in 1914. He died at Clifton in April 1919 aged 57. See also Bury p. 233.

---

23. According to Bury, the ten Kaleidoscopes were a group formed from the 1881 freshmen. They enjoyed one another's company so much that they met at an annual dinner for more than fifty years. The papers of this remarkable society are held in the College archives.

1884

ARNOLD, Alfred James, Brevet Colonel, DSO CBE FRGS (1866–1933), Manchester Regiment and Royal Welch Fusiliers. Alfred was born in Didsbury, Manchester, the son of Alfred Robert Arnold a cotton goods merchant and his wife Dumvilia née Taaffe. He was educated at Hawthorn Hall School, Wilmslow, Cheshire and matriculated into Corpus in 1884. He left the College two years later without taking a degree and subsequently enlisted in the 6th Battalion Dragoon Guards. Thereafter, he was a professional soldier. In 1893, he was gazetted into the 3rd (The King's Own) Hussars. The following year, he joined the Royal Niger Constabulary in Nigeria and between 1894 and 1899 was a Commander. He served throughout the Niger-Soudan Campaign, 1895 and 1896, was Mentioned in Despatches and awarded the DSO. He went on to serve in the South African War, 1899–1901, and was Mentioned in Despatches. Between 1899 and 1913, he was Inspecteur-Général d'Exploitation for the Mozambique Company. He served throughout the First World War as a Brevet Colonel with both the Manchester Regiment and Royal Welch Fusiliers. He was made CBE in 1919. He was a member of the Cavalry Club and listed his recreations as cricket, hunting, shooting, rackets, tennis, cycling and chess. In retirement, he lived at Plas Owen, Harlech, Merionethshire (now Gwynedd), Wales, where he died in 1933 aged 67.

LOFT, Reverend Edmund William Boswell (1865–1928), CF 4th Class, Royal Army Chaplains Department. Edmund was born at Bishop Auckland, Co. Durham and matriculated into Corpus in 1884. He graduated with a BA in 1889, ordained deacon the same year and priest in 1891. He served as a curate in Lincolnshire between 1889 and 1908 and thereafter, until 1917, held livings in Lincolnshire. After his war service, he obtained a living in Norfolk before returning to Lincolnshire, where he died in 1928 aged 63.

1886

LART, Charles Edmund, Captain (1867–1947), 4th Battalion Devonshire Regiment (Territorial Force). Charles was born in St James's Square, Notting Hill, London, the son of Edmund Lart. Educated at Westminster School, he matriculated into Corpus as a pensioner in 1886, graduating with a BA in 1889. In 1897, he married Amy Vincent née Watson in Meltham, Yorkshire. In the 1911 census, the couple were living in Charworth, Dorset, had four children, and Charles self-described as an author of private means. He was a well-known writer on French Huguenots. His works include *Huguenot Pedigrees* (2 vols.) (1924) together with several works concerning the Huguenot parochial registers (these are still in print). In 1900, he was a 2nd Lieutenant in the 1st Cinque Ports Volunteer Artillery. He saw wartime service as a Captain with the Devonshire Regiment and was also an officer instructor attached to New Zealand forces. He died in Devon in June 1947 aged 80. TNA have an officer file WO 374/40843 and a medal card WO 372/12/6596.

MARRIOTT, Reverend Herbert Marriott (1868–1943), CF 4th Class, Royal Army Chaplains Department. Herbert was born at Weston-Super-Mare, Somerset, the son of the Reverend George Herbert Marriott (1932–18) (Trinity College, Dublin, m.1857) and his second wife Angeline Elizabeth née Berry (1846–1910) both of whom were of Anglo-Irish decent. He was the elder brother of John Francis Laycock Marriott (1889–1915) (m.1907) who died during war service (see biography). Herbert was home schooled and admitted to Corpus as a pensioner in 1886. He graduated with a BA in 1889, trained at Ridley Hall, ordained deacon in 1891 and priest the following year. He served several curacies until 1901, when he became a Chaplain to the Forces in South Africa for which he was awarded the Queen's South Africa Medal. Between 1902 and 1904, he served a curacy in Newbridge, Co. Kildare, Ireland and between 1904 and 1916, at the newly created Church of the Holy Apostles, Leicester. In April 1916, he was commissioned CF 4th Class and saw service both in France and Egypt. He was thereafter, until 1940, vicar of the Church of St Margaret of Antioch, Blackfordby, Leicestershire. He died on 31 May 1943 at Ashby-de-la-Zouche, Leicestershire aged 75. He never married. He is not mentioned in either *The War List* or in Bury as having served as a Chaplain to the Forces. However, family websites have provided much of the information.

1887

WARD, Reverend Algernon, FRSL FRGS FSA Scot (1869–1947), CF 4th Class, Royal Army Chaplains Department. Algernon was born in Leamington, Warwickshire, the son of the Reverend Robert Ward of Hagworthington, Lincolnshire. He was educated at Queen Elizabeth's Grammar School, Horncastle, Lincolnshire and matriculated into Corpus in 1887. He graduated with a BA in 1890 (MA 1894), was ordained a deacon in 1892 and priest the following year. Between 1897 and 1902, after serving several curacies, he was appointed divinity lecturer at Queen's College, Birmingham. And, between 1902 and 1915, held the post of chaplain at All Saints' Church, Ramleh, Egypt (between 1904 and 1906 he was also canon of Jerusalem), then at St Mark's, Alexandria, Egypt. Thereafter, until 1922 (apart from war service), he was vicar of Sturminster Newton, Dorset and until 1926 vicar of Stowe, Shropshire. Also, between 1922 and 1936, he was rector of Church Lawford with Newnham Regis, Warwickshire. His final ecclesiastical appointment, between 1936 and 1945, was as archdeacon of the Collegiate Church of St Mary, Warwick. Algernon Ward was the author of several theological works, including *A Guide to the Study of the Book of Common Prayer* (1901). He was married to Elizabeth Mary née Waters. Algernon Ward died at Paignton, Devon in 1947 aged 78. TNA have a medal card WO 372/20/215649.

1888

COLLETT, William George, Major (b.1869), 13th Battalion (attached to the 5th Battalion) Rifle Brigade. William was born at Upper Clapton, Middlesex the son of Thomas Trusson Collett of Ringleton, Kent. Educated at Sutton Valence School, Maidstone, Kent he matriculated into Corpus in 1888 as a pensioner to read the Mathematical Tripos, graduating with a BA in 1891 (MA 1895). Thereafter, he taught at the Oxford Military College until 1897 and then, between 1897 and 1929, at Wellington College. In 1911, he was married to Ruth Lilian Collett and had three children. During the war he served as a Major in the Rifle Brigade. TNA have an officer file (though it lists the Connaught Rangers as his regiment) WO 339/19830.

DOUGHTY, Ernest Christie, Major, DSO (1868–1928), 2nd Battalion Suffolk Regiment. Ernest was born at Martlesham, Suffolk, the son of the Reverend Ernest George Doughty, rector of Martlesham, and his wife Mary. He was educated at Tonbridge School and admitted to Corpus in 1888 as a pensioner. In 1890, he left the College without graduating to join the Suffolk Regiment; in 1910, he was attached to the 3rd Battalion West Suffolk Militia. He saw combat in August 1914, was wounded and made a prisoner of war. He was also Mentioned in Despatches. In 1920, he was awarded the DSO, by which time he was employed by the War Office. He died in 1928 aged 60.

FISON, Edmund Towers, Captain (1869–1950), Royal Army Medical Corps, Sanitary Service (Territorial Force). Edmund was born at King's House, King's, Thetford, Norfolk, the son of Cornell Henry Fison JP, a merchant, and his wife Eliza. His father developed an important fertiliser business based on the processing of coprolite (which was mined mainly on Corpus-owned land). Edmund was educated at Repton School and matriculated into Corpus as a pensioner in 1888, graduating with a BA in 1891. Whilst at the College he was a three times Rowing Blue, 1890, 1891, and 1892. In 1889, he won the prestigious CUBC Colquhoun Sculls, the Rowlinson Pairs (with Henry Martin (m.1886)), and the Heywood Sculls in 1890 and Wilkinson Sculls in 1891. He was also Captain of the Boat Club in 1890. He rowed at 12 stone 10 pounds.

After graduation, he took an MB and BChir in 1895 and MD in 1898. He trained at St George's Hospital, London from 1891, MRCS and LRCP 1895 and FRCS (Edin) 1898. He served as house physician and house surgeon at St George's Hospital, as clinical assistant at the Hospital for Women, Soho Square, London and in 1910 as physician at the Salisbury Infirmary, Salisbury.

The 1901 census has him married, but no wife is listed and Edmund was living with his family in Thetford. His wife is not listed in the 1911 census, but there is a daughter aged 14. He was later Medical Officer of Health for Salisbury, Wiltshire. Edmund served as a Captain in the RAMC during the First World War. He was living in Salisbury in 1942. He was the brother of Charles Frederick Fison (1862–1926) (m.1880), who graduated in 1883 (MA 1886) and went on to become an Anglican priest.

1889

*DIXON-WRIGHT, Reverend Henry Dixon, MVO (1870–1916), Chaplain, RN. He died on 1 June 1916 of wounds received in action at Jutland on HMS *Barham* aged 46.

*DOUDNEY, Reverend Charles Edmund (1871–1915), CF 4th Class, Royal Army Chaplains Department. He died on 16 October 1915 of wounds.

1890

MASTERS, Reverend Frederick George, Captain (1871–1939), CF 4th Class, Australian Chaplains Department. Frederick was born in Cambridge the son of James George Masters. Educated at the Perse School, he matriculated into Corpus as a scholar in 1890 and became sub-librarian in 1892. He graduated with a BA in 1893 (MA 1898), ordained deacon in 1895 and priest the following year. Thereafter, he was a curate in Cornwall, before moving first to New Zealand and then Australia. In 1900, he married Alice Maude Mary née Todd and in 1917, held the living at Balaclava, Melbourne, Australia.

Between January and June 1917, at the age of 46, he served with the Australian Imperial Force as a troop ship Chaplain. An Australian internet site has the following 1939 obituary:

> The Reverend F G Masters, who died in England recently, was rector of All Souls', St Peters from 1900 to 1904. He was married there in 1900 to Miss Maude Todd, daughter of Sir Charles Todd and two of his three daughters – who are now in England – were born in the parish. In 1904 he went to Holy Trinity Church, Balaclava, Melbourne, and from there in 1920 to St Luke's, Bath England [where his contemporary Charlie Doudney (m.1889) (see biography) had been vicar]. Ten years later, he was appointed to St Mary Abchurch, London, a Wren Church, the living being in the gift of his old college, Corpus Christi, Cambridge. Mr Masters did great work among lay readers of the Diocese of London.

> He remained at St Mary until his death in 1939.

TOOGOOD, Reverend Joseph Hooker (1868–1952), CF 4th Class, Royal Army Chaplains Department (Territorial Force) attached to the Cheshire Brigade, Royal Field Artillery. Joseph was born at Hotwell, Bristol, the son of Samuel Hunter Toogood. Educated at Clifton College, he was admitted to Corpus in 1890 to read the Mathematical Tripos and became a scholar and 29th Wrangler the following year. He graduated with a BA in 1893 (MA 1897), was ordained deacon 1894 and priest the following year. Thereafter (apart from war service), he served in parishes in Cheshire. In 1901, he married Esther née Bradshaw Isherwood of Marple Hall, Cheshire (a relative of the writer Christopher Bradshaw Isherwood (m.1923)). In 1911, the couple had two children. Between 1907 and 1946, he was vicar of St Peter's Church, Plemstall, Cheshire. A skilled carver, Joseph was responsible for much of the renewal of the church woodwork. Over time, he made improvements to the chancel screen, created a new altar, the reredos, and panelling for the sanctuary. He also made the lectern, refurnished much of the north chapel, and improved the baptistry, including a new cover for the font. He worked on the choirstalls and their canopy, made figures for the sanctuary niches and an alms box. In addition, he carved a list of sidesmen on the west wall and a war memorial on the north wall. He retired in 1946 and died in 1952 aged 84. TNA have an officer file WO 374/69135.

1891

COBHAM, Reverend John Lawrence Cobham (1873–1960) CF, Royal Army Chaplains Department. John was educated at Merchant Taylors' School, Crosby, and in 1891, matriculated into Corpus as a pensioner, graduating with a BA in 1894 (MA 1898). He was ordained deacon in 1896 and priest the following year. From 1896 to 1904, he was a curate and then appointed vicar of Carshalton, Surrey (now the London Borough of Sutton). During the war, he served as a Chaplain to the Forces and Commissary for Uganda; in 1920, he was Chaplain in Entebbe, Uganda. He was later vicar of St Peter's Church, Tunbridge Wells and rector of St Mark's Church, Torwood, Torquay. His final appointment was archdeacon of Totnes between 1933 and 1947. His son the Venerable John Oldcastle Cobham (m.1919) was archdeacon of Durham. Furthermore, he was the brother of Reverend George Henry Cobham (m.1890) and uncle of Brian Cobham (see biography).

DAWES, Reverend Alfred Wilkinson (1871–1941), CF 2nd Class, Royal Army Chaplains Department. He was the son of Eliza and Alfred Dawes, a bank cashier of Clifton, Bristol. Alfred was born in Bath, educated at Bristol Cathedral School and Bristol Grammar School. In 1891, he matriculated into Corpus as a pensioner, graduating in 1894. That same year, he was ordained deacon and priest in 1896. He was a curate first in Chelsea, then at Barton Hill, Bristol. Between 1898 and 1899, he worked for the London Diocese Home Mission, Willesdon and between 1899 and 1919 was a Chaplain to the Forces, serving in both home and overseas postings as well as during the South African and First World Wars. He subsequently held various livings finally, between 1939 and 1941, at Midgham, Berkshire, where he died aged 70.

RECKITT, Frank Norman, Acting Captain (1872–1940), Middlesex Regiment attached to the Labour Corps. Frank (known as Norman) was born in Hessle, Yorkshire, the son of starch manufacturer Francis Reckitt (of Reckitt and Sons Ltd) and his wife Eliza. Norman was educated at Wellington College and matriculated into Corpus as a pensioner in 1891. He graduated in 1894 (MA 1898) and went on to train as an architect. He also saw service in the South African War (South African Infantry-Yeomanry) and during the First World War served with the Middlesex Regiment and Labour Corps. He married Beatrice Margaret née Hewitt and had a son Basil Norman Reckitt (who was later chairman of the family firm Reckitt and Colman plc). Norman died in West Somerset in 1940 aged 68. TNA have a medal card WO 372/16/170083.

STEVENS, James Algernon, Lieutenant Colonel, CIE OBE VD (1873–1934), 18th (Rangoon) Battalion, Indian Defence Force. James was born at Cuttack, India, the son of Indian civil servant John Foster and his wife Frances Stevens. He was educated at Blundell's School, Tiverton, Devon and matriculated into Corpus in 1892 as a scholar. He graduated with a BA in 1895 and in 1898 joined the Indian Police Service. In 1906, he transferred to the Indian Customs Service and between 1913 and 1921 was chief collector of customs in Burmah. From 1921, he was collector of customs in Bombay (now Mumbai). James married Ethel née Cloete in 1901 and the couple later retired to Redland, Bristol. He died in 1934 aged 61.

1892

GALER, Frederic Bertram, Captain and Adjutant (1873–1942), 24th Battalion London Regiment (The Queen's). Bertram was born in Kensington, London, the son of civil servant accountant John Maxcey Galer and his wife Louise Jane Galer. Educated at Dulwich College, he matriculated into Corpus in 1892 to read the Mathematical Tripos. He became a scholar in 1894 and graduated in 1895 (MA 1917). He went on to train as an insurance actuary, becoming an assistant actuary with the Rock Life Assurance Company in 1896 and became an FIA in 1904. Between 1910 and 1913, he was secretary of the Norwich Union Life Office and between 1914 and 1917, general manager and actuary of the Eagle Assurance Company. Between 1917 and 1921, he was manager of the Eagle Star and British Dominions Assurance Company. In 1919, after war service, he became an underwriter at Lloyd's and was senior partner in the firm of F Bertram Galer and Co., Assurance Brokers. During the interwar years, he served on the Port of London Authority and with the London and Home Counties Traffic Advisory Committee. He was, between 1937 and 1938, deputy-chairman of the London County Council. Knighted in 1939, he also held appointments as DL and JP. He died at Henley-on-Thames in 1942 aged 69. TNA have a medal card WO 372/7/187946.

HARPER-SMITH, Septimus William, 2nd Lieutenant (b.1874), Labour Corps. Formerly Quartermaster Sergeant, Royal Fusiliers. Septimus was born at Galagate House, Norham, Northumberland, the son of Septimus Harper Harper-Smith, a farmer. Educated at George Watson's College, Edinburgh he matriculated into Corpus in 1892 and graduated in 1895. Between 1896 and 1898, he was a schoolmaster at Dover College and subsequently at Timsbury School, Eastbourne. He married Mabel née Caister at Boston, Lincolnshire in 1905. In the 1911 census he was living at 'The Hall' Coningsby, Lincolnshire with his wife and a son. He gave his occupation as a farmer. He is listed in Bury as Smith. TNA have an officer file WO 374/31140.

LAWRENCE, Reverend George Henry (1874–1948), Royal Army Medical Corps. George was born at Oakleigh, Beckenham, Kent, the son of F W Lawrence, a merchant. He was educated at Charterhouse, matriculating into Corpus in 1892 and graduating with a BA in 1895. In 1897, he was ordained deacon and the following year priest. Thereafter, apart from war service in the RAMC, he held various livings. He died in 1948 aged 74.

LUCAS, Reverend Robert Holmes (1873–1949), CF 4th Class, Royal Army Chaplains Department. Robert was born in Liverpool, the son of an Anglican clergyman of Belstone, Devon. Educated at Crediton Grammar School, Devon (now Queen Elizabeth's School), he matriculated into Corpus in 1892 as a pensioner, graduating with a BA in 1895. He was ordained deacon in 1896 and priest the following year. Thereafter, apart from war service, he held a variety of livings in Devon, the last, between 1933 and 1944, as rural dean of Plympton. He married Irena Elizabeth and the couple had three children. He died in 1949 aged 76. TNA have an officer file WO 374/43164 and a medal card WO 372/12/156915.

*PATCH, Noel James Stanway, Private (2699) (1874–1917), 47th Battalion (6th Reinforcement) Infantry, Australian Imperial Force. He was killed at the 3rd Battle of Ypres.

Matriculated in 1891, this group of finalists are soon to graduate. It includes an individual who won a wooden spoon for being the lowest ranking undergraduate to pass the Mathematics Tripos. Alas, there is no key to identify the students. They include Noel Patch who was killed in action in 1917 and for whom no other photograph appears to have survived.

1893

*BOURNES, George Henry (Acting Sergeant), Corporal 6051089 (1873–1921)**, 10th (Service) Battalion Royal Fusiliers attached to the Intelligence Corps. Formerly, 1st Battalion Royal Scots (The Royal Regiment), the Royal Engineers, the 1/6th Battalion Duke of Wellington's (West Riding) Regiment and the Labour Corps. In 1921, he was in Germany as part of the occupation forces. He committed suicide on 31 March 1921 aged 47.

GRIFFITHS, Reverend Richard (known as Richie) (1867–1952), Chaplain to the Royal Navy. Formerly, CF 4th Class, Royal Army Chaplains Department. Richard was born in Pontypridd, Glamorganshire, Wales, the son of Griffith Griffiths a railway contractor and his wife Catherin. The family lived at Stonehouse, Gloucestershire. He was educated at the King's School, Gloucester and St Aidan's Theological College, Birkenhead where, in 1891, he was ordained deacon and priest in 1892. He then served as assistant chaplain at Holy Trinity Church, Nice, France from where, in 1893, aged 26, he was admitted to Corpus as a pensioner. During his time at the College, he served as curate at Holy Trinity Church, Cambridge, graduating in 1896 with a BA (MA 1902). He then held appointments in Britain and Australia and between 1901 and 1903 served as a Chaplain to the Forces in South Africa. He returned to Britain in 1903, where he remained a Chaplain with the Territorial Reserve as well as holding civilian appointments. The 1911 census shows him as vicar of All Saint's Church, West Farleigh, Kent, married to Margaret Sumarez Griffiths and the couple had two children (they had two further children, one of whom died in infancy). Richie also served as Chaplain to the 3rd (Reserve) Battalion the Buffs (East Kent Regiment).

He joined the RACD in 1914 and was posted to the 24th Field Ambulance, RAMC, a part of the 8th Division. By early November 1914, his unit was serving in France and Flanders. His almost daily letters to his wife and journal notes chronicle his activities and the battles in which he participated, for which he was Mentioned in Despatches. In May 1917, he transferred to the Royal Naval Base in Larne Harbour, Ireland (now Northern Ireland), where he served as a Chaplain until the end of the war. Between 1918 and 1920, although back in his parish, Richard remained a Royal Navy Chaplain and a Chaplain at the Mission to Seamen. In 1920, the family moved to Darley Dale, Derbyshire, where he was rector of St Helen's Church. He remained there until retirement in 1938, when he and Margaret moved first to Derby and then, in 1946, to live with their daughter Agatha Faith in Kingston, near Richmond Park, Surrey. Richard Griffiths died in 1952 aged 85 and Margaret died the following year. In 2018, his granddaughter Diana Heywood self-published *The Game of Blood and Iron* (2 vols.) containing Richard's wartime letters to Margaret, together with his journal notes and photographs. Copies of the volumes together with the collection of letters, journal notes, medals, and photographs are now preserved in the College Archives. TNA have an officer file WO 339/78937.

*LANG, Henry Astell, Major (1874–1915), Worcestershire Regiment. He was killed in action at Gallipoli on 6 June 1915.

MICHELL, Reverend Eardley Wilmot (1874–1939), CF 4th Class, Royal Army Chaplains Department. Eardley was born in Richmond, Surrey, the son of a vicar and alumni of the same name (m.1862). Educated at Cranleigh School, Surrey and Monckton Coombe School, Bath, he was admitted to Corpus as a pensioner in 1893, graduated with a BA in 1896 (MA 1900), and ordained priest in 1899. He held several ecclesiastical appointments until 1912, when he became vicar of St Mary Magdalene's Church, Bolney, Sussex where (apart from war service) he remained until his death in 1939 aged 65. TNA have a medal card WO 372/13/222703.

SMITH, Reverend Frederick Samuel (b. *c.*1893) CF 4th Class, Royal Army Chaplains Department. He is not listed in the University alumni database but is recorded in Bury and *The War List*.

Smyth, Reverend John William Wallace (1873–1935), CF 4th Class, Royal Army Chaplains Department. John was born at Steppingley, Bedfordshire, the son of an Anglican clergyman. Educated at Bedford Grammar School, he matriculated into Corpus as a pensioner in 1893 graduating with a BA in 1896 (MA 1901). In 1898, he was ordained deacon and priest in 1900. Until the outbreak of war, he served several curacies and held other appointments. During the war, he served in the RACD and was Mentioned in Despatches. He remained a Chaplain to the Forces until 1927. Thereafter, he was rector at Lamarsh with Alphamstone, Essex until his death in 1935 aged 62.

1894

*Barker, William, Major (1873–1915), 4th Battalion, attached the 9th (Service) Battalion Worcestershire Regiment. He died on 15 August 1915 of wounds received in action.

Crispin, Arthur Edward, Private (1743) (1874–1961), 28th Battalion London Regiment (Artists Rifles), Transport Division, Labour Corps (945th Employment Company). Arthur and his twin brother Ernest Henry (m.1894, St John's) were born in St James's Square, London, the sons of the late Lieutenant Colonel George Bell Crispin. The brothers were educated at Bedford School and Arthur matriculated into Corpus as a pensioner in 1894. He graduated with a BA in 1898 and in later life became a schoolmaster. The 1911 census has him as a single man living in Stevenage, Hertfordshire. He later married Elsie née Underwood and died in Sussex in 1961 aged 86. TNA has a microfilmed file WO363-4/007295152/00770 and 00771.

Gell, Reverend Edward Anthony Sydney, Lieutenant Colonel, DSO MC (1875–1941), 2/7th Battalion Lancashire Fusiliers. Formerly Lieutenant, Royal Fusiliers. Edward was born in Hereford in 1875, the son of Francis Gell (m.1849). He was educated first at Sutton School and then Sidcot School, Somerset, matriculating into Corpus as a pensioner in 1894. He graduated with a BA in 1897 (MA 1902), ordained deacon in 1898 but was not ordained a priest until 1909. During the South African War, 1899 to 1902, he served as a Private, though he was subsequently commissioned Lieutenant in 5th Battalion Imperial Yeomanry. In 1902, he married Gertrude Jennie Ryland née Bembridge. The couple had one son. Thereafter, he held several civilian ecclesiastical appointments until 1914, though he remained a Chaplain to the Forces, serving postings in Britain and abroad.

In 1918, he was wounded twice, reported missing, and made a prisoner of war. He was also Mentioned in Despatches. His DSO citation reads:

> He had just arrived on leave in England when he heard his division was engaged. He hurried back and after much difficulty got to them. Within half an hour of arrival he collected about one hundred stragglers and attached them to the

remnants of his own battalion, his vigour and fearlessness put fresh life into the defence. Next day, when the line was being driven back, he led a counter-attack with splendid dash under very heavy machine-gun fire.

His MC citation reads: 'For conspicuous gallantry. When his patrol was attacked by machine gin and rifle fire, he brought it safely back, and then returned and endeavoured to rescue a wounded man who was twice hit again whilst dressing his wounds. He has repeatedly carried out gallant work and has always set a fine example.'

In 1920, he was appointed an assistant director of graves registration at GHQ France and between 1921 and 1926, held an appointment with the Imperial War Graves Commission (now the Commonwealth War Graves Commission). He was also a member of the Anglo-Italian Committee. Edward spent his final years in Highgate, London, where he died in 1941 aged 66.

MANSFIELD, Reverend James, Sergeant (1870–1944), Royal Army Medical Corps, 2nd Southern General Hospital (Territorial Force). James was born in Shirehampton, Somerset, the son of Reverend Arthur Mansfield vicar of Aldmondsbury, Gloucestershire; his brother was Charles Mansfield (m.1890). James was educated at Weymouth College, Dorset and in 1894 matriculated into Corpus as a pensioner. He graduated with a BA in 1898 (MA 1901), ordained deacon in 1901 and priest the following year. Between 1906 and 1944, he was rector of St Augustine of Hippo Church, Clutton, Somerset, where he died aged 74.

PARKER, Reverend Herbert Leslie (1872–1947), CF 4th Class, Royal Army Chaplains Department. Herbert was born in Liverpool in 1872, the son of William a cashier. Educated at Liverpool College, in 1894, aged 22, he matriculated into Corpus as a pensioner, graduating with a BA in 1897. In 1898, he was ordained deacon and priest the following year. Between 1901 and 1910, Herbert was Chaplain to HM Cadet Ship *Conway* and the Mersey Mission to Seamen. Thereafter, he was a Chaplain to the Forces serving in Britain and overseas. During his war service, he was twice Mentioned in Despatches. He married Mary Balharry in 1904 and died at Ozier Hill, Taghmon, Co. Wexford, Ireland in 1947 aged 75.

PETTY, William, Lieutenant Colonel, DSO (b.1875), 9th Battalion Seaforth Highlanders (Ross-shire Buffs, the Duke of Albany's). William was born in Wisbech, Cambridgeshire in 1875, the son of Reverend William Petty (m.1870). Educated at St Paul's School, he matriculated into Corpus as a pensioner in 1894, graduating with a BA in 1898. Thereafter, he obtained a teaching position before military service in the South African War, which was followed by a period with the South African police. On his return to Britain, he obtained further teaching appointments. During his war service, he was wounded twice, Mentioned in Despatches twice, and awarded the DSO in the 1918 New Year's Honours.

1895

ADAMS, Reverend Newsham Peers (1861–1940), CF 4th Class, Royal Army Chaplains Department. Newsham was born in Bombay (now Mumbai), India in 1861, the son of a Bombay Army General Henry Augustus Adams, previously of Funchal, Madeira. Educated at Lymington School, Hampshire, he matriculated into Corpus as a pensioner in 1895 aged 34 and graduated with a BA in 1898 (MA 1904). In 1901, he was ordained deacon and priest the following year. Between 1904 and 1912, he held a living in Suffolk. He served as Chaplain to the Forces between 1915 and 1918 and subsequently held various livings until his death in Surrey in 1940 aged 79. He was a descendant of the Anglo-Irish ascendancy Adams family of Co. Cavan, Ireland.

DRURY, Reverend William, MC (1876–1940), CF 2nd Class, Royal Army Chaplains Department. William was born in Burton-on-Trent, Staffordshire, the son of Reverend William Frederick Drury (m.1860). Educated at Burton Grammar School (now Abbot Beyne Comprehensive School) and Christ's Hospital, Sussex, he matriculated into Corpus as a pensioner in 1895, graduating with a BA in 1898 (MA 1906). William was ordained deacon in 1899 and priest the following year. Thereafter, he held several posts as a Chaplain to the Forces, first in South Africa, then Singapore, and finally in Britain. He was wartime assistant to the principal Chaplain to the British Expeditionary Force, during which he was awarded the MC and Mentioned in Despatches three times. After the war, he was Chaplain to the Royal Hospital Chelsea and thereafter held other appointments. TNA have an officer file WO 339/114035 and a medal card WO 372/6/98680.

MAUNDRELL, Reverend William Herbert (1876–1958), Chaplain Royal Navy. He was born in Nagasaki, Japan, the son of the Reverend Herbert Maundrell archdeacon of Japan and Sarah Elizabeth, née Hobbs. William was educated at The King's School, Canterbury and matriculated into Corpus in 1895 with a Parker Exhibition. He subsequently became a scholar and graduated with a BA in 1898 (MA 1904). During his time at the College, he was President of the Chess Club and a member of the Gravediggers. He was also an Athletics Blue and post Cambridge played cricket for Hampshire. Between 1899 and 1904, William was an assistant tutor at West Wratting and in 1905 ordained deacon and priest the following year. Between 1904 and 1907, he was an assistant master at The King's School, Canterbury. Thereafter, until 1931, he was a Royal Navy Chaplain. He served on several ships including the ill-fated HMS *Bedford*, then in 1916, moved to the Royal Naval College, Osborne where he remained until 1921. He was subsequently Chaplain at several shore establishments in Britain and overseas until retirement in 1931. In 1912, he married Evelyn Helen née Furley and between 1931 and 1940 was rector of the Church of St Nicholas, Ringwould, Kent.

PEARSON, Louis, 2nd Lieutenant (1876–1944), South Staffordshire Regiment. Previously, Private 766260, London Regiment (Artists Rifles). Louis was born in 1876, the son of Francis Fenwick Pearson, a solicitor of Storrs Hall, Arkholme with Cawood, Kirkby Lonsdale, Lancashire (now Cumbria) and educated at Uppingham School. He matriculated into Corpus as a pensioner in 1895, graduating six years later with a BA. On graduation, he served as Private Secretary to Sir Arthur Stanley MP GCVO GBE CB. In 1918, during his war service, Louis was wounded. He was employed by the Ministry of Labour in 1930 and died at Torquay, Devon in 1944 aged 68.

WEATHERHEAD, Roberto, Commander RN (1878–1935), naval instructor at HMS *President*, a shore establishment and home base of the London Division of the Royal Naval Reserve. Roberto was born in Liverpool, the son of the Reverend Robert Johnstone Weatherhead and his wife Anne Bagot. He was educated at Rossall School, Lancashire, the Liverpool Institute, and Monmouth School. He matriculated into Corpus in 1895 as a pensioner and became a scholar the following year. He graduated with a BA in 1898 and then became a naval instructor. He went on to publish *The Star Pocket Book or How to Find Your Way at Night by the Stars: A Simple Manual for the Use of Soldiers, Travellers, and Other Landsmen* (1911). After war service, he lived in Heswall, Cheshire and latterly in Cambridge. Roberto died at Harborne, Staffordshire in 1935 aged 57.

1896

PAGE, Cecil Herbert Winter, Captain, BChir MD MRCS LRCP (1879–1951), Royal Army Medical Corps. Cecil was born in Norwich, the son of Charles Fountain Page, a merchant. Educated at the City of Norwich Grammar School, he matriculated into Corpus as a pensioner in 1896 and later became a scholar. He graduated with a BA in 1899 (MA 1903), became an LRCP and MRCS in 1904, BChir in 1906 and MD in 1909. He trained at St Bartholomew's Hospital, London (now Barts and the London School of Medicine and Dentistry). After war service, he practised medicine in North Walsham, Norfolk. He was an FSA, a member of the council of the Norfolk and Norwich Archaeological Society, and Honorary Secretary of the Norfolk Record Society.

TELFER, Robert George, Lieutenant (b.1877), Border Regiment. Robert was born in Nottingham, the son of Annie Marie and the Reverend Archibald Telfer. Educated at Worcester Cathedral School, he matriculated into Corpus as a pensioner in 1896, graduating with a BA in 1899. He held a series of teaching appointments until 1910, at which point he went to Dulwich College where he remained (apart from war service) until 1933. In 1913, he married Flora Mary née Gibson. During the war he was a draft conducting officer. TNA have a medal card WO 372/19/188758.

1897

SAYERS, Lorne Douglas Watson, Lieutenant Colonel (1878–1940), Royal Army Service Corps. Lorne was born in 1878 at St Peter's Square, London, the son of the artist Reuben Thomas William Sayers (1815–88). He was educated at St Paul's School and matriculated into Corpus as a pensioner in 1897, graduating with a BA in 1900. A professional soldier, Lorne was commissioned 2nd Lieutenant in the Army Service Corps in 1901, promoted Lieutenant in 1903, Captain 1906 and Major in 1914; his final rank was Lieutenant Colonel. He served with the RAMC during the First World War and in 1914 was deputy assistant director, supplies and transport, Northern Command. In 1916, he became deputy assistant quarter master general, Portsmouth Garrison and between 1916 and 1918 deputy assistant quarter master general, Scottish Command. In 1910, he married Lucile Newell née Schiff, daughter of Charles Schiff of Alston Hall, Devon, where he died suddenly in 1940 aged 62.

STEPHENS, Arthur Ralph, Staff Captain (b.1878), Royal Army Service Corps. Formerly Corporal. Arthur was the son of the Reverend James Stephens of Cambridge. His brother Alfred Metcalfe Stephens was also a Corpus alumnus (m.1892); he later became an Anglican priest. There is confusion over Arthur's place of birth. However, the 1911 census shows he was born in Cornwall, which fits in with his parents' and family location. Educated at the Perse School, Cambridge, he matriculated into Corpus as a pensioner in 1897 and graduated with a BA in 1902 (MA 1905). He was called to the Bar in 1907. On the outbreak of war, he enlisted in the RASC, before gaining a commission eventually becoming a Staff Captain. During his war service, he was wounded and post-war moved to Zanzibar where he was a partner in the law firm Wiggins and Stephens.

1898

CHURCHILL, Gordon Seton, Captain (1879–1942), 7th (Service) Battalion East Surrey Regiment. Gordon was born at Taungngu, Bago, Burmah (now Myanmar) in 1879, the son of Lieutenant Colonel Seton Churchill a military officer in the army pay department and his wife Elinor. The family lived in Staffordshire and Gordon was educated at Charterhouse. He matriculated into Corpus as a pensioner in 1898, graduating in 1901 with a BA. He was admitted to the Inner Temple in 1899, but had his name withdrawn in 1907. In the 1911 census, Gordon was living in Weston-Super-Mare, Somerset and self-described as single and 'a temporary assistant school master, usually of private means'. Apart from war service, he had a lengthy career as a Lloyds underwriter, lived in Wimbledon, and died in Surrey in 1942 aged 63.

GALER, Reginald Vincent, Reverend Captain (1879–1947), 24th Battalion London Regiment (The Queen's). Reginald was born in Kensington, London in 1879, the son of John Maxcey Galer a civil servant and his wife Louise Jane. He was educated at Dulwich College and the Merchant Taylors' School. He matriculated into Corpus as a pensioner in 1898, though he did not take his degree until 1914 (see 1914 graduation photograph below). He was ordained deacon in 1904 and priest the following year. His elder brother was Frederic Bertram Galer (m.1892), see above. Between 1904 and 1908, he was an assistant missioner at the Christchurch Cambridge Mission, Camberwell, and from 1908 to 1913, curate of St Andrew's Church, Battersea. Between 1913 and 1925, he was chaplain at King's College Hospital, Denmark Hill, London. He saw war service between 1915 and 1918. Between 1925 and 1947, he held the post of diocesan inspector of schools in Blackheath, Kent, and during these same years, he was vicar at St Germain's Church also in Blackheath. He died in Westminster in 1947 aged 70. TNA have a medal card WO 372/7/187965.

*****HAMILTON, James, 2nd Lieutenant** (1879–1916), 4th Battalion Border Regiment (Territorial Force). He was killed in action on 5 November 1916.

*****HEWITT, Reverend Frederick Whitmore** (1880–1915), CF 4th Class, Royal Army Chaplains Department. He was killed in action on 28 September 1915.

*****MARTIN, Edward Nugent Meredyth, 2nd Lieutenant** (1881–1916), 5th Battalion Royal Irish Lancers. He was killed in action on 30 September 1916.

PALMER, Reverend Reginald, MC DSO (1879–1945), CF 4th Class, Royal Army Chaplains Department. Reginald was born in Islington, London in 1879, the son of John Palmer, a merchant and exporter. He was educated at Fettes College, Edinburgh, Blundell's School, Devon, and at the University College of Wales. He was subsequently admitted to Corpus, matriculating as a pensioner in 1898. However, in 1900, like his contemporary Edward Nugent Meredyth Martin, he left the College without taking a degree to serve in the South African War as a Lieutenant with the Royal Irish Regiment. In 1903, at Bloemfontein, he was ordained deacon and the following year priest. Thereafter, before war service, he held several appointments in South Africa and Britain. The census of 1911 has him as a single man and vicar in Lee, Buckinghamshire. During the war, he was twice Mentioned in Despatches, and in 1918, became an Assistant Chaplain-General. The citation for his MC reads: 'Although wounded he rescued several wounded men with the greatest courage. He has on many occasions displayed the greatest bravery.' After the war, he held several ecclesiastical appointments including curate at St Martin-in-the-Fields, London, member of the mission of help to India, archdeacon of Egypt, and chaplain and sub-dean of All Saints' Pro-Cathedral, Cairo, Egypt. Reginald retired to live on Jersey, Channel Islands. In 1940, he was evacuated to England shortly before the Nazi occupation of the island. He returned in 1945 and died shortly afterwards aged 66.

1899

*COOPER, Henry Weatherly Frank, 2nd Lieutenant (1881–1917), 7th Battalion Royal Fusiliers. He died on 29 April 1917 of wounds received in action.

EDDOWES, Reverend Henry Cyril (known as Cyril) (1880–1967), CF 4th Class, Royal Army Chaplains Department, later attached to the RAF. Cyril was born at Sandymount, Dublin eight months after the death of his father Surgeon Major William Eddowes. He was the son of Grace Eddowes, a government pensioner of Westwick Gardens, West Kensington Park, London. His elder brother was Lieutenant Colonel William Black Eddowes (m.1896, Emmanuel) a professional soldier with the Manchester Regiment. Educated at St Paul's School, Cyril matriculated into Corpus in 1899 with a St Paul's Exhibition. He graduated with a BA in 1902 (MA 1906), was ordained deacon in 1905 and priest the following year. Between 1909 and 1913, he held two curacies before undertaking missionary work in India. He married in 1910, but during his time in India the marriage ended and in 1917 there was a nasty and very public divorce hearing. TNA have a 1917 divorce file J 77/1276/8903 and there is a 24 October 1917 *Nottingham Evening Post* report of the hearing, which granted Cyril a decree nisi with costs and the custody of the only child. In 1923, he ceased to be a clergyman. Cyril died in Dorset in 1967 aged 86. TNA have various files: an officer RACD file WO 339/51930 and a medal card WO 372/6/154649.

ELWIN, Walter Douglas, Captain (1879–1922), Kent Fortress Royal Engineers (Territorial Force). Walter was born in Dover, the son of Edward, a solicitor, and Harriet Frederica Elizabeth Elwin. Educated at Charterhouse, he matriculated into Corpus as a pensioner in 1899 and graduated with a BA in 1906. He married Eva Cissy Elwin the same year and later qualified as a solicitor. During the war, he was an instructor in explosives. On Christmas Eve 1920, after completing his military service, he became a teacher and sailed to join the Educational Service, Dominica, West Indies, where he died in 1922 aged 43. TNA have an officer file WO 374/22708.

GARDNER, Joseph, Lieutenant (b.1880), Royal Garrison Artillery (Special Reserve). Joseph was born in Berkshire the son of Joseph Gardner, a farmer of Maidenhead. Educated at Malvern College, he matriculated into Corpus as a scholar in 1899. He took First Class Honours and graduated with a BA in 1904. TNA have an officer file WO 339/68159 and a medal card WO 372/7/204712.

*LEEKE, Henry Alan, Lieutenant (1880–1915), D Company 9th Battalion Royal Warwickshire Regiment. An Olympian, he died of meningitis on 29 May 1915.

MARSHALL, Alfred Turner Lieutenant (b.1880), Suffolk Regiment (Territorial Force). The son of a clergyman, Alfred was born in Northampton and lived in Redditch. Educated at Thetford Grammar School and the King's School, Worcester, he matriculated into Corpus as a pensioner in 1899. He graduated with a BA in 1902 (MA 1907), went on to qualify as a solicitor and practised at Herne Bay, Kent. He married Matilda Rachel née Cooke in 1906. TNA have an officer file WO 374/46209.

OLDFIELD, Reverend Henry Douglas, MC (1880–1950), CF 3rd Class, Royal Army Chaplains Department. Henry was born in Allahabad, India the son of a British army general and educated at Old College, Windermere. He was admitted to Corpus as a pensioner in 1899 but does not appear to have graduated. The 1911 census shows he was a single man studying for the priesthood in the Isle of Man. He was ordained deacon in 1912 and priest the following year. He served as an Army Chaplain, being awarded an MC and Mentioned in Despatches three times. He remained a Chaplain until 1935 and was then rector of St Andrew's Church, South Warnborough, Hampshire until his death in 1950 aged 70. TNA have a medal card WO 372/15/49589.

RYOTT, Thomas Gurney, Private 30499 (1881–1965), 2/6th Battalion Machine Gun Corps. Formerly Suffolk Regiment. Thomas was born in Newbury, Berkshire, the son of Robert Charles Ryott, a chemist. Educated at Newbury Grammar School and Berkamstead School, he matriculated into Corpus in 1899 as a pensioner and holder of a Newbury Grammar School scholarship. Thomas read the Law Tripos, gaining a BA and LLB in 1902. He was admitted as a solicitor in 1905 and practised in Winchester. In 1915, he married Evelyn née Adolphus. TNA have microfilmed files WO363–4/0073678000/00701.

SKINNER, Edward Fretson, Captain (1880–1944), 3rd Battalion West Riding Field Ambulance, Royal Army Medical Corps (Territorial Force). Edward was born in 1880, the son of Edward Skinner a surgeon of Sheffield. Educated at Wesley College, Sheffield, he matriculated into Corpus in 1899 as a pensioner and graduated with a BA in 1902 (MA 1906). He became a LRCP in 1906, took an MB and BChir in 1908, MRCP in 1909, FRCP in 1922, and MD in 1935. He married in 1907 and had a son. In the 1911 census, Edward self-described as a consultant physician. He practised as an ophthalmic house surgeon at Sheffield Royal Hospital and was a lecturer in medical psychology at Sheffield University.

STEPHENS, Ernest Aitken, Corporal (b.1881), Middlesex Regiment and Machine Gun Corps. Ernest was born in Flushing, Cornwall in 1881. *The War List* says he matriculated in 1901, Bury says 1899 (both are correct). The University database says he was a non-collegiate matriculation in 1899 who migrated to Corpus in 1901. He graduated with a BA in 1903 (MA 1907), was ordained a deacon in 1903 and priest in 1905. He was a curate between 1903 and 1908, but is not mentioned in the annual ecclesiastical directory *Crockfords* after 1909. The 1911 census has him living in Hendon and is self-described as a 'student for the Roman Catholic priesthood'. During his military service he was wounded.

THOMPSON, Joshua Clibborn, Captain (b.1874), 4th Battalion The Queen's Own Cameron Highlanders. Joshua was born in 1874 at White Abbey, White, Co. Antrim, Ireland (now Northern Ireland) and educated at St Olive's Mount School, Scarborough, Yorkshire. He matriculated into Corpus as a pensioner in 1899, graduating with a BA in 1902. Ordained deacon in 1904, he was a curate at Stockwell Green, Surrey until 1905. He was later ordained priest.

1900

*BULLOCK, Gervase Frederic, 2nd Lieutenant (1881–1917), 11th Battalion South Wales Borderers. He was killed in action on 31 July 1917.

CHAPPELL, Frederick (known as Fred) Edmondson, Major and Adjutant (b.1881), 3rd Base Royal Army Service Corps. Fred was born in 1881, the son of Charles Arthur Chappell, a salesman of Paddington, London. Educated first at Kensington Grammar School and then St Paul's, he matriculated into Corpus as a pensioner in 1900 and graduated with a BA in 1903 (MA 1913). He subsequently entered the teaching profession. In 1910, Fred became founder and headmaster of Beachborough School, near Folkestone, Kent (now located in Northampton). He married and, apart from war service, spent his entire career at the school. He retired in 1957. During his war service he was Mentioned in Despatches. TNA have a medal card WO 372/4/86522.

QUENTIN, George Augustus Frederick, Lieutenant, DSO (1881–1942), King's Royal Rifle Corps. Born in Norfolk, George was the son of a clergyman and educated at The King's School, Canterbury. He matriculated into Corpus in 1900 with both a Parker Exhibition and an Open Mathematical Exhibition. He graduated with a BA in 1903. Thereafter, between 1906 and 1927 (apart from war service), he was employed in the Education Department of the Egyptian government service and, between 1925 and 1927, held the post of inspector of schools. In 1911, he married Edith Florence née Beazley. He saw war service as an assistant officer in charge of records and in 1917 was Mentioned in Despatches. TNA have an officer file WO 339/35261.

WILBERFORCE, Harold Hartley, Lieutenant Colonel, DSO (1881–1943), Royal Army Service Corps (Territorial Force). Harold was born in York, the son of William Wilkinson Wilberforce, a merchant. Educated at Aysgarth

School, Yorkshire and Malvern College, he matriculated into Corpus as a pensioner in 1900 and became a scholar the following year. He graduated with a BA in 1903, LLB 1904 (MA 1909). In 1907, he was admitted as a solicitor and went into practice in York (Messrs Ware and Wilberforce). During war service, he was awarded the DSO and Mentioned in Despatches. In 1922, he married Tessa née Trendor of Bournemouth. Harold died at Fulford, near York, in 1943 aged 62. TNA have a medal card WO 372/21/15564.

WILLIAMSON, Reverend Francis Lorrimer (1882–1946), CF 4th Class, Royal Army Chaplains Department, Woolwich. He was born at Jubbulpore, India, the son of the Reverend Henry Drummond Williamson (m.1873) of Cheltenham. Francis was educated at Rossall School, Lancashire and matriculated into Corpus with a sizarship in 1900. He rowed bow in the 1900 Lent boat and stroked the 1901 and 1902 Lent and May boats. Also in 1902, he was Second Boat Captain and trialled for the Blue Boat. In addition, Francis played tennis, football (club Secretary in 1902), and cricket for the College. He was a member of the Chess Club, Gravediggers, and Musical Society. Francis graduated with a BA in 1903 (MA 1909), was ordained deacon in 1905 and priest the following year. Between 1905 and 191, he served curacies, and between 1912 and 1938, was rector at St Mary the Virgin Church, Great Warley, Essex. Between 1938 and 1943, he was rector of St Mark's Church, Torwood, Torquay, and between 1943 and 1946, he worked for the Diocese of Exeter. In 1909, he married Eleanor Mabel née James. Francis died at Brixham, Devon in 1946 aged 64.

The militarisation of Corpus began during the South African War 1899 to 1902. This May 1901 photograph shows members of College who were part of the Cambridge University Rifle Volunteers, a precursor to the CUOTC.

1901

CAREY, Richard Stocker, Surgeon Lieutenant (1884–1957). Royal Navy. Richard was born in London; the 1911 census has him self-described as physician and surgeon. At the time, he was living at home in Suffolk with his retired surgeon father of the same name and his mother Lavina. He served on HMS *Southampton* at the Battle of Jutland, was Mentioned in Despatches and awarded an OBE in 1919: 'for skilful and untiring attention to the wounded'. He married Edith née Beauchamp in 1917 and after war service was a Bristol-based physician in general practice. He died in Bristol on 15 December 1957 aged 73.

COULCHER, Goodricke Bohun, Lieutenant (1883–1957), Royal Army Service Corps. Formerly Private 251627, Durham Light Infantry. Goodricke was the son of the Reverend George Bohun Coulcher (m.1861) and his wife Aimee Catherine Burton; his clergyman grandfather had been incumbent of the College living, St Bene't's Church, Cambridge. Educated at Marlborough College, he matriculated into Corpus in 1901 to read the Classical Tripos and was awarded the Bishop Green Cup in 1903. After graduation, he became a schoolmaster in Guildford, Surrey. At the time of the 1911 census, he was single, but later married Agnes Aimee. During his war service, he was Mentioned in Despatches. He died in Ipswich in 1957 aged 74. TNA have an officer file WO 374/15750 and a medal card WO 372/5/40998.

DURNFORD, Reverend Francis Henry, MC (1882–1969), CF 2nd Class, Australian Chaplains Department. He served first with 22nd Battalion 2nd Australian Division and later with 6th Infantry Brigade, Australian Imperial Force. Francis was the son of a clergyman and educated at The King's School, Canterbury. He matriculated into Corpus in 1901 as a sizar with a Parker Exhibition to read the Classical Tripos. He graduated with a BA in 1904 (MA 1908), was ordained deacon in 1906 and priest the following year. Francis then went to Australia where, until the outbreak of war, he held several posts. Between 1915 and 1919, he served as a Chaplain with the Australian Imperial Force, leaving Australia for France in 1916. In May 1917, he was awarded an MC:

> for conspicuous bravery and most honourable devotion to duty during the action near Bullecourt on 3rd May 1917. He continued his ministrations among the wounded throughout the 48 hours that the Brigade was engaged under very heavy Machine Gun and Artillery fire. By his fearless conduct and his cheerful bearing he helped maintain the spirit of the Troops in a most valuable manner.

In October 1917, he was wounded in the hand and in April 1918 posted to Australian HQ, London. Between 1922 and 1929, he was a chaplain in Sudan and, also in 1929, married Lucy Victoria née Carless. The couple returned to Britain where he was, between 1930 and 1959, vicar of Longhoughton, Northumberland.

*HANNA, John Henry, 2nd Lieutenant (1884–1917), 19th St Pancras Battalion London Regiment. He was killed in action on 20 September 1917.

WILLIAMS, Graeme Douglas, Lieutenant (1885–1923), Essex Regiment. Formerly Private, London Regiment, Artists Rifles. Graeme was born at Keynsham, Somerset in 1885. The 1911 census has him married with a son, living with his widowed mother and brother in Twickenham, London. He self-describes as a freelance journalist and author. His publications include *Wonders of Land and Sea* (1913) and *The World We Live In* (4 vols.) (1915–1918). TNA have a medal card WO 372/21/189344.

CCCC Chess Club serial

Corpus Christi College, Chess Club Lent Term 1901.

1902

DARE, Albert George, 2nd Lieutenant (1883–1964), St Lawrence College, Ramsgate, OTC. Albert was born in Tamworth, Staffordshire, the son of John Taylor a gardener. He was educated at Lady Manners' School, Bakewell, Derbyshire, and after graduating from Corpus became a schoolmaster. In 1911, he was living in Newport, Shropshire and a teacher at Newport Grammar School.

FINDLAY, John Galloway, Lieutenant (1883–1956), 5th Battalion Bedfordshire Regiment. John was born in Glasgow in 1883, the son of Robert Downie Findlay, a stockbroker, and his wife Margaret Findlay. John was educated at Harrow and after graduation he became a stockbroker. TNA have a medal card WO 372/7/62318.

HODDER, Francis Edwin, Lance Corporal (1883–1932), Royal Munster Fusiliers. He was born in Willesden, London, the son of Edwin (who was described in the Admissions Register simply as 'Literary'). This refers to his prodigious output of mainly religious writings. Francis was educated at Dulwich College. At Corpus he was the Senior Classical Scholar. He rowed in the 1905 Lent boat and was a member of the Honest Cods. He graduated in 1905 (MA 1917) and became a schoolmaster.

*****SMITH, Reginald George, Captain** (1883–1917), 47th Battalion 10th Infantry Brigade, 4th Canadian Division. Formerly 77th Battalion Infantry Western Ontario Regiment, Canadian Expeditionary Force. He was killed in action on 5 May 1917.

1903

ALFORD, Reverend Charles Symes Leslie (1885–1963), CF 4th Class, Royal Army Chaplains Department. Charles Alford was born in Bristol the son of the Reverend Josiah George Alford ((m.1866) see above). He was educated at Marlborough College, where he was a member of the Volunteers. At Corpus, as the Easter Term 1904 *Benedict* noted, he had taken a commission in the Auxiliary Forces, becoming Captain and instructor of musketry in the University Volunteers. The following year, he was awarded a Blue for shooting. In 1908, he was ordained deacon and priest the following year. Between 1910 and 1927, after a curacy in Barnard Castle, he held appointments with the Royal Army Chaplains Department. He was then vicar of Marshfield, Gloucestershire until 1938, when he was appointed archdeacon of Bristol. In later years, he was rector of Staple Fitzpaine, Somerset and then Rowberrow, Somerset. He died in 1963 aged 78.

DONALDSON, Christopher Herbert, Rifleman (1884–1962), London Regiment (London Rifle Brigade). Christopher was born in Cookham, Berkshire, the youngest son of the precentor of Truro Cathedral, the Reverend Augustus Blair Donaldson and his wife Amelia née Breverton. Educated at St Paul's, he matriculated into Corpus in 1903 with a St Paul's School Stock Exhibition. He graduated in 1908, later studying modern languages in France and subsequently becoming a schoolmaster. In 1915, he was wounded and erroneously posted killed in action. He died in Surrey in 1962 aged 78.

FORSE, Reverend Leslie Napier (1882–1961), CF 4th Class, Royal Army Chaplains Department, attached to the Loyal North Lancashire Regiment, 55th Division. Leslie was born in Surrey, the son of Edward John Forse, a music teacher and organist, and his wife Maria Colley. On graduation, he was ordained priest. The 1911 census shows him a curate serving in Fleetwood, Lancashire. During his war service he was made a prisoner of war. He returned to Lancashire and was for thirty-seven years rector of Holy Trinity Church, Tarleton, . He died in 1961 aged 79. TNA have an officer file WO 161/96/133 and a medal card WO 372/7/116733.

GRABURN, Godfrey Noel, Lieutenant (1886–1974), London Brigade Royal Field Artillery (Territorial Force). Godfrey was born in Burpham, Sussex, the son of Nowell Graburn, a farmer. Educated at Malvern College, he matriculated into Corpus in 1903. As an undergraduate, he rowed, played association football and was described in *The Benedict* (Michaelmas Term 1903) as having: 'played several times at left back, is a fair worker, but very unsound both in tackling and passing'. After graduation, he trained as a solicitor. During his war service, he was wounded twice, the second time was described as 'severely'. He died in Sussex in 1974 aged 88.

KEMP, Kenneth Macintyre, Captain (1884–1949), 127th Battalion Baluchis Regiment, Indian Army Reserve of Officers. He was born in Bombay (now Mumbai), India, the son of David Skinner (whose occupation was recorded in the Admissions Register as 'Gentleman'), and educated at Dulwich College. He is missing from the 1911 census, though it is possible he had returned to India to join his family. He was knighted in 1938.

NORRIS, William Henry Hobbs, Lieutenant (1884–1950), Royal Engineers. William was born in Battersea, London in 1884, the son of William Norris an art master. He was educated at Battersea Polytechnic (now part of the University of Surrey). He came to Corpus in 1903 with a Mathematics Scholarship, which was renewed in 1904 contingent on his reading the Natural Sciences Tripos. The 1911 census shows him living in Northwich, Cheshire, working as a research chemist at the Winnington Works of alkali manufacturer Brunner Mond Ltd (later part of ICI). During his war service, he was wounded and later employed by the Ministry of Munitions. TNA have an officer file WO 339/74263 and a medal card WO 372/15/7787.

1904

CRAFT, Herbert Baynes, Sergeant (1885–1964), Royal Army Medical Corps (Territorial Force). Herbert was born in Newlyn, Cornwall, the son of artist Percy Robert Craft (1856–1934) and his wife Anne Elizabeth. Herbert was educated at Wellington College and Trent College, Long Eaton, Nottinghamshire. He returned to Cornwall after graduation and, according to the 1911 census, was a single man and a teacher at Monkton Coombe School. He died in Surrey in 1964 aged 78.

CROWTHER, Wilfred Cooksey, Lieutenant (1885–1962), London Regiment (St Pancras Battalion). Wilfred was born in West Bromwich, Staffordshire, the son of Alice and George Crowther a glass manufacturers' agent (described in the Admissions Register as a 'Managing Clerk'). He was educated at King Edward VI Grammar School, Birmingham. At Corpus, he was awarded a Mawson Scholarship. He died in Cornwall in 1962 aged 77.

*DYER, Harry Frank, 2nd Lieutenant (1886–1917), 1/6th Battalion Duke of Wellington's (West Riding) Regiment. He died on 28 August 1917 of wounds received in action on 8 August 1917.

GILLIBRAND, Arthur, Lieutenant (1885–1948), 9th Battalion Duke of Wellington's (West Riding) Regiment. Formerly Private, 21st (Public Schools) Battalion Royal Fusiliers. Arthur was born in Dundee, Scotland, the son of a clergyman. Educated at The King's School, Canterbury, he matriculated into Corpus in 1904 with a Parker Exhibition. As an undergraduate he rowed, was a member of the Chess Club and graduated with a BA in 1907 (MA 1925). He became an assistant master at Lindley Lodge, Nuneaton in 1909, then assistant master and housemaster at Bromsgrove School, Worcestershire. He married Clare Arundell née Leakey in 1916. During his war service, he was wounded twice (and once posted missing). TNA have an officer file WO 339/35478 and a medal card WO 372/8/21507.

LATTEY, William Tabor, Lieutenant (1886–1965), Royal Field Artillery. He was born in Streatham, London, the son of Henry Lattey, a solicitor. He was educated at Dulwich College. In the 1911 census, he self-described as a leather manufacturer. He died in Sussex in 1965 aged 79. TNA have an officer file WO 339/62642.

*OKE, Robert William Leslie, Captain (1884–1915), 3rd Battalion (attached to the 6th) (Princess Charlotte of Wales's) Royal Berkshire Regiment. He was killed in action on 25 September 1915.

THOMAS, Tudor Gordon, Captain (1884–1960), Special List (Bombing Officer). Formerly Lieutenant, 16th Battalion The King's Regiment (Liverpool). Tudor was born in St Helens, Lancashire (now Merseyside), the son of the Reverend David A Thomas and his wife Margaret. Tudor was educated at St John's College, Leatherhead and Liverpool College. He was admitted to Corpus in April 1904 having kept three terms as a non-collegiate student. In the 1911 census, Tudor self-described as a mathematical tutor at a preparatory school for boys in Bournemouth, Hampshire. In 1914, he married Tessie née Gunston in Cambridge. He died in Hampshire in 1960 aged 76. TNA have an officer file WO 339/34978 and a medal card WO 372/19/213710.

*WILSON, Ronald Edward, 2nd Lieutenant (1885–1916), Bombay Volunteer Rifles attached to the Volunteer Maxim Machine Gun Company. He was killed in action in East Africa on 13 March 1916.

1905

CHADWICK, Reverend Charles Egerton, MC (1881–1958), CF 2nd Class, Royal Army Chaplains Department. Charles was born in Bromley, Kent, the son of Edward Chadwick a paper manufacturer. He was educated at St Mark's College, Chelsea (now part of Plymouth Marjon University). He was a Senior Chaplain (Deputy Assistant Chaplain-General). He later served in the RAF. During his service, he was wounded, Mentioned in Despatches and Mentioned in the Secretary of State's List. He was married in 1917 to Dorothy Elwin née Harris and died in Surrey in 1958 aged 77. TNA have a medal card WO 372/4/62533.

JONES, Rhys (Bury has Rees) Richard Percy, Instructor Lieutenant (b.1886), Royal Navy. Rhys was born in Bridgend, Ammanford, Carmarthenshire, Wales, the son of a clerk and was educated at Llandovery College, Llandovery, Carmarthenshire, Wales. At Corpus he was a Manners Scholar and awarded a Bishop Green Cup for his success in the Mathematical Tripos. In the 1911 census, he was living at Bury St Edmunds and an assistant master at a public school.

*KNIGHT, Ernest Alexander, 2nd Lieutenant (1886–1917), 233rd Company Machine Gun Corps (Infantry). He was killed in action on 24 September 1917.

LEAKEY, Raymond Arundell, Captain (1887–1976), Bengal-Napur Railway Traffic Officer, Indian Army. He was born at Sudbury, Suffolk, the son of

Reverend Arundell Leakey and his wife Florence née Gray. He was educated at Haileybury. He died in Essex aged 89.

MERRIMAN, Reverend Ernest Steward (1886–1970), CF 4th Class, Royal Army Chaplains Department. Ernest was born at Martham, Norfolk, the son of a clergyman, and educated at Haileybury. He died in Wiltshire in 1970 aged 84. TNA have an officer file WO 374/47421 and a medal card WO 372/12/215032.

ROWAN, Arthur, Lieutenant (b.c.1887), Special List (Staff Lieutenant, Intelligence Corps). GHQ Home Forces. Arthur was born Leipzig, Germany, the son of William Robert a civil engineer and his wife Gerdina A (The Admissions book has both the place of birth and the name of his mother were written in pencil with '??'). He was educated Bedford Grammar School. He left the College without completing his degree.

SHARP, Reverend Gordon Frank (1887–1957), CF 4th Class, Royal Army Chaplains Department. Gordon was born in Addlestone, Surrey in 1887 and educated at St John's College, Leatherhead. He matriculated into Corpus as a Spencer Scholar. After graduation, he was ordained priest and in May 1913 married Vera Eleanor née Heath. Their first child Peter was born in 1914. TNA have an officer file WO 339/113728.

1906

BELL, Robert Harman, Captain, MC and Bar (b.1888), Oxford and Bucks Light Infantry. Robert was educated at Bradfield College, Berkshire. When war broke out, he was a professional soldier, serving in India with the 2nd Battalion Leicestershire Regiment. He was wounded during his military service. The citation for the Bar to his MC (18 October 1917) reads: 'Throughout 12 days' fighting this officer rendered invaluable services, both in carrying messages and in rallying men who were falling back. Time after time he went forward at critical moments, and rallied men, re-establishing the line, always under shell or machine-gun fire.' TNA have an officer file WO 339/7681.

CAMPBELL-SMITH, Walter, Lieutenant Colonel, MC (1887–1988), previously Lance Corporal, London Regiment (Artists Rifles), attached to the 189th Company Royal Engineers (Special Brigade). Walter was born in Solihull, the son of George Hamilton Smith, a paper merchant and educated at Solihull School, Walwickshire (now West Midlands). On graduation in 1909, he won the Wiltshire Prize for mineralogy. During war service in France, he was awarded the MC and twice Mentioned in Despatches. Walter continued to serve with the Artists Rifles (TF) until 1935. In 1939, he re-joined the unit as Brevet Lieutenant Colonel.

Between 1921 and 1924, Walter was a College Fellow and later in his career became Keeper of Minerals at the British Museum. Also, in later life he was awarded a CBE and the Murchison Medal. He died in 1988 aged 101. See also Bury, p. 256, and obituary in *The Letter of the Corpus Association*, No. 68 (Michaelmas 1989), pp. 49–50. TNA have a medal card WO 372/18/181715 together with references to the British Museum Archives.

ILLINGWORTH, Oswald, Captain (b.1887), 11th Battalion West Yorkshire Regiment (Prince of Wales's Own). The son of a tea merchant, Oswald was educated at Rossall School and came to Corpus with an Entrance Scholarship worth £40 to read the Mathematical Tripos. He subsequently gained a Manners and then a Cowell Scholarship. In December 1915, during war service, he was wounded. However, he recovered and on 15 May 1917 was posted missing in action (he was initially reported killed) but later discovered to be a prisoner of war. TNA have an officer file WO 339/20285 and a medal card WO 372/10/146558.

***JAMES, Eric Samuel Pennant Kingsbury, Captain** (1887–1915), 6th (Reserve) Battalion (attached to the 4th Battalion) King's Royal Rifle Corps. He was killed in action on 17 March 1915.

LYLE, Robert Charles, Captain and Adjutant, MC (1887–1943), Royal Army Service Corps. Robert was born in Great Dunmow, Essex, where his late father had been in general practice. He was educated at Felsted School and came to Corpus with an Entrance Scholarship worth £40 to read the Mathematical Tripos. The 1911 census shows him living in Bishop's Stortford and self-described as a journalist. Robert married Daisy née Brunskill at Bishop's Stortford in 1913. During his war service, he was Mentioned in Despatches. Later in life, he became sporting editor of *The Times*. Robert died in Surrey in 1943 aged 56. TNA have an officer file WO 339/46195 and a medal card WO 372/12/168221.

***MAINWARING, Cyril Lyttleton, Lieutenant** (1887–1919), Royal Garrison Artillery, 422nd Siege Battery. He is not recorded in *The War List* as dead, but his name appears in the Commonwealth War Graves Commission database. Cyril died in early 1919 during the influenza pandemic. His name appears on the College war memorial, but out of alphabetical order.

MOUNSEY, Jasper Percy, Lieutenant (1887–1952), Lancashire Fusiliers and King's African Rifles. He was born in Madras (now Chennai), India, the son of an Indian civil servant. Prior to coming up to Corpus, Jasper was educated at Charterhouse. The 1911 census has him a single man, living at Hove, Sussex and self-described as a teacher. In later life, Jasper lived in Canterbury, where he died in 1952 aged 65. TNA have a medal card WO 372/14/192916.

ONYON, Richard Rigby, Captain (1888–1948), 6th Battalion East Surrey Regiment (Territorial Force). He was born in Hartismere, Suffolk, the son of a surgeons' dispenser. He was educated at Christ's Hospital and admitted to the College with an Entrance Scholarship. In the 1911 census, he was living at Richmond, Surrey and self-described as an assistant secondary schoolmaster. In 1920, Richard married Rosalie Maud née Hammond in Fulham. TNA have an officer file WO 339/51414 and a medal card WO 372/15/57743.

POOK, John de Coursey, Lieutenant (1887–1974), Indian Army Reserve of Officers, attached to the Supply and Transport Corps. John was born in Kidbrooke, Kent in 1887, son of a commission agent in the China and Japanese trade. He was educated at St Anne's School, Redhill (closed 1919) and admitted to Corpus as a sizar. In the 1911 census, he was living at Barnard Castle and self-described as a schoolmaster. He married Ruth née Hudson at Lewisham, London in 1929 and died at Sedgemoor, Somerset in 1974 aged 87.

RODGERS, Reverend Harold Nickinson (Bury has Nickenson) (1882–1947), CF 4th Class, Royal Army Chaplains Department. He was born at Brixton Hill, London in 1882, the son of John Rodgers, a solicitor, and his wife Elizabeth. Prior to his coming to Corpus, Harold was privately educated. In the 1911 census, he was living in Southsea and an Anglican clergyman. He later became archdeacon of the Isle of Wight and died at Winchester in 1947 aged 65.

WATKINS, Lawrence Theodore (1887–1946), Indian Army Reserve of Officers, attached to the 52nd Sikhs, Frontier Force. Lawrence was born at Bareilly, Uttar Pradesh, India, the son of Archdeacon Oscar Dan and Elizabeth Martha Watkins. Educated at The King's School, Canterbury, he matriculated into Corpus in 1906 with a Parker Exhibition. During his time at the College, he was awarded the Brotherton Prize and graduated with a BA in 1909. Thereafter, he was an assistant master at Bradford Grammar School then, between 1909 and 1913, at King William's College, Isle of Man (where Arthur Milton Lewis (m.1913) was a student – they later served together with the 52nd Sikhs), and between 1913 and 1924 (except for the war years) with the Indian Educational Service. In 1916, he married Gwendolen Noël née Brooks. Between 1925 and 1944, he taught at Radley College. His name is not included in *The War List*.

1907

CASSIDI, Francis Laird, Surgeon Lieutenant (1889–1963), Volunteer Reserve Detachment Royal Navy. Francis came from an Anglo-Irish family of physicians of Glenbrook, Magherafelt, Co. Londonderry, Ireland (now Northern Ireland). He was born in Derby and educated at Rugby School prior to coming to Corpus.

In later life, he was Surgeon Captain Royal Naval Volunteer Reserve and Honorary Surgeon to King George VI. In 1924, he married Phyllis Mary née Haviland and had three children.

DUNLOP, William Craufurd Carstares, Lieutenant (1887–1974) (later known as William Craufurd Carstares-Dunlop), Royal Scots Guards. He was born in Bromley, Kent, the son of a Bank of England employee and Scottish landed proprietor. Prior to coming to Corpus, William was educated at Cheltenham College.

HALL, Harold Octavius, Staff Captain (1887–1975). Formerly Lieutenant, Royal Field Artillery. Born in Knodishall, Suffolk, the son of a farmer, after graduating from Corpus, he was a schoolmaster. Harold was Mentioned in Despatches twice and later awarded both the OBE and Croix de Guerre. He was subsequently ordained a priest. TNA have an officer file WO 339/53553.

HUNTER, Cyril James, Lieutenant MC (1888–1965), 9th Battalion North Staffordshire Regiment (The Prince of Wales's). Cyril was born in Burton-on-Trent, Staffordshire in 1888, and prior to coming to Corpus, was educated at Burton Grammar School (now part of Abbot Beyne Comprehensive School). He was admitted to Corpus with an Entrance Scholarship to read the Mathematical Tripos. During his war service, he was wounded. He died in Victoria, British Columbia, Canada in 1965 aged 76. TNA have an officer file WO 339/30538.

KELHAM, Marmaduke Henry Cogan, Lieutenant (1888–1933), 10th Battalion Durham Light Infantry, attached to the Royal Defence Corps. Marmaduke was born in France to British parents, and prior to coming to Corpus was educated at Monkton Combe School, near Bath, Somerset. During his time at Corpus, although just 5 feet 1 inch, he was a member of the OTC. In November 1915, he was severely wounded at Ypres and suffered shell shock to the extent he spent the next two years unfit for military service. In February 1918, he finally resigned his commission. After the war, he joined the consular service and by 1927 was British Vice-Consul and Chargé d'affaires in Havana, Cuba. He subsequently held similar roles in Brazil and Honduras, where he died on 11 April 1933 aged 44. TNA have an officer file WO 339/11806.

KEMPE, Reverend Wilfred Noel (1887–1958), CF 4th Class, Royal Army Chaplains Department. Wilfred was born at Long Ashton, Somerset, the son of a school proprietor and educated at The King's School, Canterbury. He was admitted to Corpus with a Parker Exhibition. The 1911 census shows him as a theological student at Cuddeston, Oxford. After war service, he was, between 1924 and 1933, vicar of St Michael the Archangel, Flax Bourton, Somerset. He died in Gloucestershire in 1958 aged 71.

*LAING, Alexander Torrance, Reverend Captain (1889–1916), 13th Battalion Northumberland Fusiliers. He died on 24 July 1916 of wounds received in action.

*MARRIOTT, John Francis Laycock, 2nd Lieutenant (1889–1915), 7th Battalion Duke of Cornwall's Light Infantry. He died 26 January 1915 of spotted fever.

MARTINDALE, Robert Gunson, 2nd Lieutenant (1887–1952), Royal Garrison Artillery. Formerly Lance Corporal, Royal Engineers (Fortress, Territorial Force). Robert was born in Scalthwaiterigg, near Kendal, Westmorland (now part of Cumbria), the son of a bank cashier, and educated at Kendal Grammar School. During his time at Corpus, he was organ scholar. The 1911 census shows him a music master at Uppingham School, Rutland and the following year, in Cambridge, he married Dora née Sheldrick. He died in Sussex in 1952 aged 65. TNA have an officer file WO 339/80056.

NEVINSON, Guy Roger Grisewood, Sergeant (1886–1961), 28th Battalion Royal Fusiliers. He was born in Chelsea, London, the son of a barrister, and educated at Malvern College. The 1911 census show he was still living in Chelsea self-describing as being of 'private means'. He died in Worcestershire in 1961 aged 75.

1908

CHURCHWARD, Reverend Basil (1891–1971), CF 4th Class, Royal Army Chaplains Department. Basil was born in Aldershot, the son of an Anglican clergyman and Chaplain to the Forces. He was the brother of Hubert Alan Churchward ((m.1911) see biography) and admitted to Corpus as a sizar. In 1941, he married Sophie née Mandragi at Wokingham. He died in Kent in 1971 aged 80. TNA have a medal card WO 372/4/119452.

*CUNNINGTON, Edward Charles, Captain (1890–1918), 95th Field Ambulance, Royal Army Medical Corps. A physician, he was killed by a shell on 23 March 1918 whilst treating the wounded at a dressing station.

DAVIES, Reverend Percy Marr (1873–1947), CF 4th Class, Royal Army Chaplains Department. Percy was born in Newton Heath, Lancashire (now Greater Manchester) in 1873. He came to Corpus as a mature student aged 35 and was described in the 1911 census as a theological student. He died in Bolton in 1947 aged 74. TNA have an officer file WO 339/18404 and a medal card WO 372/5/194366.

HALL, Arthur Leonard, Lieutenant (1896–1983), Lancashire Fusiliers. Formerly Private Kent Cyclist Battalion. Arthur came to Corpus from the Royal Grammar School, Colchester and held the James Hewitt Exhibition. During his time at the College, he was organ scholar. In 1918, during war service, he was Mentioned in Despatches. Arthur was later ordained a priest and died in Wellingborough in 1983 aged 87. TNA have an officer file WO 339/30122.

HAVERS, Cecil Robert, Captain and Adjutant (1889–1977), Tank Corps and formerly Lieutenant, 5th Battalion Hampshire Regiment. Cecil was the son of a solicitor and educated at Norwich Grammar School. He matriculated into Corpus in 1910 with an Entrance Scholarship to read the Classical Tripos. During his time at the College, he was awarded the Latin Declamation Cup and in 1912 graduated with First Class Honours in the Classical Tripos. The following year he became an LLB. As an undergraduate, he was a Lawn Tennis Blue and subsequently played in the 1926 men's doubles at Wimbledon. During his war service, he was both wounded and Mentioned in Despatches. Cecil Havers later became a distinguished jurist, knighted, and a judge of the High Court. His daughter is Corpus Honorary Fellow Baroness Elizabeth Butler-Schloss and his son was Michael, Baron Havers (1923–92) (m.1946), who was briefly Lord Chancellor in 1987.

JEEVES, Reverend Leonard Lambert Garnet (1882–1956), CF 4th Class, Royal Army Chaplains Department. Leonard was born in Taunton, Somerset in 1882, the son of Emilia and Anthony Jeeves, a commission agent. He was educated at Devon County and Hele's School, Exeter (now part of St Peter's Church of England Aided Comprehensive School) and came to Corpus after taking three terms as a non-collegiate student. After graduating from Corpus, he was ordained priest and in 1911 served at St Mary's Church, Stepney. In 1919, after war service, he married Beatrice née Wilson; the couple had a daughter Coralie. Thereafter, family spent time in St John's, Newfoundland, Canada. He died in Worcestershire in 1956 aged 73. TNA have an officer file WO 339/75535.

JORDAN, George Paul, Lieutenant (1888–1966), Labour Corps. Formerly 2nd Lieutenant, Essex Regiment (Territorial Force). George was born in Victoria, Hong Kong in 1888. Prior to coming to Corpus, he was educated at Dulwich College. In 1911, he was a Corpus undergraduate and living with his widowed mother, a brother, and five sisters in Hampton, Surrey. He died in London in 1966 aged 78. TNA have an officer file WO 339/104738 and a medal card WO 372/11/73043.

*LEEMING, Alfred Johnson, Captain (1889–1917), 6th Battalion Royal Fusiliers. Alfred was Mentioned in Despatches and killed in action on 31 July 1917.

MORTON, Harold Swithun, Major, OBE (1889–1919). Formerly Staff Captain. During the war, Harold was deputy assistant director of quartering at the War Office. He came to Corpus in 1908 to read the Natural Sciences Tripos, was a scholar and a chapel clerk. He was also Captain of Boats in 1910. King's College, Cambridge *Annual Report, 1919* has the following obituary:

> Harold Swithun Morton, MA, OBE, died on February 28 [1919], in his 30th year. He was at Oundle School, and then a Scholar at Corpus Christi College. In his second year, 1910, he was in the 1st Class in Part I of the Natural Sciences Tripos, and in 1911 he obtained the diploma in Agriculture. He then entered a land agents office in order to obtain training in the business. In 1913 the College [King's] established a new office, that of Assistant Bursar, and to this, on November 25, Mr Morton was appointed, the expectation being that he might become a Bursar when Mr Grant retired. He entered upon his duties with vigour and ability, and in March 1915 was elected to a Fellowship. He was unfit for combatant military service on account of defective eyesight; but in May 1915 he obtained a commission in the Army Service Corps and left Cambridge. From October 1916 until January 1919, he was at the War Office in the department of the Director of Quartering, where he became Deputy Assistant Director of Quartering, with the rank of Major, and was chiefly responsible for the 'Quartering Regulations' which were issued in 1917. From about December 1917, he had practically entire charge of the work of hiring premises for the accommodation of troops, and of questions of compensation throughout the United Kingdom. He returned to Cambridge in the Lent Term 1919, eager to devote himself to College work, but a few weeks later a virulent attack of influenza caused his death. He was greatly beloved by his friends here and at Corpus, and the College has lost a very capable and loyal officer.

TNA have an officer file WO 339/587.

MURRAY, Donald Cecil Laird, Lieutenant, MC (1891–1938), Middlesex Regiment. Donald was born in India and educated at Charterhouse. At Corpus, he read the Natural Sciences Tripos and trained as a chemist. After war service, he married and travelled widely. He died in Washington, DC in 1938. His half-brother Malcolm George Murray, an undergraduate at Trinity College, committed suicide a week later. Their father was Sir Hugh Murray, deputy controller of timber supplies in 1917 and a forestry commissioner 1924 to 1934.

RESKER, Reverend Basil Alfred, Lance Corporal (1889–1969), London Regiment (Artists Rifles). Basil was born in Purley, where his father was vicar and was educated at Whitgift School, Croydon. He was subsequently archdeacon of Koot, Canada. He died in 1969 aged 80 at Nelson, British Columbia, Canada.

SEDDON, Alan Douglas, Captain (1889–1976), 2nd Battalion King's Own Royal Regiment (Lancaster). Alan was born in Las Palmas, Canary Islands, Spain, the son of William (a colliery manager) and Catherin Georgina, D'Arcy née Doorly. He was educated at Uppingham School and matriculated into Corpus in 1908. As an undergraduate, he was a member of the OTC and in 1911 commissioned 2nd Lieutenant (probationary), 4th Battalion North Staffordshire Regiment (The Prince of Wales's), Special Reserve of Officers. In 1913, he obtained a regular army commission as 2nd Lieutenant, 2nd Battalion King's Own Royal Regiment (Lancaster). During the early phase of the war, he served in France and Belgium and promoted Captain. However, in the spring of 1915, he was both wounded and made a prisoner of war. In April 1918, he was repatriated back to Britain. Between 1919 and 1920, he served as an intelligence officer in the Black Sea and was Adjutant between 1924 and 1927; thereafter he was engaged in various intelligence activities with the rank of Major. Between 1942 and 1943, he was a GSO2 creating and running the SOE Russian Section. Alan was a British Resident during the post-war military occupation of Germany. He was awarded the Russian Order of St Stanislaw and the White Russian Cross of the Archangel Michael. He retired as a Lieutenant Colonel and died at his home in Las Palmas in 1976. TNA have a medal card WO 372/14/157339.

1909

BUCK, George Reginald, Lieutenant (b.1881), 4th (Special Reserve) Battalion Bedfordshire Regiment (Territorial Force). Formerly 3/5th Battalion Bedfordshire Regiment. George was born at Chesterton Hall, Cambridge in 1881, the son of a primary school head teacher, and educated at the Perse School, Cambridge. His unit landed in France in July 1916 during the Somme Campaign and formed part of the 190th Brigade of the 63rd (Royal Naval) Division. Between 1916 and 1918, he saw active service during major engagements in France and Flanders. TNA have an officer file WO 374/10497 and a medal card WO 372/3/151367.

*CONINGHAM, William Francis Meyrick, 2nd Lieutenant (1888–1920), Royal Army Service Corps (Mechanical Transport). William was one of thousands of unrecorded casualties of war; he took his own life on 4 April 1920 aged 32. William's service is remembered on the war memorial at All Souls Church, Brighton.

*HARSTON, Frank Northey, Brigade-Major, MC (1890–1918). 11th Infantry Brigade East Lancashire Regiment. General Staff, 3rd Grade Headquarters, 4th Division. Formerly 9th Battalion Leicestershire Regiment. He was killed in action on 22 April 1918.

JAMESON, Reverend Cecil William (1880–1977), CF 4th Class, Royal Army Chaplains Department. He was born in Dublin, the son of a land agent, and educated at Monkton Combe School, near Bath, Somerset. During his time at Corpus, Cecil was Captain of the 1912 Lawn Tennis team who were winners of the division two championship. TNA have an officer file WO 339/37064 and a medal card WO 372/10/199012.

KIRKPATRICK, Roger Maning, Captain (1890–1937), 3rd Battalion Rifle Brigade and General Staff. Roger was born in Cambridge, the son of the Dean of Ely. He was educated at Marlborough College and admitted to Corpus with a Classics Scholarship. During his war service he was wounded. He died in London in 1937 aged 46.

LAMBERT, William, Major (b.1891) (Kite Balloon officer), RFC/RAF and formerly Captain, Royal Fusiliers. The son of a postmaster, he was educated at the Perse School, Cambridge. William was Mentioned in the Secretary of State List. TNA have an officer file in its burnt collection (microfilmed) WO 363/L400.

LA MOTHE, Hugo Dominique (1891–1956), Nigerian Field Force, West African Frontier Force. Hugo was born in Broughton, Preston, Lancashire, the son of the Reverend Frederick La Mothe (m.1863) and his wife Mabel Clare. Before Corpus, he was educated at Rossall School, Lancashire. Although he is not listed in Bury, Hugo La Mothe matriculated in 1909 as a sizar. During his time at Corpus, he played cricket and graduated with a BA in 1912. In November 1914, he was wounded during the Cameroons Campaign in West Africa. In 1919, on his return to Britain, he married Christine née Wallace at Bolton, Lancashire (now Greater Manchester).

LAPORTE-PAYNE (Payne), Archibald Aldridge, Major (1888–1980), 175th Brigade Royal Field Artillery. Archibald was born at Strood, Kent in 1888, the son of a clergyman. His brother was Reginald (see below, m.1910). He was educated at Cheltenham and the family lived at Herne Bay, Kent. During his time at Corpus, he was a sizar; he also rowed and trialled for the University Boat. On graduation, he went to Ridley Hall to train for the priesthood. However, on the declaration of war, he left Cambridge after obtaining a commission in the Royal Field Artillery; he was promoted Captain in 1917. During war service, Archibald was twice Mentioned in Despatches and in May 1918 he was wounded. Shortly after the Armistice, he returned to France to command a battery. In March 1919, as a Major with the 155th Army Brigade Royal Field Artillery, he moved to Cologne and Klein Vemich in the Rhineland with the 3rd Division attached to the 76th Army Brigade Royal Field Artillery. Demobilised in September 1919, he worked for the Ministry of Labour until 1920. In May 1929, he married Muriel née Cross, who died in 1963 at Yateley (gross estate of £430,746). In 1973, Archibald, solicitor of Carrick House, Yateley, Camberley, gave up his practice to become a barrister. He died on 15 May 1980 aged 92 whilst on holiday, leaving £548,374. On his death, family papers were dumped at a tip, but were subsequently rescued. Many of Archibald's letters written from the trenches are held by the Imperial War Museum where they are catalogued as Documents.12930. A few found their way to the Bay Museum on Canvey Island. In the early 1990s, a descendant of Archibald left a significant bequest to the College which formed part of the student hardship fund. TNA have a medal card WO 372/12/3245.

LITTLE, Andrew Hunter, Captain (b.1890), 11th Field Ambulance Royal Army Medical Corps. Andrew was born in Aylsham, Norfolk in 1891, the son of Frederick Little, a surgeon. He was educated at Oundle School before coming to Corpus. During his time at the College, he played lawn tennis and in 1912 was part of the winning division two championship team.

*NELSON, Ernest Bertram, 2nd Lieutenant (1890–1916), Indian Army Reserve of Officers, attached to the Indian Infantry, 1st Battalion 8th Gurkha Rifles. On 15 March 1916, he died of wounds received in action in Mesopotamia and has no known grave.

PATTESON, Cyril, Captain (Acting Major), MC Air Force Cross (1888–1932), RAF, 65th Field Company Royal Engineers. Formerly South Wales Borderers. He was born the son of a planter at Batcham in the Malacca Straits and educated at the King's School, Canterbury. During his service, he was wounded and Mentioned in Despatches twice. He remained in the RAF until October 1919 and died in London in 1932 aged 44. TNA have officer files AIR 76/393/90, WO 33911847 and a medal card WO 372/15/152444.

*READ, Reverend Eric Oswald (1888–1918), CF 4th Class, Royal Army Chaplains Department, attached to the 5th Battalion Dorsetshire Regiment. He was killed on 3 October 1918.

SELWYN, Very Reverend Dr Edward Gordon (1885–1959), CF 4th Class, Royal Army Chaplains Department. Edward was educated at Eton and King's College, Cambridge; his brother was John Selwyn (m.1911, see below). Edward was elected to a Fellowship in Classics in 1909, ordained in 1910, and left the Fellowship in 1913. He was made an Honorary Fellow in 1942. During his war service, he was Mentioned in Despatches. After a distinguished career as a writer and priest in the Anglican church, he served between 1938 and 1958 as dean of Winchester Cathedral. His father-in-law, Sir Edwyn Hoskyns (see below) was also a Fellow of Corpus. See also Bury, pp. 239–40. TNA have an officer file WO 374/61307.

VIGGARS, Reverend Spencer Hollins (1888–1935), CF 4th Class, Royal Army Chaplains Department. Spencer was born in Wolstanton, Staffordshire, the son of a brick manufacturer. He was educated at the High School, Newcastle upon Tyne. During war service, he was Mentioned in Despatches. He died in Kent in 1935 aged 47. TNA have an officer file WO 374/70618 and a medal card WO 372/20/149855.

1910

BOOTH, Walter Reynolds, Acting Captain (1891–1963). Royal Field Artillery (Territorial Force). Formerly Wellington College OTC. He was the son of James, a company secretary, and Martha née Illingworth, and prior to coming to Corpus was educated at Bradford Grammar School. During his time at Corpus, Walter was a scholar, though he changed subjects part way through his course of study. He also received a college gratuity. He saw active service in 1917 and was taken prisoner of war. He was later high master of Dulwich College. Walter died in Cockermouth, Westmorland (now Cumbria) in 1963. The school have a link to his biography www.bellhouse.co.uk/dc-masters-house.

*****BOWER, Charles Francis, Captain** (1891–1917), 16th (Service) Battalion Sherwood Foresters (Notts and Derby Regiment). He was killed in action on 13 September 1917.

CAVE, Thomas Storrar, Captain (1891–1966), Royal Garrison Artillery. He was born in Nottingham, the son of Thomas William Cave, vice principal, Agricultural College, Wye and Matilda née Storrar. Thomas was educated at The King's School, Canterbury and matriculated into Corpus in 1910 with a Parker Scholarship to read the Natural Sciences Tripos. In 1913, he was awarded a prize for his Tripos results and the following year a £20 College grant. Thomas graduated with a BA in 1914. He was wounded during war service and subsequently employed by the Ministry of Munitions until he retired in 1925. He married Doris Mary.

*****CLARKE, John Percy Dalzell, 2nd Lieutenant** (1891–1915), Royal Fusiliers attached to the 10th (Service) Battalion Worcestershire Regiment. He was killed in a riding accident in 1915.

*****DUCKWORTH, Walter Clarence, 2nd Lieutenant** (1889–1918), 1st Battalion Welch Regiment, attached to the 1st Battalion King's Shropshire Light Infantry. He was killed in action on 8 October 1918.

FARNSWORTH, Reverend Charles Roy (1887–1972), CF 4th Class, Royal Army Chaplains Department. Charles was born in Didsbury, Lancashire (now

Greater Manchester) in 1887, the son of a dentist. Prior to coming to Corpus, he was educated at the King's School, Rochester, Kent. In 1913, he received a College gratuity of £15 to help with his studies. Between 1939 and 1951, he was vicar of St George's Church, Ramsgate. He died in Hampshire in 1972 aged 85. TNA have an officer file WO 399/63403.

FARRER, Edward Richard Blackburne, Major, OBE MC Chevalier Légion d'honneur (1891–1959). Royal Army Service Corps, DAD Supplies. Edward was born in Rathfarnham, Co. Dublin, Ireland, the eldest child of the Reverend Henry Richard William Farrer, later canon at Salisbury Cathedral, and Georgina Beatrice née Blackburne. He was the grandson of Edward Blackburne KC of Rathfarnham Castle, Co. Dublin, Ireland. Edward was educated at Sherborne School, matriculated into Corpus in 1910, played in the cricket XI in 1911, and graduated in 1913.

During war service, he was Mentioned in Despatches and awarded an MC, the citation of which reads:

> He remained at his post during a withdrawal, keeping in touch with corps head-quarters and forward railheads, and carrying out the supply services. He carried out his duties under most difficult conditions, being continually subjected to bombing and machine-gun fire from enemy aircraft. It was due to his initiative and presence of mind that the supply services were so successfully carried out.

Edward's younger brother, Captain (Acting Major) Henry Wyndham Francis Blackburne Farrer MC and two bars (1894–1918), 30th Battalion Royal Field Artillery, was killed in action on 30 October 1918 (twelve days before the armistice), aged 24. After the war, Edward described himself as a company director and merchant. He was married to Cynthia Betty née Stanton and the couple had three children. During the Second World War, Edward served as a Lieutenant Colonel in the Royal Army Service Corps (Special Reserve) and awarded the MC and Mentioned in Despatches twice. In 1945, one of his children, John Richard Stanton Farrer, was commissioned in the Grenadier Guards and killed in action whilst serving in Malaya in 1949.

GREEN, Thomas Reginald, Lieutenant (b.1891) (Kite Balloon officer), RAF. Formerly Private, Public School Battalion Royal Fusiliers. He was the son of Thomas Willoughby, and prior to coming to the College was educated at Charterhouse. Thomas returned to Corpus in 1919 to complete his degree. TNA have an officer file AIR 76/194/51.

HARVEY, Godfrey Thomas Benedict, Captain (1892–1957), Calcutta Rifle Volunteers, attached to the Corps of Indian Army Reserve of Officers. Godfrey was born at Romsey, Hampshire in 1892. He came to Corpus to read the Historical Tripos and in 1913 was given a College grant of £50 to assist him.

He was later made a Companion of the Indian Empire (CIE) and in 1936 wrote a novel *Duet in Kerath*. He died in Tunbridge Wells in 1957 aged 65.

LAST, Frederick William, 2nd Lieutenant (b.1891), Lincolnshire Regiment. He was born in Wimbledon, the son of a solicitor, and educated first at Eastbourne College and then at Uppingham School. TNA have a medal card WO 372/12/7548.

MILLS, Eric, Lieutenant (b.1892), 8th Battalion Bedfordshire and Northamptonshire Regiment. Eric was born in Harlesden, the son of a schoolmaster, and educated at Dame Alice Owen's School, Islington, London. He was admitted to Corpus with an Entrance Scholarship to read the Mathematical Tripos and was subsequently awarded a Cowell Scholarship. During war service, he became a staff Captain, then a Major and was Military Governor of Gaza. He was also wounded, gassed, and Mentioned in Despatches. He was later awarded the OBE and CBE. TNA have an officer file WO 339/184 and a medal card WO 372/14/16379.

PAYNE, Reverend Reginald Merac (later Laporte-Payne), MC (1891–1972), CF 4th Class, Royal Army Chaplains Department. Reginald was born in Warwickshire, the son of a clergyman at Herne Bay, Kent. Prior to coming to the College, he was educated at Monkton Combe School, near Bath, Somerset. His elder brother Archibald (m.1909) also saw war service (see above). Reginald married Olive née Hart in 1917. After graduating from Corpus, he was ordained deacon and then priest. Between 1939 and 1941, he was vicar of the College living St Mary Abchurch, in the City of London, which was damaged by enemy action in 1941. He died in Bedfordshire in 1972 aged 81. TNA have a medal card WO 372/15/162168.

POIGNAND, George Clive Irving, Captain (1891–1925), Royal Army Service Corps. Formerly 2nd Lieutenant, Leinster Regiment. George was born in Sandhurst, Kent, the son of an army major (later retired colonel), and educated at Radley College. He was admitted to Corpus with an Entrance Scholarship to read the Classical Tripos. He died in 1925 unmarried aged 34.

PULLINGER, Sidney Russell, Captain (1891–1971), 5th Battalion Leicestershire Regiment (Territorial Force). Sidney was born at Bow, East London, the son of a rate collector, and educated at St Olave's Grammar School, Southwark, London (now located in Orpington). During his time at Corpus, he was first awarded a Classics Exhibition then a scholarship worth £20. He was also the winner of the Latin Declamation Cup in 1912 and the following year a prize for his Tripos results. Sidney married Evangeline née Schofield at Morpeth, Northumberland in 1919. He was headmaster of Loughborough Grammar School between 1926 and 1955. TNA have a medal card WO 372/16/107831.

ROYLANCE, Philip, Lieutenant (1892–1935), Duke of Lancaster's Own Yeomanry. The 1911 census shows he was born in Altrincham, Cheshire and self-describes as 'independent means'.

*****SHAW, Robert, Captain** (1892–1917), 1/7th Battalion The King's Regiment (Liverpool) (Territorial Force). He was killed in action on 20 September 1917.

TEBBS, John Archibald, Lieutenant (1891–1982), Royal Field Artillery. John was born in Cambridge where his father was an estate agents' clerk and lay clerk. At Corpus, John studied music and was a choral exhibitioner. In 1914, he married Grace née Swain. TNA have a medal card WO 372/19/186872.

WARD, Dudley Cuthbert Leslie, Staff Captain (1891–1945), 1/23rd Battalion (County of London) The London Regiment. Dudley was born in Hampstead in 1891, the son of a managing director. Prior to Corpus he was educated at St Paul's School. He matriculated in 1910 to read Divinity. In 1913, he was awarded a prize for his Tripos results. The 1/23rd Battalion formed part of the 142nd Brigade, 47th (2nd London) Division and fought on the Western Front between 1915 and 1918. The Battalion was involved in the Battles of Festibert, Loos, the Somme, Messines, Ypres, Cambrai, and Tournai. During his war service, he was wounded, Mentioned in Despatches, and Mentioned in the Secretary of State's List. In September 1921, Dudley married Muriel Alice née Bolus in Surbiton; the couple had two children. He died in London in December 1944 aged 53. TNA have a medal card WO 372/20/17404.

WILLS, Arthur Gerald Philip (officer file has Phillips), Captain, MC (1890–1969), Royal Army Medical Corps. Arthur was born in Halton, Leeds the son of a general practitioner. Prior to coming to the College, he was educated at Oundle School. TNA have an officer file WO 339/67613.

1911

BRUCE, Adam Douglas, Lieutenant (b.1893), 8th Battalion (Princess Louise's) Argyll and Sutherland Highlanders, 3rd Battalion Hussars and Machine Gun Corps, attached to the Royal Engineers (Signals). He was born in Edinburgh, the son of a clergyman and educated at Middlesborough High School (now closed). According to TNA medal card WO 372/1/12099, Adam was awarded the 1914–15 Star and served in the Gallipoli Campaign. TNA have an officer file WO 374/180.

*****CHURCHWARD, Hubert Alan, 2nd Lieutenant** (1891–1917), 2nd County of London Yeomanry (Westminster Dragoons); attached to the 9 Squadron Royal Flying Corps. He was killed in action on 16 August 1917.

Clark-Kennedy, Archibald Edmund, Captain (1893–1985), RAMC and formerly Lieutenant, 5th Battalion The Queen's (Royal West Surrey Regiment). He was born in Sevenoaks, Kent, the son of a clergyman and educated at Wellington College. As an undergraduate, he read the Natural Sciences Tripos and held an exhibition worth £30. It was the start of a long and distinguished association with Corpus. He saw active service in India and Mesopotamia before completing his medical training and finished the war as a doctor on the Western Front. He was later a College Fellow and the first Director of Studies in Medicine, and was later Dean of the London Hospital. See also Bury, pp. 253–4.

Culley, George Charles Henry, Captain (1893–1982), 4th Battalion Norfolk Regiment, later Machine Gun Corps, Royal Flying Corps and RAF. George was educated at the City of Norwich School and matriculated into Corpus in 1911 to read the Historical and Law Triposes. During his time at the College, he held a Parker Exhibition. He was also a member of both the Chess Club and Boat Club, and between 1912 and 1914, rowed in many First Boats. George also trialled for the University Boat.

On 24 August 1914, he was commissioned 2nd Lieutenant, Norfolk Regiment. In April 1915, he was gazetted Lieutenant (Acting Captain) and saw service in the Gallipoli Campaign. In 1916 and 1917, he served in Egypt with the Machine Gun Corps. In June 1916, he was promoted Captain and in September joined the Royal Flying Corps (23 Training Squadron). In 1917 at Aboukir, he was badly injured and hospitalised in a flying accident in which a trainee pilot died. In 1918, he was transferred to France and became an RAF Captain. In November 1918, he was again hospitalised, first in France and then in London, and the following month he 'relinquished his commission on account of ill-health'. In early 1919, George returned to the College to complete his law degree, graduating in October 1919. He passed his final examinations in 1920 and thereafter practised as a solicitor. During the 1930s, he spent time in East Asia. However, he returned to the RAF during the Second World War, first as a Pilot Officer in the Administrative and Special Duties Branch and then, in 1940, as a Flying Officer. In 1941, he became a Flight Lieutenant, and in 1944, resigned his commission. In 1946, he was appointed a judge advocate for the Singapore war crimes trials. Following war service, he returned to practice at Little Shelford, Cambridgeshire until his retirement in 1957. He died in 1982 aged 89. A photograph album of his time at Corpus is held in the Cambridgeshire Collection. TNA have an officer file AIR 76/117/59 and a medal card WO 372/5/120212.

Gates, Sidney Barrington (Barry), Private (1893–1973), Public Schools Battalion Royal Fusiliers. In his unfinished memoir, Sidney wrote: 'The atmosphere [at Corpus was] altogether warmer and friendlier than at [City of Norwich] school. In his own words, "It would be rather more realistic to say that my years at Corpus lifted me into a happiness I had never known in my childhood and have only rarely known since".' At Corpus, he read the Mathematical Tripos, took a double first and was a Wrangler. Like George Paget Thomson (see below), he spent much of the war in the Aerodynamics Department of the Royal Aircraft Factory, known later as the Royal Aircraft Establishment (RAE) at Farnborough. It proved to be the beginning of a long and distinguished career working in this field. He was elected a Fellow of the Royal Society in 1950. See FRS obituary.

HALL, Alexander Ferneau, 2nd Lieutenant, MC (b.1893), 6th Battalion Gloucestershire Regiment. Formerly Lance Corporal. He was born in Clifton, Gloucestershire, the son of a director of public companies. He was admitted to Corpus with an Entrance Scholarship of £50 to read the Historical Tripos. He subsequently changed to Natural Sciences and was awarded the Science Prize of £5 in 1914. The MC citation reads: 'During an enemy attack, he held a position most gallantly with a number of men of his battalion throughout the day, and finally throughout the night, held his position at the rear with his party and a Lewis gun. He behaved splendidly and caused heavy casualties to be inflicted on the enemy.'

HARRISON, Frank Eric, Captain and Adjutant, MC and Bar (1891–1966), C/165th Brigade Royal Field Artillery. Frank was born in Salford, Lancashire (now Greater Manchester), the son of a clergyman, and educated at Manchester Grammar School. He served in France from March 1916, was Mentioned in Despatches, and awarded the MC and a Bar. He died in Berkshire in 1966 aged 75. TNA have an officer file WO 339/28717 and a medal card WO 372/9/49627.

ISON, Arthur Jesse, Lieutenant (1891–1958), 13th Battalion Northumberland Fusiliers and Welch Guards, attached to the Royal Horse Guards Machine Gun Regiment and Commandant, School of Instruction. Arthur was born in Howden-on-Tyne, Northumberland in 1891, the son of a clergyman, and educated at the Royal Grammar School, Newcastle upon Tyne. He was later ordained a priest and died in Lincolnshire in 1958 aged 67. TNA have a medal card WO 372/10/165955.

JONES, Bernard Collier, Acting Captain (b.1893), RFC/RAF. Formerly 5th Battalion Officer Cadet Corps. Prior to coming to the College, Bernard was educated at Lancing College. During his time at Corpus, Bernard was organ scholar. He was wounded during war service and Mentioned in Despatches. TNA have an officer file AIR 76/262/81.

*KEATING, George Henry, Lieutenant (1893–1918), 2/1st Battalion Cambridgeshire Regiment. Formerly Private 16th Public Schools Battalion Middlesex Regiment. He was killed in action on 18 September 1918.

KENDALL, John Michael Angerstein, Captain (1892–1960), The King's Own Royal Regiment (Norfolk Yeomanry). John was the son of a clergyman of Richmond, Surrey. After Marlborough College, he came to Corpus to read the Historical Tripos and held an exhibition worth £30. TNA have an officer file WO 374/39151.

*MACINTOSH, Henry Maitland, Captain (1892–1918), 1/8th (Argyllshire) Battalion Princess Louise's (Argyll and Sutherland Highlanders). He died of wounds on 26 July 1918.

MAWDESLEY, John Leyland, Captain (1893–1974), Royal Army Ordnance Corps. He was formerly Private 2373, then Sergeant, 1st Battalion London Scottish Regiment. John was born in Dewsbury, Yorkshire in 1893, the son of a solicitor who was a town clerk (in 1901 at Croydon, Surrey). Prior to matriculating into Corpus, John was educated at Gresham's School, Holt, Norfolk. TNA have a medal card WO 372/13/180666.

MONTAGU, George Henry Simon, Lieutenant (1892–1977), 7th Battalion City of London Regiment. George was born in Kensington, London, the son of a surveyor, and educated at Clifton College. During war service, he was wounded. He died in St Marylebone, London in 1977 aged 85. TNA have an officer file WO 374/48414 and a medal card WO 372/14/59618.

PALLISER, Wray Frederick Cecil, Lieutenant (1892–1938), 13th Battalion Worcestershire Regiment. Wray was the son of Charles Wray Palliser of the New Zealand Commissioner's Office and Bessie née Proctor. He was educated at The King's School, Canterbury and matriculated into Corpus in 1911. He married (1) Iris Elaine Bickford in 1915 and (2) Mary Freda, daughter of Ralph Yardley Sidebottom in 1927.

PENZER, Norman Mosley, 2nd Lieutenant (1892–1960), 2nd Garrison Battalion Essex Regiment. Norman was born in Maudesley, Lancashire, the son of a clergyman, and educated at Marlborough College. After war service, he became an independent scholar, a Fellow of the Royal Asiatic Society and the Hakluyt Society. His interests encompassed economics, geology, comparative anthropology, folklore, the history of exploration, and old silver. He was primarily an Orientalist and an authority on the British explorer, scholar, and ethnologist Sir Richard Francis Burton (1821–90). His obituary in the *Geographical Journal* states that:

> he was chiefly known at the RGS for his interest in Sir Richard Burton. He edited a volume of selected papers by Burton and he founded, with Dr F Grenfell Baker, the Richard Burton Memorial Lecture at the Royal Asiatic Society... Penzer's gifts of scholarship were never as fully developed as many thought they might have been and it will always be a matter of regret that he did not write the definitive biography of Burton it was so well within his power.

He was also a LittD FGS FRGS and FSA.

SELWYN, John, (Temporary) Major (1893–1959), S02 RAF. Formerly Captain, 7th Division Royal Field Artillery, 170th Brigade, ADC and Staff Captain. His father was the Reverend Canon Edwyn Carus Selwyn (1853–1918), between 1887 and 1907 the headmaster of Uppingham School, and his mother was Lucy Ada née Arnold (1858–1894). His brother was the Very Reverend Dr Edward Gordon Selwyn (College Fellow 1909–13, see above). John and his family lived at Undershaw, Hindhead, Haselmere, Surrey. He was born in Uppingham and educated at Eton and awarded a Corpus Entrance Scholarship worth £50 to read the Classical Tripos. In 1913, he was awarded the English Literature Prize. During his time at the College, he was Secretary and subsequently Captain of the Boat Club and rowed in many Corpus boats during the years 1911 to 1914. In 1914, he drove the gun team at the Royal Military Tournament as part of the Oxford and Cambridge OTC artillery driving competition. On 15 May 1915, he was wounded but recovered, remaining with the RAF until October 1919. TNA have an officer file AIR 76/454/50 and a medal card WO 372/17/223843.

SWANSTON, Eric Romilly, Lieutenant (1892–1929), Motorcyclists Corps, Royal Engineers. Eric was born in Kensington, the son of Edward Shenland (self-described as a Gentleman) and educated at St Paul's School. He matriculated into Corpus in 1911 to read the Natural Sciences Tripos and held an exhibition worth £30. On the outbreak of war, he enlisted as a Corporal in the Royal Engineers and in July 1916 commissioned 2nd Lieutenant. He saw active service and after the Armistice remained in the army; in 1921, he transferred to the Royal Corps of Signals. In the mid-1920s, he left the armed forces and went to Nigeria as a deputy director of education. In 1927, he became editor of the *Bulletin of Educational Matters* and was His Majesty's Inspector of Education. He left Nigeria in 1929 and died shortly afterwards aged 36.

VAUGHAN, John Henry, Lieutenant, MC (1892–1965), 3rd Battalion Royal Inniskilling Fusiliers attached to the Royal Engineers (Signals). John was the son of a brewer and educated at Eastbourne College, he matriculated into Corpus as a sizar, holding a Spencer Scholarship to read the Law Tripos. In October 1914, he was awarded the Spens Essay Prize worth £3. During his military service, he was wounded and awarded the MC, the citation for which reads: 'While acting as Signal Officer, he showed great courage and determination in carrying out his duties. On his own initiative he rallied a party of men in the vicinity, and succeeded in leading them to a fresh position.' After military service, he went on to serve as Attorney General of Zanzibar and later as Attorney General and subsequently Chief Justice of Fiji. He was also a noted ornithologist. TNA have an officer file WO 339/53746 and a medal card WO 372/20/139810.

***WEBB, Arthur Henry, 2nd Lieutenant** (1891–1917), 4th Battalion (attached to the 8th Battalion) the Buffs (East Kent Regiment) (Territorial Force). He was killed in action on 23 June 1917.

G C H Culley album

Corpus Christi College, Matriculation 1911.
Four of the cohort did not survive the war, Webb, Churchward, Macintosh, and Keating. In all, twenty-one of the twenty-nine matriculating students are known to have undertaken military service.

1912

*BROWNLEE, Wilfred Methven, 2nd Lieutenant** (1890–1914), 3rd (Special Reserve) Battalion Dorsetshire Regiment. Wilfred died of pneumonia on 12 October 1914.

CHURCHILL, Harold Edwin, Lieutenant (1892–1976), Royal Army Service Corps (Motorised Transport). He was born in Stanford Hill, London, the son of an engineer, and educated at University College School, London. In later life, Harold was a company director and lived in Enfield. He died in Somerset in 1976 aged 84.

*DAVIES, Trevor Arthur Manning, Lieutenant** (1893–1916), 4th North Midland (Howitzer) Brigade, Royal Field Artillery (Territorial Force). Trevor was killed in action on 1 July 1916.

DAWBARN, Graham Richards, 2nd Lieutenant (1893–1976), RFC. Formerly Lance Corporal, Royal Fusiliers. Graham was the son of Robert Arthur (an engineer) and Mary Louisa Dawbarn. He was educated at The King's School, Canterbury before matriculating into Corpus with a Parker Exhibition. At Corpus, he read Part I of the Mathematical Tripos before changing to Architectural Studies. His time at the College was bisected by the war and he was in uniform before he could begin his third year; in June 1916, having completed Part I of the Tripos, he took a wartime BA. In September 1917, he was declared permanently unfit for military service and invalided out of the armed forces. In 1919, he returned to the College to complete Part II of his Tripos (MA 1920). During this time, he published, jointly with John Dunning Macleod (see below) *Vade Mecum or the Freshers A.B.C.* (1919). Thereafter, he assisted Professor Edward Schroeder Prior in the School of Architectural Studies. He went on to become a distinguished Modernist architect, FRIBA FRAeS MIStructE, and between 1921 and 1923, worked in the Hong Kong Public Works Department. He designed the Golden Gates at Corpus and was architect for the remodelling of the Stable Yard area of the College. Among the many buildings he designed was the BBC Television Centre. In 1923, he married Olive Ellen Elizabeth née Topham. He was awarded the CBE in 1948 and died on 30 January 1976 aged 83. TNA have various files WO 339/60334, AIR 76/127/282 and a medal card WO 372/5/214258.

FOULSTON, Samuel Vernon, Corporal (1893–1939), Royal Engineers, Special Brigade (Chemists). Samuel was born in Hull the youngest of three children of William Lawson Foulston and Elizabeth née Rushworth and educated at Hayman's College, Hull. His father was the owner of W. L. Foulston & Co., glass manufacturers, 41 Cumberland Street, Hull. At Corpus, he held an Entrance Scholarship to study the Natural Sciences Tripos and in 1914 received a College grant of £30. He was a noted chess player and died in Hull in 1939 aged 46.

HALL, John Thornton, Lieutenant (b. c.1893), 7th Battalion Loyal North Lancashire Regiment attached to the King's Royal Rifle Corps. He was born in Blackpool, the son of a builder, and privately educated. During his war service, John was wounded twice, first in November 1915 and then again in February 1916. TNA have an officer file WO 339/1649.

HELY HUTCHINSON, James, Air Mechanic (b.1893), RAF. James came from a prominent Anglo-Irish family related to the Earl of Donoghmore. He was born in Cockermouth, Cumberland (now part of Cumbria), the son of a physician, and educated at Eastbourne College. TNA have an officer file AIR 79/686/75308.

HINDERLICK, Albert August William, Captain and Adjutant (1894–1955), Royal Garrison Artillery. He was born in Holloway, London, the son of a businessman, and educated at University College School, London. During his war service, he was wounded and Mentioned in Despatches. He returned to Corpus after the war to complete his degree, graduating with a BA in December 1919. Thereafter, he was a radio engineer.

HOLT, Francis Neville, Major (*The War List* **has Captain**) (1893–1980), 7th Battalion The Queen's (Royal West Kent Regiment). Francis was born on 12 September 1893 in Maidstone, Kent, the son of a clergyman. He was educated at The King's School, Canterbury and matriculated into Corpus as a sizar with a Parker Scholarship. He was an active member of the Boat Club and rowed in the 1914 Lent and May bumps. During the war, he was employed at the Ministry of Labour. In January 1919, he returned to the College to complete his studies and was the first post-war Captain of Boats. He graduated with a BA in December 1919 (MA 1924). He married (1) Irene Thirza Thompson in 1921 (d.1929); (2) Nellie A Earl in 1934; (3) Alice M Weller in 1948. He later became headmaster of the Belmont School, Falmouth (which has subsequently closed). Francis died in Cornwall in 1980 aged 87. TNA have a medal card WO 372/10/19138.

HOOLEY, Leonard Joseph, Corporal 113151 (1894–1996), 187th Battalion Royal Engineers (Chemicals Corps). Leonard was born on 11 November 1894 in Blackpool, Lancashire, the son of a schoolmaster and educated at Macclesfield Grammar School. In 1912, he matriculated into Corpus with an exhibition to read the Natural Sciences Tripos and in 1914 received a College grant of £45. On the outbreak of war, despite pre-war membership of the OTC, his application for a commission was rejected on health grounds. Leonard responded by enlisting in the 187th Battalion Royal Engineers, 3rd Provisional Corps. In October 1915, he was seriously wounded in action. He lost a hand and was discharged from the armed forces. In December 1916, Leonard, having completed Part I of the Tripos, took a wartime BA (by proxy). In 1919, he returned to the College to take Part II of the Tripos and graduated in June 1920. He married Barbara née Walsh in 1921. He died in 1996 aged 102. At the time of his death, he was the last known living member of Corpus to have served in the First World War. See obituary in *The Letter of the Corpus Association*, No. 77 (Michaelmas 1998), pp. 80–1. TNA have an officer file WO 363–4/007299671/00710.

JOMARON, Adolphe (**Bury has Adolph**) **Charles, Captain** (1893–1963), 11th Brigade Royal Field Artillery. Formerly Lieutenant and Adjutant. Adolphe was born in Yeovil, Somerset, but grew up in Islington, London, the son a French language teacher (in the 1911 census, his father self-described as a Professor of French Language and a French national). He was educated at University College School, London and awarded an Entrance Scholarship to Corpus and in June 1914 appointed sub-librarian. Adolphe was wounded during his war service. He returned to Corpus in 1919 to complete his degree, graduating with a BA in June 1920. He went on to become a Malay civil servant (a colleague described him 'as a nice chap, but not very bright') and died in London in 1963 aged 70. TNA have an officer file WO 339/18183.

Pryor, George Hawser Deen, Lieutenant (1894–1963), 12th Battalion King's Royal Rifle Corps. Born in Cambridge, the son of a fishmonger, George was educated at Haileybury. He was wounded during his war service.

Raven, Geoffrey Earle, Lieutenant, MC (1893–1987), 7th Battalion West Yorkshire Regiment (Prince of Wales's Own). ADC to GOC, West Riding Division. Geoffrey was born the son of a clergyman who was also a master at Uppingham School, where Geoffrey was educated. The family were distinguished members of the Church of England and academics. At Corpus, he held an exhibition and was, in 1914, awarded a College grant of £20. During war service, he was wounded and awarded the MC. He later became a teacher and subsequently ordained priest. See obituary in *The Letter of the Corpus Association*, No. 67 (Michaelmas 1988), p. 74. TNA have an officer file WO 374/56319 and a medal card WO 372/16/155276.

*****Terrell, Frank William, Lieutenant** (1893–1916), 8th (Service) Battalion Gloucestershire Regiment, attached to the 3rd Battalion Worcestershire Regiment. He was killed in action on 3 September 1916.

Thouless, Robert Henry, 2nd Lieutenant (1894–1984), Royal Engineers (Signalling). In December 1914, he was elected to a Colman Exhibition and in June 1915 awarded a prize of books on being placed in the First Class of Part I of the Natural Sciences Tripos. On the outbreak of war, he enlisted in the Royal Engineers and was made Sergeant-Instructor. He was subsequently commissioned and served as a Signals Officer in the Salonica campaign, where he suffered the effects of poison gas. After war service, Robert returned to Corpus, took an MA in June 1920 and in 1923 became one of the first graduates to complete a Cambridge research-based PhD. He was a Fellow of the College and enjoyed a long and distinguished career as a psychologist. See also Bury, pp. 256–7, and *The Record*, No. 100 (Michaelmas 2021). TNA have an officer file WO 339/124167 and a medal card WO 372/20/23344.

Wells, Harold Marty, Lieutenant (b.1890), Motor Cyclists Corps Royal Engineers; employed by the Ministry of Munitions. Born in Birmingham, Harold was the son of an engineer and educated at Rossall School. A non-Collegiate import, he read the Mechanical Sciences Tripos at Corpus and in 1914 received a College grant of £20. TNA have an officer file WO 339/48096.

*WHITTAM, Matthew John Goldborough, Lieutenant (1893–1915), 8th (Service) Battalion Duke of Wellington's (West Riding) Regiment. Matthew died on 2 August 1915 of wounds received in action at Gallipoli.

WILSON, Reverend Thomas, Private (b. *c.*1892), King's Own Yorkshire Light Infantry. He was born in Loftus, Yorkshire, the son of a merchant, and educated at Guisborough Grammar School (now part of Prior Pursglove and Stockton Sixth Form College).

YENCKEN, Edward Druce, Captain (1891–1964), Royal Army Service Corps. Edward and his brother Arthur were born in Australia and educated at Melbourne Church of England Grammar School. Although there was a three-year difference in their ages, both matriculated in April 1912. During their time at the College, the brothers were members of the Chess Club and the Strawberries. In 1914, they were both Lawn Tennis Blues and won the Varsity lawn tennis open doubles. Edward's war duties included service in Salonika, where he was Mentioned in Despatches. In January 1919, he returned to Corpus, graduating with a BA in June of that year. He returned to Australia where he took up various positions in the family manufacturing business. TNA have an officer file WO 339/18050.

YENCKEN, Arthur Ferdinand, Major, MC (1894–1944), 6th London Brigade Royal Field Artillery (Territorial Force). Before matriculating into Corpus, Arthur Yencken was educated at Melbourne Church of England Grammar School. He came to the College in the same year as his elder brother Edward (see above). In August 1914, Arthur enlisted in the British Army and became a Major in the Royal Field Artillery. During his war service, he was wounded, gassed, awarded the Military Cross, and twice Mentioned in Despatches. He returned to Corpus in 1919, graduating with a BA in June of that year. He then joined the Foreign Office and after several appointments was made British Minister in Madrid in 1940. He was appointed CMG in 1941. Arthur Yencken was killed in an air crash south of Barcelona, Spain on 18 May 1944. His name is not currently recorded on the College Second World War memorial. Both of Arthur's sons came to Corpus and went on to enjoy distinguished careers in Australia. See also https://en.wikipedia.org/wiki/Arthur_Ferdinand_Yencken. TNA have a medal card WO 372/22/113619.

GCH Culley album

The first Corpus May Ball, June 1912.

Yencken album

A group of friends in Old Court *c.*1914. Note the railings and the ivy-covered walls (it was being removed when war broke out). (l to r) Wilfred Methven Brownlee (1890–1914), Archibald Edmund Clark-Kennedy (1893–1985), Harold Edwin Churchill (1892–1976), George Charles Henry Culley (1893–1982), Edmund Druce Yencken (1891- 1964), Arthur Ferdinand Yencken (1894–1944) and possibly George Henry Keating (1893–1918).

Corpus tennis teams 1914: colourised

Corpus Christi College contingent at the Cambridge University OTC camp
Farnborough 1912.

1913

BERNARD, Douglas Vivian, Lieutenant (1894–1958), The Queen's (Royal West Surrey Regiment), formerly 2nd Lieutenant, Duke of Wellington's (West Riding) Regiment. Douglas was born in Madras (now known as Chennai), India, the son of an Indian civil servant. He was educated at St Paul's School. At Corpus, he read the Mechanical Sciences Tripos and was awarded the Sykes Exhibition. He returned to the College in 1919 to complete his degree. Also in 1919, he married Elizabeth née Gibbs. Douglas died in 1958 aged 64. TNA have an officer file WO 339/33679.

BOULTBEE, Beauchamp St John, Acting Captain, MC (1895–1956), Lieutenant, 1st Battalion Northamptonshire Regiment, seconded to RFC and subsequently RAF. Beauchamp was born in Huntingdon, the son of a clergyman and educated at the King's School, Ely. He served with his regiment in France and in 1915 was seconded to the RFC. He was Mentioned in Despatches three times and awarded the Military Cross in June 1917. The citation reads: 'For conspicuous gallantry and devotion to duty while on contact patrol. He descended from a height of 400 feet and attacked a large party of the enemy. He subsequently effected a safe landing in spite of very adverse weather conditions. He has on many previous occasions done fine work.' During his RFC/RAF service, he flew many types of aircraft and became an experienced night flyer. However, he was injured several times and suffered other health problems requiring hospitalisation, including a spell at Netley. In March 1918, he was posted for home service, ending the war as part of the pilot training unit at RAF Yatesbury, Wiltshire. In 1919, he took a regular commission in the Royal Northamptonshire Regiment seconded to the RAF, but was invalided out in 1922. On leaving the armed forces, he became a tea-planter in India. In 1929, he married Eve Mary Boland in Madras (now known as Chennai). His brother Arthur Elsdale Boultbee (1897–1917), although not a member of College, also served in the RFC and was killed by the Red Baron. TNA have an officer file AIR 76/47/140 and a medal card WO 372/2/227182.

*BUDGEN, Robert Gordon, Lieutenant (1894–1915), 5th (Service) Battalion King's Shropshire Light Infantry. Robert was killed in action on 24 August 1915.

BUTLER, Ralph Lewis Giberne, Captain (1883–1967), Special List. He served with VI Corps and in 1915 was Town Major of Ypres. A Fellow of the College between 1913 and 1916, in 1914 he was, according to Bury (p. 248): 'given leave of absence, since he had joined the Headquarters staff of the 6th Division of the BEF in France'. During his war service, he was wounded three times and invalided out of the army in 1916.

CHRISTIE, Robert Gilner, Captain (b.1893), 128th Field Corps, Royal Electrical and Mechanical Engineers. He was the son of a businessman and educated at Bedales School. In 1914, Robert was awarded a Mawson Scholarship worth £30. He also rowed in the 1914 Lent and May bumps. In 1918, he was twice Mentioned in Despatches and in 1919 returned to Corpus to complete his degree. He was one of those returning students who helped re-establish the Boat Club.

COLLINS, Eric George William, Lieutenant, MC (1892–1969), 8th Battalion The Duke of Edinburgh's (Wiltshire Regiment). He was the son of a clergyman and educated at Monkton Combe School, near Bath, Somerset. During his war service, Eric was wounded twice. The citation for his MC reads: 'For conspicuous gallantry and devotion to duty. He showed great coolness and ability in leading his company under heavy fire. He had previously directed the brigade on a difficult night march with accuracy and coolness prior to the attack.'

CRICK, George Hilary, Lieutenant (b.1894), 9th Battalion Royal Scots Fusiliers. He was the son of a clergyman and educated at Glenalmond School, Edinburgh. In 1913, he was appointed a choral exhibitioner. During his war service, George served as an assistant instructor in gunnery and subsequently Captain (Temporary), RAF. In 1919, he returned to Corpus to complete his degree and was later ordained priest. TNA have officer files AIR 76/113/25 and WO 339/3736.

***CROSSE, Robert Grant, Lieutenant** (1894–1916), 7th Battalion The Queen's (Royal West Kent Regiment). Robert died of wounds on 14 July 1916.

***DAY, Norman Leslie, 2nd Lieutenant** (1894–1916), 'C' Company, 14th (Service) Battalion The King's Regiment (Liverpool). Norman was killed in action on 14 September 1916.

***DEVEREUX, Humphrey William, Lieutenant** (1894–1916), 1/5th Battalion South Staffordshire Regiment (Territorial Force). Humphrey was killed at the Somme on 26 June 1916.

FAWCETT, Albert Wellesley L'Estrange, Major MC (1894–1961), Machine Gun Corps. Formerly Captain, 9th Battalion Gloucestershire Regiment. Albert was born in Southport, Lancashire (now Merseyside), the son of a clergyman, and educated at Cheltenham College. He came to Corpus with an exhibition to read the Historical Tripos and in June 1914 was awarded a grant of £25. On the declaration of war, he left the College and was commissioned in the Gloucestershire Regiment. During his military service, he was wounded. The citation for his 1917 MC reads: 'Owing to the intense barrage his company suffered heavy losses. He however, got the remainder in front and succeeded in occupying the enemy's position. He then reconnoitred the whole position and was able to send back valuable information.' In January 1919, he returned to Corpus to complete his degree, graduating in June 1920. He subsequently became a screenwriter and film producer, notable for his work at Gainsborough Pictures in films such as *Bed and Breakfast* (1930). He was also a journalist and film critic. As an author he wrote *Films: Facts and Forecasts* (1927), which had a preface by Charlie Chaplin, and *Writing for the Films* (1932). In 1920, he married Cecilia Mary Herklots Jerwood (née Powles), the widow of Major John Hugh Jerwood MC and mother of John Jerwood. They had two sons. He died in 1961 aged 67.

HARVEY, Hugo Morgan, 2nd Lieutenant (1895–1965), 7th Battalion Northamptonshire Regiment and Royal Garrison Artillery. Hugo was born in Melton Mowbray, Leicestershire, the son of a bank manager, and educated at Oundle School. In October 1914, he was awarded the Perowne Theological Prize worth £5. TNA have an officer file WO 339/3694 and a medal card WO 372/9/71337.

JACKS, Mervyn, 2nd Lieutenant (1894–1933), East Lancashire Regiment. Mervyn was later Lieutenant and Adjutant with the RFC and RAF. He was born in Clifton, Gloucestershire, the son of a linen merchant. He matriculated into Corpus during the Lent term 1913, and in June 1914, he was awarded a Spencer Scholarship. TNA have two officer files WO 339/49097 and AIR 76/251/43.

JENKINS, George Edwin, Lieutenant (b.1890), 3rd Battalion East Yorkshire Regiment and The Queen's (Royal West Surrey Regiment). He was the son of a merchant and educated at the Friends' School, Kendal, Westmorland (now Cumbria). George returned to Cambridge after war service to study for the priesthood at Westcott House. He subsequently served in several parishes and, between 1941 and 1947, was vicar of St Thomas the Martyr, Newcastle upon Tyne.

KAIN, Hubert Gerard (TNA have Gerrard), Lieutenant (1894–1964), Royal Garrison Artillery. He was the son of a banker and educated at the King's School, Canterbury. During his time at Corpus, Hubert was a sizar and, in October 1914, awarded a grant of £25. He died in 1964 aged 69. TNA have an officer file WO 339/53082.

KIRKCALDY, Grange Inglis, Captain (b.1895), Royal Highlanders. Formerly Lieutenant 4th Divisional Supply Column, Royal Army Service Corps and Black Watch. He was born in Dunedin, New Zealand, the son of William Melville Kirkaldy, an underwriter, and educated at Waitaki Boys' High School, Oamaru, Otago, New Zealand and Bradfield College, Berkshire. George was erroneously reported missing in action in October 1918, but then discovered to be a prisoner of war. In 1920, he married Mildred née Nicoll in Chelsea. TNA have a medal card WO 372/11/185595.

LA BROOY, Maynert Victor Theodore Johnstone, Lieutenant (b.1892), 83rd Siege Battery Royal Garrison Artillery. Maynert was born in London, the son of Amelia Fanny and Justin Theodore La Brooy, a senior civil servant at the War Office, and educated at Shrewsbury School. His war service saw him employed at the Ministry of Munitions. He returned to Corpus in 1919 to complete his History degree, graduating with a BA in June 1920. He married Phyllis née Lewis in 1921 and went on to have a business career in various South American countries.

*LEWIS, Arthur Milton, Acting Captain (1894–1919), 1st Battalion 52nd Sikhs (Frontier Force), Indian Army Reserve of Officers. He was formerly Lieutenant, 9th (Service) Battalion Devonshire Regiment and previously Private, Public Schools Battalion Royal Fusiliers. Arthur was killed in Mesopotamia on 8 August 1919 and has no known grave.

LIDDELL HART, Basil Henry, Captain and Adjutant (1895–1970), 2nd Battalion King's Own Yorkshire Light Infantry. Basil Liddell Hart was born in Paris, the son of Henry Bramley Hart a Wesleyan Methodist minister and his wife Clara Adeline Kate Beatrice née Liddell. Educated at St Paul's School, he matriculated into the College in 1913 to read the Historical Tripos. During his year in residence, he was a keen games player and although he passed Prelims to Part I of the Tripos, he only achieved third-class marks. Commissioned early in the war, he arrived in France in September 1915. At the end of that year, he suffered concussion from an exploding shell in the Ypres Salient; however, he recovered sufficiently to return to his unit for the Somme Offensive in July 1916. On 16 July, his war service abruptly ended when he was severely gassed. He never returned to the College to complete his degree, but after the war became a seminal figure in military writing. In 1965, he was knighted, became an Honorary Fellow of the College and received a Hon DLitt (Oxford). His papers form part of the Liddell Hart Centre for Military Archives at King's College London. See also Professor Sir Hew Strachan, "Sir Basil Liddell Hart", an address given in the College Chapel at the Commemoration of Benefactors, 2 December 1994, *The Letter of the Corpus Association*, No. 74 (Michaelmas 1995), pp. 30–44.

*LOCKHART, Norman Douglas Stuart Bruce, Lieutenant (1894–1915), 7th Battalion Seaforth Highlanders, 9th Highland Division. Norman was killed in action on 25 September 1915.

*MACKAY, Claude Lysaght, 2nd Lieutenant (1894–1915), 5th Battalion Worcestershire Regiment (Special Reserve), attached to the 2nd Battalion Manchester Regiment. Claude died on 7 June 1915 of wounds received in action on 28 May 1915.

Macleod, John (Jock) Dunning, Captain (1894–1957), 2nd Battalion The Queen's Own Cameron Highlanders and Machine Gun Corps. Jock was born the son of a university teacher of Indian law in Naini Tal in India, and educated at Rugby School. He came to Corpus with an Entrance Scholarship worth £60 to read the Classical Tripos. He left the College on the outbreak of war, serving on the Western Front and in the Salonika campaign. Jock returned to Corpus in 1919 to complete his degree. During this period, he published *Macedonian Measures and Others* (1919), a book of poems written during and drawing on his experiences of the Salonika campaign. He also published, jointly with Graham Richards Dawbarn (see above), *Vade Mecum or the Freshers A.B.C.* (1919). His wartime letters and papers are held at the University of Leeds Library, special collections. TNA holds various files about Jock Macleod. These are an officer file WO 339/46139, a medal card WO 372/13/46578 and a pension file PIN 26/22047. According to the latter, Jock suffered from dementia praecox (schizophrenia). He died in 1957 at the psychiatric unit of Crichton Royal Infirmary, Dumfries, Scotland.

*Mathews, Arnold, Lieutenant** (1894–1915), 14th (Reserve) Battalion Cheshire Regiment. Arnold died of wounds in Mesopotamia on 14 April 1916.

Neale, Francis Seward, Lieutenant (1895–1962), Machine Gun Corps. Formerly Private (Public Schools Battalion) Royal Fusiliers. Francis was the son of a farmer and educated at Haileybury. He returned to Corpus after war service to complete his History degree, graduating with a BA in June 1920.

Nisbet, Alan George, 2nd Lieutenant (1895–1969), Motor Transport, Royal Army Service Corps. He was born in Newton Abbott, Devon, the son of Adam Thomson Nisbet a medical practitioner and privately educated. After war service, he emigrated to New Zealand and trained as a dental surgeon. He married Ivy Auchterlonie and there were children. During the Second World War, Alan was appointed Captain (Temporary) in his local Greytown, New Zealand, Home Guard Battalion; he lived and died in Greytown aged 73.

*Sandford, Clement Richard Folliott, Captain,** MC (1893–1917), 5th Battalion King's Own Yorkshire Light Infantry (Territorial Force). During his war service, Clement was first wounded and subsequently killed in action on 22 February 1917.

*Wynne, Edward Ernest, Captain** (1895–1917), 1/5th Battalion Leicestershire Regiment (Territorial Force). Formerly, Private 11th (Public Schools) Battalion Royal Fusiliers. In 1915, Edward was wounded and gassed, and on 8 June 1917 killed in action.

Yencken album

Corpus Christi College, Strawberries dinner Lent Term 1914.

G C H Culley album

Corpus Christi College Second Boat, Lent 1914.
Cox, S L R Sharp; stroke, R G Christie; 7, B St J Boultbee; 6, F N Holt; 5, N D S B Lockhart;
4, R G Budgen; 3, L J Hooley; 2, N L Day and bow G I Kirkcaldy. On the bank is coach,
G C H Culley and on the balcony with the College banner is coach, J T Smith.

G C H Culley album

In June 1914, Corpus Christi College made two trips to the Senate House to graduate its students, the first was on 20 June. This photograph forms part of the G C H Culley album and features ten of the eleven students graduating on that day. Unfortunately, there is no accompanying key to the names. However, the Praelector lists the following:

C Breay, A D Bruce, C K Burton, H A Churchward (standing far right)
G C H Culley (standing third left), R V Galer (m.1898) (probably standing second left),
B C Jones, J M A Kendall, H M Macintosh (seated second left),
J L Mawdesley, N M Penzer, A E Clark-Kennedy (seated far right);
the Dean, Edmund Courtney Pearce is seated centre.

G C H Culley album

G C H Culley album

Corpus Christi College Graduation, June 1914: six weeks later Britain was at war.

1914

*BARNES, John Edward Templeman, 2nd Lieutenant (Acting Captain) (1895–1917), 7th (Service) Battalion Gloucestershire Regiment. He was killed in action on 3 February 1917.

EVERETT, Clifford Ernest Foster, Lieutenant (1896–1976), 8th Battalion Loyal North Lancashire Regiment. Formerly Private, Royal Fusiliers. Clifford was born in Colchester, Essex, the son of a building contractor and town councillor. During his war service, Clifford lost an arm and sustained other life-changing injuries that left him permanently disabled. Although admitted to the College and awarded a sizarship, he never came into residence. His award is listed in the Chapter Book but is not in the Admissions Book, nor is he listed in Bury. Clifford died in Worcestershire in 1976 aged 80. TNA have an officer file WO 339/44972 and a medal card WO 372/6/239532.

GAITSKELL, Maurice Howard, Lieutenant (1895–1987), Hampshire Fortress, Royal Engineers. Maurice was born in Paddington, London, the son of Captain Sidney Howard of the Royal Military Academy and his wife Harriet Edith Hamilton née Mayne. Educated at Cheltenham College, he came up to Corpus in October 1914 with a sizarship and an exhibition to read the Mathematical Tripos. *The War List* has 1914 as the date of his matriculation whilst Bury mistakenly has 1915; according to the Boat Club minute book, he rowed for the College in the Michaelmas Term 1914. Maurice returned to Corpus in 1919 to complete his degree. In 1921, he married Peggy née Ellis in Cambridge and in 1987 died at Olney, Buckinghamshire aged 92. TNA have an officer file WO 374/26200.

GALLOWAY, Alexander, Captain, MC (1895–1977), 1/4th Battalion King's Own Scottish Borderers. Formerly 2nd Lieutenant 1st Battalion Cameronians (Scottish Rifles). Although there is no certainty, the data suggests he was Lieutenant General Sir Alexander Galloway KBE CB DSO MC. He was born in Minto, near Hawick, Scotland on 3 November 1895, the son of a Church of Scotland minister, and educated at King William's College, Isle of Man. Although admitted to the College, he never matriculated nor did he come into residence. On the outbreak of war, he obtained a commission with the Cameronians and saw action at Gallipoli, in Egypt and Palestine, and on the Western Front. In 1917, Alexander obtained a regular commission, promoted Captain and posted back to the Scottish Rifles. In 1918, he was awarded the MC and Mentioned in Despatches. During the Second World War, he served in several theatres of operation and was a GSO3. He was subsequently knighted and retired as Lieutenant General. His name does not appear in Bury. TNA have a medal card WO 374/7/192313.

Gledhill, Alan, Lieutenant, MC LLD (London) (1895–1983), 2nd Battalion Monmouthshire Regiment. Alan was the son of Owen Gledhill, a schoolmaster, and his wife Anne née Watson. He was educated at Rugby School and came to Corpus with an Entrance Scholarship (Archbishop Parker's City of Norwich Scholarship) to read the Natural Sciences Tripos. According to the Admissions Register, he matriculated on 27 October 1914, although Bury mistakenly says 1915 (this is difficult to equate with him rowing in the Michaelmas Term 1914). He went to the same battalion as William Mandeville Sankey (see biography) and on the same day. During war service, he was wounded and awarded an MC, the citation for which reads: 'As intelligence officer to his battalion he was frequently entrusted with important missions, the carrying out of which entailed great danger. It was largely due to his untiring zeal and courage that it was possible to effect the withdrawal of the Battalion, which at the time was extended over a frontage of 1,000 yards.' After the Armistice, Alan returned to Corpus to complete his degree, graduating with First Class Honours in June 1920. That same year, he joined the Indian Civil Service and in 1927 was appointed a district and sessions judge. Thereafter, he held several judicial appointments including Special Judge, Tharrawaddy 1930 to 1933; Deputy Commissioner, Cachar, Assam 1942 to 1943; Deputy Chief Judicial Officer, British Military Administration, Burmah 1944 to 1945 (Mentioned in Despatches), and Acting Judge High Court Rangoon (now Yangon, Myanmar) October 1945. He was later Professor of Oriental Law at London University and an Honorary Fellow, School of Oriental and African Studies.

*Glegg, Arthur Livingstone, 2nd Lieutenant (1895–1915), 6th (Reserve) Battalion (attached to the 9th (Service) Battalion) King's Royal Rifle Corps, 42nd Brigade part of the 14th (Light) Division. Arthur was killed in action on 10 August 1915.

*Goolden, Donald Charles, 2nd Lieutenant (1896–1916), 6th (Reserve) Battalion (attached to the 4th Battalion) City of London Regiment, Royal Fusiliers. Formerly Private, 16th (Public Schools) Battalion Middlesex Regiment. Donald was commissioned in April 1915 and killed in action on 14 August 1916.

*Hill, William Reginald, Lieutenant, MC and Bar (1896–1918), 4th Battalion (attached to the 12th) Durham Light Infantry. In 1918, he was wounded and made a prisoner of war. He died of blood poisoning at Stralsund, Germany on 6 November 1918.

McGregor, D G The Chapter Book records he was awarded an exhibition to read the Mathematical Tripos in 1913 and should have matriculated in October 1914. Although admitted to the College he never matriculated. No further information has been found.

MEDLEY John (known as Jack) **Dudley Gibbs, Major** (1891–1962), 6th (Glamorgan) Battalion Welch Regiment. A graduate of New College, Oxford, Jack was due to come to Corpus in October 1914 to undertake graduate work but never came into residence. In later life, he was Vice-Chancellor of the University of Melbourne and knighted. He is not mentioned in either Bury or *The War List*.

PICKTHORN, Kenneth William Murray, Captain (1892–1975), 15th Company London Battalion London Regiment (Civil Service Rifles). In 1914, Kenneth was elected as a College Fellow in history. During his active service in both France and Macedonia, he was wounded twice and later in the war served at the War Office as an RAF Captain. On his return to the College, he served as Dean between 1919 and 1927, as Tutor between 1927 and 1935, and as President between 1937 and 1944; the College has a portrait of him from this time. In 1935, he was elected Member of Parliament for Cambridge University and when in 1948 university seats were abolished, he became MP for the Carlton Division of Nottinghamshire in the subsequent 1950 general election. He was created a baronet in 1959, a Privy Counsellor in 1964, and retired in 1966. TNA have officer files AIR 76/404/15 and WO 374/54061. See also Bury, pp. 250–1.

***PIERSON, Leslie Dilworth, Lieutenant** (1896–1916), 10th (Service) Battalion East Yorkshire Regiment. Leslie was killed in action on 30 October 1916.

***ROXBURGH, John Hewitt, Major** MC (1895–1918), 63rd Battalion Royal Naval Division, Machine Gun Corps (Infantry). John was killed in action on 2 October 1918.

***SANKEY, William Mandeville, Lieutenant** MC (1895–1918), 2nd Battalion Monmouthshire Regiment. He died on 23 March 1918 of wounds received in action.

STUART-PRINCE, Dudley, Captain (1895–1968), Indian Army, Reserve of Officers, attached to the Indian Army Munitions Board. Dudley Stuart-Prince was born in Turkey, the son of Colonel William Charles Stuart-Prince (1867–1951) an officer in the Indian Army and his wife Magdalen née Fosbrooke (1867–1952). Educated at Sherborne School between 1909 and 1914, Dudley became a sixth form scholar, school prefect, and head of school. He was also awarded the Latin Verse prize in 1913 and the following year the Sherborne Classical Medal, the Greek Verse prize, and the Leweston prize (Classics). During his time at Sherborne, Dudley played rugby and was a medium bowler (he played for the School 1st XI in 1913 and 1914). In the March 1914 edition of *The Shirburnian*, his skills at rugby were described as: 'A wing three-quarter who, largely through accidents and ill health, failed to fulfil the expectations raised by his brilliant form against Tonbridge. Is a strong runner with a powerful hand-off.' The July 1914 edition of the same journal commented on his cricketing prowess explaining that he was a: 'Slow medium pace bowler who has been rather disappointing, as his length and direction have been too erratic. A fair field.' At Sherborne, he was a contemporary of John Edward Templeman Barnes (see biography) and appears as the character 'Harding' in Alec Waugh's novel *The Loom of Youth* (1917). Admitted to Corpus with an Entrance Scholarship he should have matriculated in October 1914. Because of the war, he never came into residence. He is, however, listed in Bury's wartime appendix. In May 1915, he was commissioned into the Indian Army and remained on active service until 1920. After he left the armed forces, he could have taken up his Corpus scholarship but clearly decided not to. Instead, between 1922 and 1929, he worked as a planter (probably in Malaya) and after 1931 as an engineer. During the Second World War he served in the Home Guard. Dudley Stuart-Prince died in Buckinghamshire in 1968. TNA have an officer file WO 372/16/90121 and WO 372/28/4577.

1915

ALLIN, Eric Kenelm, Lieutenant (Acting Captain) (1895–1985), Royal Welch Fusiliers. Eric was born in Romsley, Worcestershire, the son of William Allin, an Anglican clergyman. He was educated at Rossall School, Lancashire and, according to the Chapter Book, awarded an Entrance Exhibition in Classics and History in January 1915. The Admissions Book shows he did not come into residence in 1915, matriculating instead in 1919 after military service. He served in France, suffering gun-shot wounds as a result of which he claimed a disability pension. He died in Denbighshire in 1985 aged 90. TNA have a pensions file PIN 26/21096 and a medal card WO 372/1/65449.

ARUNDEL, Eric Shelton, 2nd Lieutenant (1896–1970), 2nd Battalion East Surrey Regiment and 2nd Lieutenant, the Worcestershire Regiment. Eric was born in Marple, Cheshire, the son of a travelling salesman in confectionary. He was brought up in Leyton, London and educated at Innovation College, London. In January 1915, he was awarded an Entrance Scholarship to read the Natural Sciences Tripos but did not come into residence, having joined the armed forces on the outbreak of war. On 19 January 1915, his Battalion landed at Le Havre and in April saw action during the 2nd Battle of Ypres where it experienced heavy casualties, some falling victim to the first use of poison gas. In September 1915, the Battalion was again in action, this time at the Battle of Loos, where they formed part of the defence of the Hohenzollern Redoubt. The following month, Eric and his Battalion went first to Egypt then Salonika. He spent the remainder of the war on the Struma Valley Front and east of Lake Doiran. The Battalion saw action at the Battle of Doiran in January 1918, the surrender of Bulgaria, and, after the Armistice, formed part of occupying forces in Turkey. In 1919, he returned to England and matriculated into Corpus. In 1931, he married Almey née Adcock and died in Worcestershire in 1970 aged 74. TNA have an officer file WO 339/36671 and a medal card WO 372/1/124172.

BARBER, Thomas Clive Quinton (known as Clive), 2nd Lieutenant (1895–1960). He served in an unknown infantry regiment. Clive was born in Bedford and attended Woodbridge School. In December 1914, he was elected to a Colman Exhibition. He was, according to Bury (possibly mistakenly), a 1915 matriculation but is not listed as such in the Admissions Book. He survived the war and in 1929 he and his wife Kathleen Audrey were living in Heacham, Norfolk with a daughter. Clive died in Cambridge in 1960 aged 65.

BANKES-WILLIAMS, Ivor Meredydd, 2nd Lieutenant (1896–1974), Royal Field Artillery. In 1911, Ivor was living in Acton, Suffolk, where his father William was vicar. Educated at Radley College, he was awarded a Corpus Entrance Scholarship in 1915 to read the Classical Tripos. He did not come into residence and instead, according to Bury, matriculated in 1919 after war service. In 1924, he married Winifred née Barnes at Risbridge, Suffolk. A note in the Admissions Book suggests he was later a senior master at Harrow School. He died in Dorset in 1974 aged 78.

BOLD, Thomas Arthur, Lieutenant (b.1894), 1st Battalion Loyal North Lancashire Regiment and Royal Sussex Regiment. Thomas was born in Brixton, London in 1894, the son of William Prosser Bold, a secretary, and his wife Anne Susan née Swain. He was educated at the Mercers' School, City of London (which closed in 1959). The Admissions Book and *The War List* has him matriculating in October 1914 whilst Bury has 1915. Thomas returned to Corpus in 1919 to complete his degree. TNA have a medal card WO 372/2/199071.

BOSWELL, A The Chapter Book records he was admitted to the College in 1914 and awarded an exhibition. He should have matriculated in October 1915 but never came into residence. His name does not appear in the Admissions Book. No further information has been found.

BROWN, Walter (known as Bill) Graham Scott (later Scott-Brown), Lieutenant (1897–1987), 2nd Battalion Royal Horse Artillery. Bill was born in Upper Tooting, London, the son of George Andrew Scott-Brown, an insurance company manager, and his wife Annie Louis née Tindall. He was educated at Whitgift School, Croydon. Although admitted to the College in 1915, he did not matriculate until 1919 when he became a Shuter Scholar. He served in France between 1916 and 1918, was wounded and Mentioned in Despatches. Bill took his MB in 1925 and after a period in general practice became a leading ENT surgeon; in 1945, he was made a Commander of the Royal Victorian Order (CVO). A noted artist, he died in Hampshire in 1987 aged 90. See obituary in *The Letter of the Corpus Association*, No. 66 (Michaelmas 1987), pp. 79–80. His son George Graham Scott-Brown (1929–2018) came to Corpus in 1948; he also studied medicine, during which he was awarded the Cunning Prize. George had a career as a medical missionary in Nepal and subsequently as a general practitioner.

Colthurst Alan St George, Lieutenant (1897–1983), Royal Field Artillery. Alan was born and died in Pershore, Worcestershire where his father the Reverend Richard Charles James Colthurst was vicar. His mother was Constance née Browning. Educated at Haileybury, he was admitted to the College in 1915 but did not matriculate until 1920. He served in France between 1916 and 1918 and was Mentioned in Despatches. TNA have a medal card WO/4/218807.

Cullen, William Godfrey, 2nd Lieutenant (Temporary) (1896–1961), RFC and subsequently RAF. William was born in Smethwick, Staffordshire (now West Midlands) and educated at Clifton College. Bury has him matriculating in 1915 whilst the Admissions Book and *The War List* has 1914.

***Digges La Touche, Denis, Captain** (1895–1915), 8th (Service) Battalion Welch Regiment. Formerly 2nd Lieutenant, King's Shropshire Light Infantry. Denis was killed in action at Gallipoli on 8 August 1915.

Haslam, James Alexander Gordon, 2nd Lieutenant, MC DFC (1896–1990), Royal Field Artillery and Lieutenant Royal Flying Corps (later Royal Air Force). Educated at Rugby School, James was awarded a Corpus Exhibition in 1915 to read the Natural Sciences Tripos, but never came into residence. Instead, he entered the Royal Military Academy, Woolwich. After active service with the Royal Field Artillery, he was attached to the RFC and trained as a pilot. During James's service on the Western Front, he was wounded. His MC citation reads:

> On August 10 [1918] this officer performed a very gallant action. While carrying out a contact patrol he was attacked by seven enemy scouts. Although wounded in the leg at the outset of the engagement, Lt Haslam, with rare courage and determination, continued to serve his machine gun. One of the enemy aeroplanes was driven down, and the remainder dispersed.

His DFC citation relates to several engagements with the enemy and concludes: 'Throughout the operations their work in cooperation with our artillery was always of the greatest value, and their expertise in attacking enemy troops and transport with bombs and machine gun fire was splendid.' In 1927, after obtaining a regular RAF commission, he finally came to Corpus as a Fellow Commoner taking an ordinary degree in Engineering Science. He returned in 1933 to undertake flight research and was later appointed University Lecturer in Aeronautics. After war service, 1939 to 1945, he retired with the rank of Group

Captain and was, in 1949, elected to a College Fellowship. His obituary appears in *The Letter of the Corpus Association*, No. 70 (Michaelmas 1991), pp. 67–8.

HEATON, Ralph, Lieutenant (b. *c*.1896), Royal Field Artillery. His name appears in the Admissions Book as matriculating in May 1915 but there is no further information. In October 1918, Ralph was wounded. TNA have an officer file WO 339/49419 and a medal card WO 372/9/125657.

HOSKYNS, Reverend Edwyn Clement, MC (1884–1937), CF 3rd Class, Royal Army Chaplains Department. Edwyn Hoskyns was born on 9 August 1884 in Notting Hill, London, the son of Bishop Edwyn Hoskyns and his wife Mary Constance Maude née Benson. In 1916, Edwyn (who had been an undergraduate at Jesus College, trained at Wells Theological College and the University of Berlin) was elected to a Corpus Fellowship and remained Dean of Chapel until 1932, when he moved to Liverpool. Edwyn served as an army Chaplain first in Egypt and subsequently in France. He was described as: 'A capable chaplain. Hard worker. Has made a good SCF [Senior Chaplain to the Forces]'. During his war service, he was wounded and Mentioned in Despatches. He was also awarded a Military Cross; the citation reads:

> For conspicuous gallantry and devotion to duty. Under heavy shell fire he personally placed wounded in a safe place and was solely responsible from preventing them falling into the hands of the enemy. He remained with them until all had been evacuated, being slightly wounded himself. Next day he showed conspicuous courage in tending wounded in an exposed position under heavy shell and machine-gun fire for nine hours without a break.

In 1925, he inherited the baronetcy (as 13th Bart) and in 1927 married Mary Trym née Budden. Sir Edwyn was an eminent interwar Anglican theologian and writer within the Anglo-Catholic tradition.

JONES, Keith Franklin, Lieutenant (1896–1975), 10th Battalion (Duke of Cambridge's Own) Middlesex Regiment, attached to the Hertfordshire Regiment. Keith was born in Newcastle upon Tyne where his father, the Reverend William George Jones, was an Anglican priest. His mother was Minnie Florence née Turner. Educated at St Paul's, Keith was admitted to the College in May 1915 with a Stock Exhibition. He is listed in both *The War List* and the *Cambridge Review* but, according to Bury, matriculated in 1919. His military service in France began in December 1917. He married Alice Winifred née Thorndike in 1930 and died in 1975 aged 79. TNA have an officer file WO 374/38363 and a medal card WO 372/11/68969.

*LING, Leonard Simpson, 2nd Lieutenant (1893–1917), 3rd Battalion (attached to the 1st Battalion) Norfolk Regiment. Leonard was killed in action on 23 April 1917.

PORTEUS, Joseph, 2nd Lieutenant (b.1898), Lancashire Fusiliers. Joseph was born in Newcastle upon Tyne, the son of James Porteus a commercial traveller, and educated at Bede College School, Co. Durham. He was admitted to the College in 1915 but did not matriculate until January 1919. His name is not recorded in *The War List* but does appear in the *Cambridge Review*. In 1918, he was erroneously reported missing in action. TNA have an officer file WO 339/88779.

*ROBERTS, William Arthur, Lieutenant (1897–1917), 19th Battalion Royal Fusiliers attached to the 30th Training Reserve Battalion, Dover, Kent. William was seriously wounded in action and died in hospital of a fractured skull on 20 August 1917.

STURT, Horace Holford, Lieutenant (1896–1962), The Duke of Edinburgh's (Wiltshire Regiment). Horace was born in Hampstead, the son of the Reverend Horace Surt, an Anglican clergyman. Educated at Marlborough College, he was admitted to the College in January 1915 with an Entrance Scholarship to read the Classical Tripos but did not come into residence. The Admissions Book and Bury both have him matriculating in March 1919. He is not mentioned in *The War List* but appears in the *Cambridge Review*. He died in Poole, Dorset in 1962 aged 66. TNA have an officer file WO 374/66286.

THOMSON, George Paget, Captain (1892–1975), The Queen's (Royal West Surrey Regiment). George Paget Thomson was born in Cambridge, the son of physicist and Nobel laureate J J Thomson and his wife Rose Elisabeth née Paget, daughter of George Edward Paget. Educated at the Perse School, Cambridge before reading mathematics and physics at Trinity College, Cambridge. On the outbreak of war, he obtained a commission with the Queen's (Royal West Surrey Regiment). After military service in France, he transferred to the RFC (later the RAF) and spent much of the war undertaking research into aerodynamics at the Royal Aircraft Establishment, Farnborough and elsewhere. He was elected to a College Fellowship in 1915 and after taking positions at Aberdeen and Imperial College, London was elected Master in 1952. In later life, he was a Nobel Laureate, an FRS and knighted. During his tenure as Master, the Leckhampton estate was returned to the College as a graduate campus and the modernist George Thomson Building was named in his honour. He died in 1975 aged 83. TNA have a medal card WO 372/20/9742. See also Bury, pp. 249–50.

*THRING, Ashton Edward, 2nd Lieutenant (1896–1917), 'D' Battery, No. 1 Reserve Brigade, Royal Field Artillery. Ashton died of pneumonia on 9 February 1917.

WALLIS, Aidan Arnold, Captain (1896–1949), RNAS/Royal Air Force. He was formerly Temporary Flight Sub-Lieutenant and subsequently Flight Lieutenant,

Royal Naval Air Service. Aidan was born in Cambridge where he lived with his mother Mary Ann Wallis née Buyen at 5 Belvoir Terrace. His father was Arnold Joseph Wallis (1856–1913) a College Fellow and Bursar. Educated at Marlborough College, Aidan was awarded an Entrance Exhibition in 1915 to read the Classical Tripos but did not come into residence. However, on 8 August 1915 he joined the Royal Naval Air Service and gained his pilot's licence in December 1915. During his subsequent active service, he experienced several air accidents, suffered burns and fractures and was hospitalised over an extended period. He was described as: 'Extremely keen, hard-working and zealous'. Due to his injuries, he spent much of his service as an instructor and was described as: 'a good pilot. As an officer he lacks experience. Good at looking after pupils.' He was discharged from the RAF in June 1919 and matriculated in October that same year. According to Bury, Aidan went on to become a successful preparatory school headmaster. In 1926, he married Joan Musgrave Middleton née Wilson and died in Lewes, Sussex in 1949 aged 53. He is not mentioned in *The War List* but is included on the *Cambridge Review* list. TNA have several files, AIR 76/527/63, ADM 273/6/296 and ADM 273/30/22.

1916

*BLYTH, Alick Frederick, Lieutenant (1897–1917), Northern Cyclists Corps (attached to the 2/5th Battalion Gloucestershire Regiment), 19th Division. Alick was killed in action on the Ypres front on 23 August 1917.

*COBHAM, Frederick George Brian, Lieutenant (1897–1918), 2nd/1st (Territorial Force) Battalion Cambridgeshire Regiment. Brian was killed in action on 8 August 1918.

MACCOBY, Simon (1898–1971), No. 2 Aldershot Company, Non-Combatant Corps. Simon was born in Spitalfields, London. Extraordinary for someone of his background, in December 1915, he was awarded a Corpus Entrance Scholarship to read the Historical Tripos. Simon's great nephew is The Rt Hon. the Lord Etherton QC Kt PC (m.1969), Honorary Fellow of the College, former Master of the Rolls, and a distinguished jurist. He has written:

> He was a person of exceptional intellect and ability who rose from a poor upbringing to achieve at Corpus the highest academic standard. He was a person of moral courage and conviction, intellectual rigour, energy and determination.
>
> Simon was the son of Jewish immigrants from a small town in the Pale of Settlement (in Western Russia), who came to England probably in the early 1870s to seek refuge from persecution and pogroms. They were poor and settled in Whitechapel in the East End of London.

Simon attended the Central Foundation School in Shoreditch in East London, which was established by the Reverend William Rogers, a social reformer. In 1916 Corpus awarded him an Entrance Scholarship to study history. In the same year he was called up for military service but was a conscientious objector. He was sentenced to six months imprisonment with hard labour. He subsequently served with the Quakers' War Victims Relief Service and with the Red Cross in France, for which he was awarded a certificate by the French Red Cross.

He eventually took up his place at Corpus in 1919, in Part I of the Tripos he achieved a First-Class degree, for which the College awarded him a Foundation Scholarship. In his Finals in 1922 he achieved a starred First. Corpus awarded him the Bishop Green Cup. I still have this beautiful silver trophy with the College crest, inscribed *Simon Maccoby AB Philosophiae Premium*. In the same year he was awarded a Whewell Scholarship by the University.

He had studied under Sir Geoffrey Butler (1887–1929) who was a Fellow of Corpus, MP for Cambridge University (1923–29), a distinguished historian and an expert on the recently created League of Nations. The Butler Room, formerly the Butler Library, underneath the Parker library is named after him. Together with Sir Geoffrey Butler, Simon Maccoby co-authored a large work *The Development of International Law* which was published in 1928. The work was described in the *Yale Law Review* as 'one of the most valuable contributions to the history of international law yet made'. In the meantime, Simon Maccoby had taken up a post as a history master at Wolsingham Grammar School in County Durham in 1927. He remained there for the rest of his working life until his retirement in 1962, serving as deputy headmaster from 1948.

It is not known why, despite his outstanding academic achievements at Corpus, he was not appointed to a Fellowship. This may possibly be explained by the fact he was not only a Jew but had once been a conscientious objector in the First World War and had served a sentence of imprisonment. Corpus was well known between the wars as a conservative Anglican institution. In addition, Sir Geoffrey Butler died suddenly and unexpectedly in 1929, and so Simon Maccoby lost his mentor and protector.

Simon Maccoby's academic achievements and intellectual brilliance continued throughout his working life. He was awarded a PhD. by the London School of Economics in 1934. In 1939 he was granted a Leverhulme Fellowship for research on the character and influence of radicalism 1768–1832. Among several other works which he wrote after leaving Cambridge, he published between 1935 and 1961 six volumes on *English Radicalism 1832–1886* and was editor of *The English Radical Tradition 1763–1914* published in 1952.

I have no doubt that, had Corpus in the 1920s been as it is today, Simon Maccoby's achievements in later life would have been as spectacular as his early academic success. He inspired me to apply to Corpus and my time there has led to all the success I have enjoyed in the law and as a member of the judiciary.

There is a TNA digital folder relating to Simon's service as a non-combatant WO 363–4/007377919/00654.

READ, Selwyn 2nd Lieutenant (b.1896), Royal Garrison Artillery. Selwyn was born in Eastbourne, Sussex, the son of Isaac Read, a watchmaker and jeweller. Educated at Eastbourne College, he was admitted to Corpus in December 1915 with an Entrance Scholarship to read the Mathematical Tripos. He did not come into residence but matriculated in April 1919 after completing military service. TNA have an officer file WO 339/67768.

*STOKES, Louis Mander, 2nd Lieutenant (1897–1916), 2nd Battalion Royal Marine Light Infantry, Royal Naval Division. Louis was killed on the Ancre on 13 November 1916.

1917

BARRY, Gerald Reid, Captain (1898–1968), RFC and RAF. Gerald was born in Norfolk, the son of a clergyman. Educated at Marlborough College, he was admitted to the College in 1916, awarded a Corpus Entrance Scholarship, and should have matriculated in 1917, but never came into residence. During his war service, he served as an RFC/RAF observer and was wounded. In 1919, he obtained a regular RAF commission. On leaving the RAF, he went into journalism, later becoming editor of the *News Chronicle* (1936–47). He was a founder of Political and Economic Planning (PEP) and later in his career Director-General of the 1951 Festival of Britain. For services to the latter, he was knighted. TNA have officer files AIR 76/25/32 and AIR 76/634/68697.

*BRAY, Frank, Flight Sub-Lieutenant (1898–1917), 8th (Naval) Squadron Royal Naval Air Service. Frank was first posted missing, then on 15 July 1917 reported killed in action.

CRUTTENDEN, Courtney, Lieutenant (b.1898), 1st Battalion Grenadier Guards. Courtney was born at St Asaph, Denbighshire, Wales, the son of Ernest Henry Cruttenden, a gentleman farmer, and his wife Ethel née Gossage. Educated at Marlborough College, Courtney was admitted to the College in December 1916 with an Entrance Exhibition to read the Classical Tripos. He matriculated into Corpus in October 1919 after completing his military service. Commissioned in the Grenadier Guards, he was posted to France on 26 October 1917. According to the Admissions Book, he later had a teaching career at St Paul's School.

*GASKELL, Lawrence Norris, 2nd Lieutenant (1898–1918), Royal Flying Corps and General List (1/7th Battalion Middlesex Regiment). Lawrence died of wounds on 1 March 1918.

MARKS, Norman Percy, 2nd Lieutenant (b.1895), the Buffs (East Kent Regiment). Norman was born in East Dulwich, the son of John Percy Marks, a shipping clerk, and his wife Mary née Wilson. Educated at Aske's School, Hatcham, he was admitted to Corpus in December 1916 with an Entrance Exhibition to read the Natural Sciences Tripos. However, according to the Admissions Book, he did not matriculate until October 1920. Norman later became a clergyman. TNA have an officer file WO 374/46037.

THORNTON, George Kennedy, 2nd Lieutenant (1898–1990), 14th (Reserve) Battery, Royal Field Artillery. George was born in Holt, Norfolk, the son of George Liscock Thornton, a physician. Educated at Sherborne School, he was admitted to Corpus in December 1916 with an Entrance Exhibition to read the Classical and Historical Triposes but did not matriculate until January 1919. Instead, he was commissioned in November 1917 and sent to France on 2 January 1918. George died in Hampshire in 1990 aged 92.

*TITCOMB, Francis Holt Yates, Lieutenant (Probationary Flying Officer) (1898–1917), Royal Naval Air Service. Francis was killed in a flying accident on 15 April 1917.

WEIGHTMAN, Hugh, Lieutenant (1898–1949), RFC and subsequently RAF. Hugh was born at Newark-on-Trent, the son of William Weightman, a maltster. He was educated at Hymer's College, Hull and was admitted to Corpus in December 1916 with an Entrance Scholarship to read the Classical Tripos. Hugh joined the RFC at Oxford in April 1917 and trained as a pilot with No. 18 Training Squadron. He went to France to serve with 70 Squadron and was wounded in action in September 1917. Hugh was demobilised on 20 January 1919 and later that year matriculated into Corpus. He subsequently had an important Colonial and India Office career. Between 1937 and 1940, he was political agent in Bahrain and later the last British Secretary for External Affairs of India for which he was made a Companion of the Indian Empire (CIE) and a Companion of the Star of India (CSI). Hugh Weightman was knighted in 1948 and died the following year aged 51. TNA have several files AIR 79/626/67843, AIR 76/537/84 and WO 339/111323.

WOOD, S E He was educated at Aske's Hatcham School. According to the Chapter Book, he was admitted to Corpus in December 1915 with an Entrance Exhibition to read the Historical Tripos. He never matriculated or came into residence. There is no additional information, but it is possible he was the S E Wood who served as a pilot with 202 Squadron, RNAS. If this is the man, then TNA have an officer file AIR 76/559/65. This man survived the war.

1918

Bishop, William Alfred, 2nd Lieutenant (1899–1991), Royal Engineers. William was born in Croydon, the son of Alfred, a broker specialising in colonial stocks. Educated at Whitgift School, he was admitted to Corpus in December 1917 with an Entrance Scholarship to read the Natural Sciences Tripos. He matriculated in March 1919, after completing war service. On graduating, he began a long and distinguished Royal Naval career, during which he reached the rank of Instructor Rear-Admiral and was awarded both a KBE and a CB. His obituary can be found in *The Letter of the Corpus Association*, No. 71 (Michaelmas 1992), pp. 67–8.

Brown, James Alexander Spence, 2nd Lieutenant (b.1899), Royal Garrison Artillery. James was born in Normanton, Yorkshire, the son of Mary Brown, a widow of independent means. The 1911 census shows the family in Bristol, where James was educated at Clifton College. In December 1917, he was admitted to Corpus with an exhibition to read the Natural Sciences Tripos. In 1919, he matriculated into the College after completing his military service. He subsequently trained as a physician and emigrated to Australia in 1950. TNA have an officer file WO 339/105362.

Carlisle, Geoffrey Townsend 2nd Lieutenant (1899–1985), Cheshire Regiment. Geoffrey was born in Alderley Edge, Cheshire, the son of Charles Stewart Carlisle JP, a merchant exporter, and his wife Mary née Royds. Educated at Radley College, Geoffrey was admitted to Corpus in December 1917 with an Entrance Scholarship to read the Classical Tripos. He matriculated in March 1919, having completed his war service. After graduation, Geoffrey was ordained priest and subsequently served in South Africa. On his return to Britain, he became a vicar in Buxton, Derbyshire. Between 1953 and 1970, he was Master of the Hospital of St Cross, Winchester. Geoffrey died in Kent in 1985 aged 86. TNA have an officer file WO 339/118786.

Crompton, James Aubrey, 2nd Lieutenant (b.1899), Royal Garrison Artillery. James was born in Bristol, the son of a municipal accountant, and educated at Clifton College. In December 1917, he was awarded an Entrance Scholarship to read the Mathematical Tripos. He matriculated in January 1919, after completing his military service. TNA have an officer file WO 339/110463.

Dixon, Murray Deighton, 2nd Lieutenant (1899–1971), Royal Engineers (Signal Depot). Formerly Private 95332 Middlesex Regiment. Murray was born in Newcastle upon Tyne, the son of James Dixon, a surgeon, and his wife Kate Margaret née Clarke. Educated at Sherborne School, he was admitted to Corpus with an Entrance Exhibition in December 1917 to read the Classical Tripos.

He matriculated in January 1920 after completing his military service. His TNA medal card WO 372/6/40169 indicates the war had ended before he became operationally active. He died in London in 1971 aged 72.

PARRY, Ronald Ernest Lambert, 2nd Lieutenant (1899–1946), Oxfordshire and Buckinghamshire Light Infantry. Ronald was born at Hampton Hill, Middlesex, the son of Ernest John Parry, an analytical chemist. Educated at Rossall School, Lancashire, he was admitted to Corpus in December 1917 with an Entrance Exhibition to read the Mathematical Tripos. He matriculated in May 1919 after completing his military service. TNA have an officer file WO 339/102029.

TOMPKIN, J Educated at the Central Foundation School, London, his name does not appear in Bury's supplementary list but he was, according to the Chapter Book, admitted to the College in December 1917 with an Entrance Exhibition to read the Mathematical Tripos. He did not matriculate or come into residence and no further information has been located.

WITHAM, Frank Barnard (1899–1973), Royal Army Service Corps. Frank was born at Grange-over-Sands, Lancashire, the son of Alfred Witham, a shopkeeper. The 1911 census indicates that Frank's father was deceased and the family lived in Lancaster. Educated at Lancaster Grammar School, he was admitted to Corpus in December 1917 with an Entrance Scholarship to read the Mathematical Tripos. He matriculated into the College in 1919 after completing his military service. In 1925, he married Mona née Bower and died in Lancaster in 1973 aged 74. TNA have an officer file WO 363/4/007283456/01479 and a pension claim held on microfilm WO 364/4806 (frames 1494–9).

College Servants

COOPER, the College clerk. The Governing Body minutes for 5 February 1915 record he was away on military service. It was agreed he should receive four shillings per week during the continuance of his service.

*CRACKNELL, Edwin George, Private 16641 (1890–1917). 11th (Cambridgeshire) Battalion the Suffolk Regiment (see biography).

HAMMOND, an under porter. The Governing Body minutes for 17 August 1914 record him as being engaged in military service. No further information.

PILLSWORTH, an under porter. The Governing Body minutes for 25 January 1915 record him having been called up for military service. It was agreed he should receive ten shillings per week in lieu of his ordinary wages, and that the Bursar arrange for his work being done by someone else.

Glossary

Praelector = The College Fellow who formally presents students during matriculation or graduation ceremonies, especially when degrees are conferred during Congregations of the Regent House.

Scholarships, exhibitions, and other awards

During the middle years of the nineteenth century, the College consolidated many of its awards and by the end of that century, there were a total of twenty-five scholarships and eight exhibitions. This process of consolidation has continued into the modern era. In addition to College awards, schools, local authorities, and others gave scholarships and exhibitions tenable at Corpus.

Bishop Green Cup = Awarded to those undergraduates who gained the top grades in Tripos.

College Prizeman = Awarded a prize (usually books or cash) for outstanding Tripos results.

Entrance Exhibitions = Before the First World War, the College awarded four such exhibitions based on College-based written entrance examinations.

Entrance Scholarship = Before the First World War, the College offered six Entrance Scholarships based on the results of College-based written examinations.

Foundation Scholar = Awarded to those undergraduates with outstanding Tripos results.

Open Exhibition = Admitted to the College with this award tenable in any subject. The award was based on College-based written entrance examination results.

Open Scholarship = These were awards tenable in any subject based on the results of College-based written entrance examinations.

Senior Optime = An undergraduate who has achieved a Second Class in the Mathematical Tripos.

Senior Wrangler = An undergraduate being the person with the highest marks in the Mathematical Tripos.

Wrangler = An undergraduate placed in the First Class in the Mathematical Tripos.

Classes of students

Pensioner = An undergraduate admitted to the College without a scholarship or exhibition.

Sizar = An undergraduate who received some form of assistance such as meals, lower fees, or lodging, in some cases in return for doing a defined job.

Corpus societies and clubs

The later Victorian and Edwardian periods were the age of College societies and clubs. Many sported uniquely striking blazers; they also developed elaborate rules and sometimes even had their own regalia. They were often short-lived and most did not survive the First World War. Below is a list and description of some of the pre-1914 Corpus societies mentioned in the text.

Chess Club = Founded in 1871, it claimed to be the oldest College society but was wound up in the 1990s. It did play chess in its earliest years and in 1881 whist was introduced. After 1892, it began to become a more convivial social group. At some point, the rule was introduced that members of the Chess Club were forbidden to lose at chess and so they ceased to play the game and it became a drinking society. Members of the Chess Club had their own distinctive blazers. After 1907, it took on the role formerly held by the Honest Cods (see below). Its termly photograph has names attached. This has enabled many of those whose biographies appear in this book to be identified.

Classical Society = Founded in 1906, students met each term to give papers and listen to the ideas of the many eminent early twentieth-century Cambridge-based Classical scholars who were among its speakers.

Cobwebs = Founded in 1908 as an archaeological society. It was not revived after the war.

Gravediggers = Founded *c.*1879 and is the oldest extant College society. Originally founded as a Shakespearian play-reading society, after 1906, it started to develop a much wider remit. It was revived soon after the war ended.

Honest Cods = Founded in 1904 but wound up in 1907. It was created by Llewellyn Powys and Robert Oke as a small, exclusive drinking and dining society made up of the College 'bloods'. The society had its own distinctive green blazers and golden drinking goblets. Its punch recipe (which still exists) was particularly lethal. Members of the Honest Cods used to enjoy shocking the seminarian wing of the College. One of the latter wrote years later: 'in one corner of the Old Court one party would be getting drunk while in the opposite corner another party would be praying for them'. The Honest Cods was wound up in 1907 when Powys, Oke, and the rest of the society finally graduated.

Pious Pelicans = Founded in 1910 as a literary and play-reading group. It was not revived after the war.

Staunton Club = Founded in 1890 and reconstituted in 1897. It really did play chess but was not revived after the war.

Strawberries = Founded in 1908 with the object of establishing a 'permanent social club among Corpus men', or, in the words of one of its members writing thirty years later, to meet regularly to have 'a good time'. The Strawberries had a striking scarlet velvet blazer and held elaborate formal dinners (see photograph in the appendix, p. 207). It was not revived after the war.

Bibliography

R A BARLOW & H V BOWEN (eds.) *A Dear and Noble boy: the Life and letters of Louis Stokes 1897–1916* (1995).

PATRICK BURY *The College of Corpus Christi and of the Blessed Virgin Mary: a history from 1822 to 1952* (1952).

GORDON VERO CAREY *The War List of the University of Cambridge 1914–1918* (1921).

MARTIN AND TERESA DAVIS *For Club, King and Country: the story of the Gloucestershire County Cricketers and the Gloucestershire Rugby Club players as soldiers of Gloucestershire in the Great War 1914–1918* (2014).

ROGER GIBBONS, *In memoriam, Gloucestershire County cricketers killed in the Great War* (2015).

DIANA HEYWOOD *The Game of Blood and Iron* (2 vols self-published 2018).

J HORNE, (ed.) *Best of Good Fellows: the Diaries and Memoirs of the Reverend Charles Edmund Doudney, MA CF (1871–1915)*, (1995).

NIGEL MCCRERY, *Final wicket: test and first-class cricketers killed in the Great War* (2015).

HEW STRACHAN *History of the Cambridge University Officers Training Corps* (1976).

WISDEN *Cricketers' Almanack* (1914–1918 editions).

A GEOFFREY WOODHEAD *The College of Corpus Christi and of the Blessed Virgin Mary: a contribution to its history from 1952 to 1994* (1995).

Journals

The Benedict (published by the students of Corpus Christi College, Cambridge, 1897–1928).

The Cambridge Review: a journal of university life and thought (vol 1–119, 1879–1998) 1914 to 1919 editions (Published by the students of Cambridge University).

Letter of the Corpus Association later *The Record* (1914 to present).

Index of names

Numbers in **bold** refer to images.